Writing for *The New Yorker*

Critical Essays on an American Periodical

Edited by Fiona Green

EDINBURGH
University Press

Edinburgh University Press Ltd
The Tun – Holyrood Road
12(2f) Jackson's Entry
Edinburgh EH8 8PJ
www.euppublishing.com

Typeset in 10.5/13 pt Sabon by
Servis Filmsetting Ltd, Stockport, Cheshire,
and printed and bound in Great Britain by
CPI Group (UK) Ltd, Croydon CR0 4YY

A CIP record for this book is available from the British Library

ISBN 978 0 7486 8249 2 (hardback)
ISBN 978 0 7486 8250 8 (webready PDF)
ISBN 978 0 7486 8251 5 (epub)

Writing for *The New Yorker*

Contents

Acknowledgements

The first debt of thanks in this book is due to its contributors, for their research and writing, and for their collaborative thinking at the Cambridge *New Yorker* Symposium in 2013. We are grateful to the Centre for Material Texts, Faculty of English, University of Cambridge, for hosting that event. We were fortunate also in having the research assistance of Victoria Beale, and grateful to the Cambridge Humanities Research Grants Scheme for funding her post.

Richard Gooder first prompted me to think about *The New Yorker*. Paul Giles, Lee Jenkins, Robin Schulze, and Andrew Thacker commented helpfully on early plans for the volume, as did the reviewers for Edinburgh University Press. Research for this book would not have been possible without the assistance of the librarians at the Manuscripts and Archives Division, New York Public Library, The Berg Collection, New York Public Library, The National Library of Scotland, The Pierpont Morgan Library, and the Reading, Pennsylvania Public Library. Thanks are due also to Jackie Jones and Dhara Patel at Edinburgh University Press; and to Sam Dean and Jen Pollard at the Cambridge English Faculty for their help with the preparation of images.

I am particularly grateful to my colleagues Tamara Follini, Kasia Boddy, and Ned Allen, and to Bharat Tandon, for their comments on draft chapters of this volume, to Tim Clark for his meticulous copy-editing, and to Joanne O'Leary for proofreading.

Lastly, I thank Peter, Joseph, Molly, and Martha Rodgers, for their patience.

Permissions

Permission from the John H. Updike Literary Trust to quote John Updike's poems, 'Duet, with Muffled Brake Drums', 'Player Piano', 'The

Newlyweds', 'Why the Telephone Wires Dip and the Poles are Cracked and Crooked', and from Updike's unpublished correspondence, is gratefully acknowledged.

Permission for the use of quotations from the unpublished letters of Marianne Moore to David Wallace, dated December 17, 1957 and February 7, 1958 respectively and from 'People's Surroundings', 'Critics and Connoisseurs', and 'Four Quartz Crystal Clocks', is granted by the Literary Estate of Marianne C. Moore, David M. Moore, Successor Executor of the Literary Estate of Marianne Moore. All rights reserved.

Abbreviation

New Yorker Records   New Yorker Records, Manuscripts and Archives Division, the New York Public Library, Astor, Lenox and Tilden Foundations.

Notes on Contributors

Kasia Boddy is a Lecturer in the Faculty of English at the University of Cambridge. She has published widely on American fiction, especially on the short story, and on sport. She is author of *Boxing: A Cultural History* (2008) and *The American Short Story Since 1950* (2010), and editor of the *New Penguin Book of American Short Stories* (2011).

Deborah Bowman is a Fellow and College Lecturer in English at Gonville and Caius College, Cambridge. Her research centres on early and mid-twentieth-century writing in English and French.

Sarah Cain is a College Lecturer and Director of Studies in English at Corpus Christi College, Cambridge. Her research interests include Anglo-American modernism, the history of modern aesthetics and literary theory, and the intersections between intellectual history and material culture.

Tamara Follini is a Fellow and Senior Lecturer in English at Clare College, Cambridge. She is General Editor, with Adrian Poole, Philip Horne and Michael Anesko, for the forthcoming Cambridge Edition of the *Complete Fiction of Henry James*.

Linda Freedman is a Lecturer in British and American Literature at University College, London. She is author of *Emily Dickinson and the Religious Imagination* (2011).

Fiona Green is a Senior Lecturer in American Literature at the University of Cambridge, and a Fellow of Jesus College. Her research interests and publications centre on American poetry and history. She serves on the steering committee of the Cambridge Centre for Material Texts.

Faye Hammill is Professor of English at the University of Strathclyde. She established the AHRC-funded 'Middlebrow Network' in 2008, and her most recent monograph is *Sophistication: A Literary and Cultural History* (2010).

Thomas Karshan is a Lecturer in Literature at the University of East Anglia. His *Vladimir Nabokov and the Art of Play* was published in 2011. He is the editor of Nabokov's *Collected Poems* and the co-translator of Nabokov's *The Tragedy of Mister Morn*. He wrote a defense of Updike which appeared in the *London Review of Books* in 2005.

Duncan Kelly is a Reader in Political Thought at the University of Cambridge, and a Fellow of Jesus College. His books include *The Propriety of Liberty: Persons, Passions and Judgement in Modern Political Thought* (2010). He is the editor of *Lineages of Empire: The Historical Roots of British Imperial Thought* (2009).

Tom Perrin is Assistant Professor of English at Huntingdon College. He is completing a book on the aesthetics of US middlebrow fiction.

Bharat Tandon is a Lecturer in Literature at the University of East Anglia. His publications include *Jane Austen and the Morality of Conversation* (2003) and an annotated edition of Jane Austen's *Emma* (2012). He has written extensively on American fiction and non-fiction for *The Times Literary Supplement*, and was a member of the judging panel for the 2012 Man Booker prize for fiction.

Introduction

Fiona Green

In December 1943, *New Yorker* editor Harold Ross fired off a memo
to Messrs. Stryker and Truax, intermediaries between the magazine's
editorial and business departments. It ended:

> I herewith presume to give you gentlemen a tip: Everybody in the business
> office that I have ever had dealings with is an arrant incompetent, save
> Stebbins and two or three members of the staff who were cruelly steamroll-
> ered out of this business after gallantly but hopelessly butting their head
> against a stone wall of stupidity that is thicker than the Japanese defenses on
> a South Sea atoll. You should be on your guard [. . .][1]

Like the unvarnished wit of the magazine's irascible editor, the standoff
between editorial and business sides is the stuff of *New Yorker* legend; the
wall of separation between them had been in place almost from the start,
when Harold Ross founded the magazine, with Raoul Fleischmann's
financial backing, in 1925.[2] This particular 1943 memo was the parting
shot in a series of exchanges prompted by Ross's discovery of two mistakes in the layout of the magazine shortly before it went to press. Both
of them, but for his intervention, might have jeopardised the immunity
of editorial from advertising. One error involved the placement of two
advertisements featuring drawings by prominent *New Yorker* cartoonists
– the kind of juxtaposition, Ross thought, that 'should be avoided'. 'In
the other instance', he wrote, 'an ad of the Boston & Maine Railroad was
run, featuring a railroad train, and on the opposite page, which was a full
page of text, was a drawing which also prominently featured a railroad
train. It was a very bad conflict.'[3] In both cases, as in the numerous other
ill-tempered exchanges preserved and recalled in *New Yorker* memos and
memoirs, Ross's complaint is that advertisements might be mistaken for
editorial, or that editorial could be misread as endorsement: two trains
on facing pages, and heading, as it happened, in the same direction,
might well have looked to be running on parallel lines.[4]

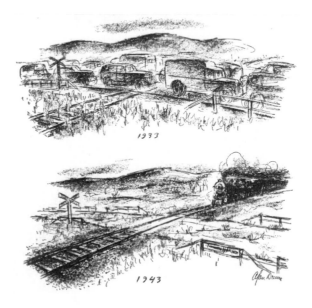

Figure I.1. Alan Dunn, Cartoon, *The New Yorker*, 27 November 1943, p. 58. © The New Yorker Collection.

Figure I.2. Boston and Maine Railroad advertisement, *The New Yorker*, 27 November 1943, p. 69.

In the issue of *The New Yorker* published on 27 November 1943, Alan Dunn's drawing of a railroad crossing appears on page 58, and the Boston and Maine ad on page 69; a last minute switch, and eleven pages, intervened to prevent the 'very bad conflict' that Ross had foreseen (Figs I.1, I.2). If there were any doubt in the advertisement over the freight train's purpose and direction, the slogan spells it out: 'One of America's railroads – all united for victory'. Alan Dunn's drawing, however, repays slower reading in relation to its historical moment. Most obviously, it is about the difference a decade makes: since Pearl Harbor, rubber and fuel rationing has erased auto traffic, and the highway has gone to seed. But Dunn is thinking about figurative journeys too – about the degree to which private pleasures and itineraries give way in wartime to collective plans. And one further thought perhaps hovers over this wordless cartoon: the duplicate drawing might tempt its reader to ponder what would happen if its two frames were overlaid. From a bird's-eye perspective – were it not for the passage of time – highway and railroad traffic would be on collision course; given that potential overview, it seems uncannily apt that Ross's timely adjustment to *The New Yorker*'s layout averted the accident he'd seen coming.

This moment in late 1943, along with the paper trail that preserves it, offer a wider perspective on *The New Yorker*, and a point of entry to the project of this book. The Second World War drained *The New Yorker* of staff, as it did other 'non-essential' industries: as Ross put it in his irate memo, 'Stebbins went to war and Weekes went to war, and the system broke down.'[5] Yet at the same time, global conflict afforded the magazine a business opportunity that would contribute significantly to its midcentury prosperity: the so-called 'Pony' edition distributed to the armed services gained for *The New Yorker* a following that stayed loyal after the war. Ross's biographer Thomas Kunkel and cultural historian Ben Yagoda have documented this, among other turning points in the magazine's fortunes, in their authoritative narratives of *The New Yorker*'s evolution from 'feather-light' humour magazine to American icon.[6] In beginning with Ross, this book starts where the magazine began, and where scholarly histories and personal memoirs have also found their points of departure and return.[7] But the 1943 memos provide an opening to this collection of essays for other reasons too. The story of a periodical is not, or not only, the story of its editors; it is also a narrative of intersections and adjacencies, of timeliness and accident, and of labour behind the scenes that is not visible in the finished product. It is to such matters as these, and particularly to their bearing on the crossing points between literary texts and periodical culture, that the essays collected in *Writing for 'The New Yorker'* variously attend.[8]

A magazine is, to repurpose a phrase of Tamara Follini's in this volume, an 'unstable compound', a shifting terrain of verbal, visual and historical contingencies that arise from its internal workings (decisions over acceptance and rejection, procedures for editing, checking, and production); in its published form (juxtapositions of editorial, cartoons, and advertising, arrangement into 'departments', visual constituents and page layouts); and in its external relations (readership, affiliations, and competition with other media).[9] The essays in this book converge on *The New Yorker* from a variety of such angles, in arguments conducted in several scales of magnitude. We read across and between *New Yorker* departments, with particular weighting towards fiction and poetry. One thing that brings the chapters together, and sometimes holds them apart, is the shifty preposition involved in 'writing *for*'. Whereas Sylvia Plath, for example, studied her markets and made a deliberate *New Yorker* pitch – her journal recalls 'the Watercolor of Grantchester meadows which [she] wrote bucolically "for" them'[10] – the letters exchanged between Marianne Moore and the Ford Motor Company ended up in the magazine almost by accident, yet seemed unmistakably to belong there. Between those extremes, writing 'for' *The New Yorker* encompasses a range of reciprocal adaptations, conscious or otherwise, between writer and periodical context. One thing that 'writing for' does not mean, in the case of this magazine, is writing under contract or to commission. The first-reading agreements between *The New Yorker* and a number of the writers discussed in this book were carefully named to distinguish them from contracts. They offered a yearly fee and increased per-line rates in exchange for the magazine's having first refusal on whatever a writer of fiction or a poet might produce, so allowing a degree of commitment and security on both sides.[11] Yet too long an attachment of this kind, or too close an identification with the magazine, presented its own risks, as, for example, in the case of John Cheever. In another instance, the exemption of novels from the first-reading agreement distinguished what John Updike wrote for *The New Yorker* from fiction of his that belonged elsewhere, and which might therefore seem differently weighted. Yet for these major figures, as also for Philip Roth, a whole writing career, and so the map of twentieth-century American fiction, might have turned out quite differently had they not in the first place found themselves writing for *The New Yorker*.

A weekly magazine is arguably no more than the sum of its ephemeral issues and its constituent parts, yet with *The New Yorker* a singular style and a recognisable ethos famously transcend its time-bound particulars: whether sharply urbane or stodgily complacent, brilliantly polished or superficial in its gloss, precise and exacting or pedantic and fussy, *The*

New Yorker seems, to its admirers and detractors alike, to have assumed a distinctive character, or characters, over time. Indeed it's hard to think of another twentieth-century magazine whose name transforms so readily into an adjective: *New Yorker* style, the *New Yorker* short story, *New Yorker* humour, have evolved, some readers have said, to the point of formulae, and have thereby restricted rather than fostered writerly talent and experiment.[12] The chapters in this book do not pretend to offer a complete history, survey or evaluation of *The New Yorker*, but they do test out in several dimensions the reciprocal relation of part to whole, some essays emphasising the part played by the magazine in the making of an individual writer, others examining the constitutive role of a writer or writers, an organising system, or a department, in the make-up of the magazine.

At certain intersections, a query hangs over one *New Yorker* character in particular: is there such a thing as a – or even 'the' – *New Yorker* reader? Mary Corey's study of the midcentury *New Yorker* cites reader surveys of 1949–59, which documented a loyal readership consisting of 'people who were likely to hold passports, drink alcohol, own binoculars, enjoy gardening, smoke cigarettes, and, if they lived outside of Manhattan, visit the city'.[13] Beyond these choice particulars, Corey rightly cautions against the fabrication of a readership on the basis of inferences from the magazine.[14] As Bharat Tandon points out in his chapter on Philip Roth, the routes plotted by individual *New Yorker* readers are too various for the magazine to have anticipated, or for criticism to track. Whether eagerly awaited and consumed from cover to cover, or idly browsed and put aside, *The New Yorker*, like other 'slick' or 'smart' weeklies, presents grounds for numerous kinds of legibility, including that entailed in its sometimes being allowed to pile up unread.[15] One aim of this book is to develop critical reading practices which, while they cannot hope to recapture the experience of any one – let alone every single – reader of the magazine, might go beyond the digital archive's binary of 'flip mode' and 'read mode' to inspect that range of mixed attentions, absorptions, and distractions practised by readers of this magazine, and by extension or contrast, of others.

The contributors to this book have situated their own readings of *The New Yorker* in relation to a variety of sources and contextual materials: we draw frequent comparisons, for example, with other magazines and newspapers that constitute the twentieth-century media ecology of which *The New Yorker* is part. Most of the eleven chapters also refer to unpublished archival material, and especially to documents held in the New York Public Library's New Yorker Records collection. When it opened its archive in 1994, *The New Yorker* gave remarkable access to its own inner workings, so making possible the scholarly volumes and articles referred to in this introduction, which have followed, and sometimes offered correctives to, the many memoirs and reminiscences published by *New Yorker* insiders. And by digitising in 2005 its entire back catalogue, the magazine has produced another vital resource for research – as well as one of its commercially profitable spinoffs. All the essays in this book have relied on facsimiles in the digital archive, and have benefited from the work of previous scholars whose labours seem all the more impressive for having been conducted before *The Complete New Yorker* was available in digital form.

The digital archive introduces yet more variables as regards readerly activity: with optical character recognition (aptly named, given the magazine's monocled mascot) the minutiae of advertisements as well as editorial are searchable, and available for close inspection.[16] Even so, it's vital to remember that searching high quality facsimiles is quite different from browsing the pages of the magazine in its pre-digital form. As with Michel de Certeau's administrative view of the city from the top of a skyscraper, the panoptic gaze of the digital archive and the strategic searches it enables can sometimes erase rather than illuminate the tactical manoeuvres and surprise encounters of those readers accustomed to browsing their magazines without a search engine.[17] Ultimately, this book reads *The New Yorker* as a print publication; we make no attempt to consider the still further set of contingencies in play for readers of, and writers for, the online *New Yorker*, nor to decide whether our operative definitions of 'magazine' and 'periodical' would continue to serve for a purely screen-based medium.

In drawing on unpublished and digital archive materials, and developing in relation to them an historicised close reading practice that is specific to magazine culture, this book participates in the expanding field of periodical studies, and in the larger material turn in literary and textual scholarship, and in modernist studies in particular. The three-volume *Oxford Critical and Cultural History of Modernist Magazines* is the most prominent and comprehensive publication among many recent monographs, essay collections, journal articles, and journals newly devoted to magazine culture.[18] Though the American volume of the *Oxford History* has an incisive chapter on 'Quality Magazines' that includes *The New Yorker*, the emphasis of the three volumes remains for the most part on 'little magazines'.[19] The character, longevity, and finances of early twentieth-century avant-garde periodicals differ in conspicuous ways from those of enduring, profitable, 'smart' publications such as *The New Yorker*. Yet in recent years too, long-held distinctions between the small, mid- and mass circulation press have begun to erode, and with them any straightforward set of oppositions between mainstream taste and modernist experiment, middlebrow culture and intellectual prestige, aesthetic value and commercial enterprise.

More so than many periodicals, *The New Yorker* recalls the shared etymology of magazine and *magasin*. In 1962 Seymour Krim lamented 'the descent of *The New Yorker* into an advertising showcase', and others have identified it as much with the luxury consumables as with the artistic and intellectual products it carries.[20] The first section of *Writing for 'The New Yorker'* concerns the magazine as both market-place and commodity. Faye Hammill begins at the beginning, focusing on *The New Yorker*'s first year, and on its positioning in relation to, and mediation for its readers of, 'the whole range of the [New York] press'. One important claim of this chapter is that by enabling its readers to become effortless insiders to low and highbrow cultures circulating elsewhere, *The New Yorker* established itself as a decidedly middlebrow product. For Harold Ross, as we've seen, the relation of magazine to market was deeply conflicted; as he well knew, the separation of business from editorial could not prevent – indeed, might even have exacerbated – the accidents occasioned by their coming together on the page.[21] Ross's 1943 memos witness his faith in systems that might pre-clude such contingencies, and his impatience with those who could not grasp or chose not to abide by them. Having pointed out the errors he had spotted, and roundly decried 'the present fantastically incompetent saphead procedure' that had led to them, Ross worked up to this:

> The suggestion that things go on as they are is ridiculous and incompetent, and to me at this moment it is heart-breaking, for it evidences the same old lazy, slovenly, muddling inertia which has characterised the management of this property for the last seventeen years.[22]

Sarah Cain reads Ross's organisational anxieties and fantasies in rela-tion to new sciences of management theory and information storage and retrieval, and proposes that the most notorious of *New Yorker* systems, its legendary fact-checking department, makes accuracy itself into a form of luxury commodity. The first section of the book closes with a contrastingly unsuccessful product, the marketing catastrophe that was the Ford Edsel, and the part played in it, as witnessed in a *New Yorker* 'Department of Amplification' column, by Marianne Moore.

Unlike the Ford Motor Company, *The New Yorker*'s first two editors, along with E. B. White, set little store by 'tipsters, pollsters, motivation-alists and dream-mongers';[23] rather than fashioning the magazine to meet the supposed desires of a certain kind of consumer, their purpose was to identify and foster writerly talent. Readers would follow. Yet despite this resistance to shaping itself to serve a particular market, self-fashioning has always been part of the *New Yorker* enterprise, and it is to this that section two of *Writing for 'The New Yorker'* turns. In the magazine's heyday, claims Renata Adler, 'it was just silly to imagine that a reader would be distracted from a piece [. . .] by the ads'. Later in her book, she returns, exasperated, to that 'silly notion, as though it were not possible to read if you are wearing nice clothes, or on a train, with billboards going by'.[24] Yet as Bharat Tandon's and Tamara Follini's chapters each suggest, the possibility of reading between commercial environments in the landscape and on the page, and the infiltration of reading consciousness by peripheral vision, may be exactly what underlies and entwines itself with fictions of selfhood in Philip Roth and John Cheever. Tandon examines the intersections of bodies, texts, and commerce in early twentieth-century metropolitan spaces such as Times Square, and finds them replete with the kinds of readable social indicator that would offer a setting, at midcentury, for the young Philip Roth's self-fashionings. Follini's essay on Cheever explores 'the beguiling vistas magazines offered for the wandering mind', and argues that Cheever's fictions take up from their print environment the possibility that 'being waylaid [. . .] may offer liberating, inspiriting ways by which to appropriate experience'.

In the case of Muriel Spark it was not so much the commercial milieu in and of *The New Yorker*, but its publishing systems and checking procedures, that had a shaping influence on fiction and autobiography. Deborah Bowman suggests that Spark 'experienced the process of publication itself as an experience of proof and proofing', and discovers in the archives evidence of the extent to which memory, selfhood, and the mechanisms of fiction involve for her their own kinds of archival storage and retrieval. *The New Yorker* was the making of Sylvia Plath in another way again: Plath's conscious bids for admission, Linda Freedman demonstrates, were shadowed by a less conscious set of tropes, of thickness and thinness, smoothness and transparency, that found their way into Plath's poetry, letters, and posthumously published journals.

It is generally agreed that after the war there was a sizable shift in the gravity of *The New Yorker*, and that it was due, in part, to groundbreaking pieces of journalism such as John Hersey's 'Hiroshima' (1946). In what would turn out to be the last year of his life, Harold Ross wrote,

War doesn't buffalo me professionally, everything being black and white in wartime, and peace doesn't, although journalistically it's not as simple as war, but I'm baffled by this in-between business. I started to get out a light magazine that wouldn't concern itself with the weighty problems of the universe, and now look at me . . .[25]

The last section of this book is about lightness and gravity, and the 'in-between business' that characterised *The New Yorker*, especially under the thirty-five year editorship of Ross's successor, William Shawn. Thomas Karshan takes seriously John Updike's light verse as well as his fictional and other writings for *The New Yorker*, and finds in them a kind of 'cartooning with words', a converse match for the writerly drawings of *New Yorker* artist Saul Steinberg. Of the many departments for which Updike wrote, it is sportswriting and its larger field of play that Kasia Boddy examines. As with Updike, celebrated columnists such as A. J. Liebling and Roger Angell learned from sports and brought to sportswriting particular forms of grace, lightness, and distance. Questions of spectatorship also come into Duncan Kelly's chapter on one of the weightiest *New Yorker* reporters, Hannah Arendt. The 'Reporter at Large' feature gave Arendt room to explore, in 'Eichmann in Jerusalem', the imperative to see things from another point of view, so bringing into focus larger currents in her thinking on political judgement. That William Shawn ran Arendt's five-part report untouched as far as substance was concerned, argues Kelly, testifies to the magazine's willingness to take risks with the writers it admired. The closing chapter of *Writing for 'The New Yorker'* brings the collection full circle, in returning to what Tom Perrin calls 'middlebrow culture's defining ambivalence toward modernism'. Perrin coins the term 'blustering' to characterise the in-between style of Dwight Macdonald, and finds in it 'an example of the modernism seemingly conspicuous by its absence from *The New Yorker*'.

At one point in the exchange of memos with which this introduction began, Harold Ross writes,

> Anyone who tries to lay out the ad pages without knowing what is on the opposite editorial pages is a fool, just a plain, helpless, asinine fool. Yet that is the practice that is being followed around here, I learn to my amazement from Mr. Fleischmann's memo. Was any effort made to find out what was going on on page 58? Nope. They just, by God, planted that Boston & Maine ad there and left the rest to chance. How, may I ask, did Mr. Bowen think that the proof of page 58 was going to get to him? Did he think I was going to bring it up and put it on his desk, or that some omnipotent pigeon, reading his mind, was going to fly into his office with it, or what?[26]

The time-consuming labours, eccentric personalities, and complex systems of production that lie behind the faultless surface of *The New Yorker* belong as much to the magazine's reality as to its mythology.

Yet no system of proofing, no God-like editor, nor omnipotent pigeon, can avert the accidents and contingencies of historical time and readerly liberty to which *The New Yorker*, like all periodicals – indeed all written texts – is subject. In that perspective, writing for *The New Yorker* means submitting fiction, verse, reportage, drawings, and in some sense also the writing self, to an irremediably accident-prone setting. The collaborative project of this book is to make that environment newly legible.

Notes

1. Harold Ross, memo to Lloyd Stryker and Hawley Truax, 6 December 1943, p. 2. New Yorker Records, box 1286, folder 6.
2. For the history of the separation between business and editorial – 'what staffers from both sides have always called church and state' – and the 'mortal antipathy' between Ross and Fleischmann, see Thomas Kunkel, *Genius in Disguise: Harold Ross of 'The New Yorker'* (New York: Random House, 1995), pp. 211–27 (pp. 212, 211).
3. Harold Ross, memo to Ik Shuman, copied to Raoul Fleischmann and Hawley Truax, 19 November 1943, New Yorker Records, box 1286, folder 6.
4. As Trysh Travis writes, 'not even a book-length work could do justice to Ross's heroic and hilarious struggles to keep the magazine's editorial and ad content pure and separate'. She goes on to quote from a number of office memos on this subject. See 'What We Talk About When We Talk About *The New Yorker*', *Book History*, 3 (2000), 253–85 (pp. 281–2, n. 21). *Letters From the Editor: The New Yorker's Harold Ross*, ed. Thomas Kunkel (New York: Modern Library, 2000) includes a sampling of Ross's office memos as well as letters to colleagues and contributors.
5. Ross, memo to Stryker and Truax, 6 December 1943, p. 1. According to this memo, Stebbins was in charge of advertising layout. Hobart Weekes was among the magazine's arbiters of style, grammar and facts. 'Almost every able-bodied man who wasn't drafted enlisted', writes Kunkel (*Genius in Disguise*, p. 353).
6. Ben Yagoda, *About Town: 'The New Yorker' and the World it Made* (New York: Scribner, 2000). Yagoda identifies the magazine's 'most revolutionary change' with its first decade, 1925–35 (p. 23), and his narrative proper begins with Ross's taking up residence in New York in 1919. Significantly, though, the prologue to this authoritative critical and cultural history opens with a wartime reminiscence (p. 11). 'Feather-light' is Kunkel's description (*Genius in Disguise*, p. 127).
7. The best-known memoir of the magazine's early period is James Thurber, *The Years with Ross* (Boston: Little, Brown, 1959). Several polemical accounts of the midcentury *New Yorker*, under William Shawn's quieter editorship (1952–87), revert to the Ross years as a golden age. For a particularly pointed example, see Seymour Krim, 'Who's Afraid of *The New Yorker* Now?', *Village Voice*, 8 November 1962, repr. in *Shake it for the World* (London: Allen & Busby, 1971). Renata Adler's controversial

Gone: The Last Days of 'The New Yorker' (New York: Simon & Schuster, 1999) identifies the start of the magazine's decline with Shawn's editorship. Whereas Adler regards Tina Brown's controversial period as editor (1992–98) as an egregious betrayal of Rossian principles, Judith Yaross Lee allows some credence to Brown's own claim that her editorship had 'revived the years with Ross'. See *Defining 'New Yorker' Humor* (Jackson: University of Mississippi Press, 2000), p. 19. For an excellent, comprehensive account of books and articles about *The New Yorker*, see the 'essays on sources' in Iain Topliss, *The Comic Worlds of Peter Arno, William Steig, Charles Addams and Saul Steinberg* (Baltimore: Johns Hopkins University Press, 2005).

8. As Iain Topliss points out, the extant scholarship on *The New Yorker* has come for the most part from historians, and historians of journalism. Topliss goes on: 'the large, complex questions *The New Yorker* raises offer an unusual opportunity for a scholar familiar with twentieth-century literature, recent literary theory, cultural history, and critical theory' (*The Comic Worlds*, p. 314). *Writing for 'The New Yorker'* takes up this opportunity, in offering interventions from literary scholars.

9. Here I am indebted to the summary of '*periodical codes* at play in any magazine', according to *The Oxford Critical and Cultural History of Modernist Magazines*, ed. Peter Brooker and Andrew Thacker, 3 vols (Oxford: Oxford University Press, 2009–13), vol. I, Britain and Ireland 1880–1955 (2009), p. 6. Brooker and Thacker acknowledge debts, in turn, to the 'bibliographic codes' identified by Jerome McGann in *The Textual Condition* (Princeton, NJ: Princeton University Press, 1991), p. 13.

10. *The Journals of Sylvia Plath 1950–1962*, ed. Karen V. Kukil (London: Faber, 2000), p. 477. Langdon Hammer notes that Plath doubly underlined the instruction 'study your markets' in her copy of *The Writer's Handbook*. See 'Plath's Lives: Poetry, Professionalism, and the Culture of School', *Representations*, 75 (Summer 2001), 61–88 (p. 77).

11. Trysh Travis seems to conflate the two in her informative and detailed note on what she terms '"first-look" contract[s]' ('What We Talk About', p. 284, n. 60); Langdon Hammer notes Plath's first-reading agreement, yet claims, because of it, that her late poems were produced for *The New Yorker* 'under contract' ('Plath's Lives', p. 84). Renata Adler puts it this way: 'it was in the nature of *New Yorker* contracts, under Shawn, that they were not really contracts. A typical agreement would consist of four points' (*Gone*, pp. 104–5). According to Kunkel, first-reading agreements with fiction writers differed from the 'drawing accounts' enjoyed by *New Yorker* fact writers: 'John Cheever and some of *The New Yorker*'s other fiction stars came to resent the fact that their journalistic counterparts were considered employees and received [. . .] reassuring weekly checks' (*Genius in Disguise*, p. 320). In neither case was writing commissioned; in the nuanced parlance of *New Yorker* arrangements, an idea 'suggested' to a writer differs from a commission as a contract does from an 'agreement'.

12. Brendan Gill, for example, claimed in a book timed to coincide with the magazine's fiftieth anniversary, that *New Yorker* fiction had now reduced itself to a formula. See *Here at 'The New Yorker'* (New York: Random House, 1975), p. 264. Janet Carey Eldred discusses fiction editor Katharine

White's grievances with this claim, and with Gill's book as a whole, in *Literate Zeal: Gender and the Making of a 'New Yorker' Ethos* (Pittsburgh: University of Pittsburgh Press, 2012), pp. 61–2. Seymour Krim holds the refinement of '*New Yorker* "style"' responsible for formulaic pieces such as 'the numberless "profiles" written by anonymous human machines who almost reduced art to science' ('Who's Afraid', p. 172).

13. Mary F. Corey, *The World Through a Monocle: 'The New Yorker' at Midcentury* (Cambridge, MA: Harvard University Press, 1999), p. 12.
14. Ibid., p. 16.
15. On not having time to read *The New Yorker*, see *Sex and the City*: Carrie (columnist for the *New York Observer*, fictionalised as the *New York Star*) and Miranda (lawyer, 'intellectual') are on the bus going to Atlantic City for the weekend. Miranda: 'I am so excited! I have been dreaming of being alone with these for months.' Carrie: 'I love that *The New Yorker* is your porn.' *Sex and the City*, Season 5 (2002), Episode 3, 'Luck Be An Old Lady'.
16. *The Complete New Yorker* DVD differs from the online archive available to subscribers as far as searching is concerned. DVD searches can be fine-tuned with limits to author/artist, department, year, and issue, with key words searched in the article abstracts that have been assembled over the years by the *New Yorker* librarians. In this format, the advertisements are visible, but not searchable. The online archive is searched through a combination of article abstracts and OCR, making the advertisements searchable, though it is not possible to refine the search by department, year, or artist/author.
17. See Michel de Certeau, 'Walking in the City', *The Practice of Everyday Life*, trans. Steven Rendall (Berkeley: University of California Press, 1984), p. 92.
18. *The Oxford Critical and Cultural History of Modernist Magazines*, ed. Peter Brooker and Andrew Thacker, 3 vols (Oxford: Oxford University Press, 2009–13), vol. I, Britain and Ireland 1880–1955 (2009); vol. II, North America 1894–1960 (2012); vol. III, parts 1 and 2, ed. Peter Brooker, Andrew Thacker, Sascha Bru, and Christian Weikop, Europe 1880–1940 (2013). The *Oxford History* evidences the established position of periodical studies in modernist scholarship, while Robert Scholes and Clifford Wulfman, *Modernism in the Magazines: An Introduction* (New Haven: Yale University Press, 2010), aimed primarily at students, testifies to its currency in pedagogy. Notable precursors to these volumes include Lawrence Rainey, *Institutions of Modernism: Literary Elites and Public Culture* (New Haven: Yale University Press, 1998), and Suzanne W. Churchill and Adam McKible's sharply prescient edited collection, *Little Magazines and Modernism* (Aldershot: Ashgate, 2007).
19. Faye Hammill and Karen Leick, 'Modernism and the Quality Magazines: *Vanity Fair* (1914–36); *American Mercury* (1924–81); *New Yorker* (1925–); *Esquire* (1933–)', in Brooker and Thacker, ed., *Oxford History*, vol. II, chapter 7. Churchill and McKible's working definition of 'little magazines' still serves: 'non-commercial enterprises founded by individuals or small groups intent upon publishing the experimental works or radical opinions of untried, unpopular, or under-represented writers. [...] these

journals are characteristically but not exclusively small-budget operations with short runs. Whatever the format, scope, or preferred topics of conversation, little magazines tend to share two features: a vexed relationship to a larger, mainstream public, and an equally vexed relationship to money' (*Little Magazines and Modernism*, pp. 6–7).

20. Krim, 'Who's Afraid', p. 175.
21. At one point in the 1943 exchange of memos, Ross 'recommend[s] the consolidation of the two make-up rooms, editorial and advertising, [. . .] if that were done it would go a long way to overcome the lack of liaison that exists between the two rooms'. The suggestion was not taken up, but it evidences Ross's attempts to pinpoint and manage the vital moment of encounter on the page between the magazine's separate departments. Harold Ross, memo to Fleischmann, Stryker, and Truax, 26 November 1943, p. 4, New Yorker Records, box 1286, folder 6.
22. Ibid., p. 3.
23. E. B. White, 'Letter from the North', *The New Yorker*, 5 April 1958, pp. 34–8 (p. 38).
24. Adler, *Gone*, pp. 21, 44.
25. Harold Ross, letter to Howard Brubaker, 22 January 1951, in Kunkel, ed., *Letters From the Editor*, p. 405.
26. Harold Ross, memo to Fleischmann, Stryker, and Truax, 26 November 1943, p. 2. Ray Bowen was the magazine's advertising director.

I Magazine and Marketplace

Chapter 1

The New Yorker, the Middlebrow, and the Periodical Marketplace in 1925

Faye Hammill

During the autumn of 1925, *The New Yorker*'s circulation and advertising revenues were increasing, following a financially troubled first summer. The 'Talk of the Town' column in the issue for 14 November included this paragraph:

> Observed on the elevated newsstand at Forty-second Street was *The New Yorker* prominently displayed between *True*, and *Snappy Stories*. This, says the circulation manager, is very, very, good news. Suicide Day for sincere members of the staff has been set for next Tuesday.[1]

Positioned beside a confession magazine and a girlie pulp, on a street which was at once spectacular and seedy, *The New Yorker* finds itself in a lucrative but unrespectable region of the city's cultural marketplace.[2] Its new visibility provokes both joy and despair amongst the magazine's staff. Their split reactions show up the tensions – between art and profit, ideals and fashions, exclusiveness and popularity – which animate, and also threaten, middlebrow publishing enterprises.

Forty-second Street would soon be described, in the finale to the eponymous 1933 musical film, as the place 'where the underworld can meet the elite'. It is an apt location for a magazine which traversed these different worlds. Reporters 'read' the city not only by visiting cultural sites and crime scenes, parties and prize fights, but also by surveying and quoting from the New York press. During the interwar period, *The New Yorker* was saturated with references to other magazines and newspapers, and with gossip about editors, columnists and press magnates. Its engagement with contemporary print media had a special significance during the earliest months of publication, as Harold Ross and his staff established the new magazine and negotiated its relationship with the American periodical scene. This chapter concentrates on *The New Yorker* in its first year, exploring its mediation of the whole range of the city's print culture. Balancing between fascination and ironic detachment in its attitude to the celebrity gossip and sensation disseminated in the tabloids, and similarly in its attitude to the high culture disseminated in avant-garde and smart magazines, *The New Yorker* adopted an intermediate position which affiliates it with middlebrow culture.

As multi-authored collages, incorporating a diverse mix of content and evolving over time, magazines are always difficult to position in relation to cultural hierarchies. *The New Yorker* has been classed, in different critical accounts, as modernist, as mass market, and as middlebrow. Trysh Travis understands it as part of a 'sophisticated popular literary culture' addressed to 'upper-middle-class men and women', and suggests that 'for lack of a better term, we might call [this] high middlebrow culture'.[3] Her unexpected conjunctions of 'popular' with 'upper-middle-class' and 'high' with 'middlebrow' reveals the way that the smart magazines force us to re-evaluate conventional cultural categories. Daniel Tracy connects *The New Yorker* firmly with the 'new middlebrow culture' which appeared in the interwar years and which, he argues, 'was not synonymous with mass culture but used the productive capacities of mass culture to capitalize on the new and growing obsession with cultural legitimacy'.[4] Expanding on this definition, 'middlebrow' may be taken to refer to a mode of circulation, reception, and consumption of cultural products. In more affirmative terms, middlebrow culture can be understood as a space where art encounters consumerism, and pleasure combines productively with self-improvement. But I also want to invoke what John Guillory refers to as the 'nervous ambivalence' of the middlebrow.[5] The word implies aspiration to membership of an elite, and all the modern 'smart' magazines, including *The New Yorker*, sell themselves through an appeal to the desire for social and verbal privilege. They overtly address an audience which is already sophisticated, yet covertly provide lessons in sophistication. The notion of 'middlebrow' also implies the existence of a recognisable high culture, and here, it begins to take on national as well as class-based inflections. Guillory argues that in America, 'there is no common culture (apart from mass culture) corresponding to the political entity of the American nation-state'. He proposes the Algonquin Round Table as an example of an attempt to create an American analogue for high culture: 'the self-destruction of the Round Table', he writes, 'gives birth to *The New Yorker*, lodged just at the interface of the middlebrow and a non-existent high culture'.[6] This chapter explores the precise ways in which the magazine 'lodged itself' in the American cultural scene of 1925.

The New Yorker and the popular press

In their influential article, 'The Rise of Periodical Studies', Sean Latham and Robert Scholes note, 'anyone who studies periodicals soon discovers that they are frequently in dialogue with one another'.[7] To illustrate this claim they choose the first issue of *The New Yorker*, dated 21 February 1925, which reprints a recent table of contents for *Hearst's International* magazine and describes it sardonically as 'the plot of America's great novel'.[8] According to Latham and Scholes, periodicals 'create and occupy typically complex and often unstable positions in sometimes collaborative and sometimes competitive cultural networks'.[9] The early *New Yorker* commented regularly on three broad categories of publication: first, the popular press (including pulps, mass market magazines, daily and Sunday papers, and cheap weeklies); second, its competitors (the 'slick' or 'smart' magazines such as *Vanity Fair*, and intellectual monthlies such as *The American Mercury*); and third, 'little' or avant-garde magazines.[10] By far the most attention was paid to the popular press, which was the source of many stories pursued in *The New Yorker*, as well as the object of its continual critique.

During the 1920s, Ralph Barton drew a regular full-page cartoon feature entitled 'Heroes of the Week' for *The New Yorker*. His contribution for 24 October 1925 includes a picture of Frank Hause, managing editor of the *New York Daily News*, which was the first successful American tabloid newspaper (Fig. 1.1). The caption reads:

> Colonel Frank Hause – Who, as editor of the *Daily News*, produces a newspaper which (along with its sister luminaries of the Fourth Estate, the *Graphic* and the *Mirror*) presents the news in the luscious form in which it is discussed over our best dinner tables by the people who read the *Times*.

High-society New Yorkers, Barton suggests, may only ever be *seen* reading quality papers, yet they know a surprising amount about the contents of the tabloids. Despite this mockery, *The New Yorker* itself offers readers access to daily papers and lowbrow magazines by frequently quoting from them and re-presenting their most remarkable stories. Readers of columns such as 'The Talk of the Town' and 'A Reporter at Large' could discover the sensational events and sordid places of the city without having to compromise their reputation as sophisticates by actually buying the *Daily News* or the *Mirror*. In addition, their sense of superiority to the readers of those newspapers is reinforced by *The New Yorker*'s continual sending-up of the melodrama and cliché which characterises tabloid reporting.

Heroes of the Week

SIGNOR GIULIO GATTI-CASAZZA—Who, as is usual with him in the Fall of the year, is being called a business man with no ear for music by a number of people who would rather like to be singing at the Metropolitan but aren't, but who, nevertheless, possesses an ear so finely attuned to sound that he can tell, nine times out of ten, the difference between the screech of an elevated train rounding a curve and the neighborhood soprano taking her lesson.

COLONEL FRANK HAUSE —Who, as editor of the *Daily News*, produces a newspaper which (along with its sister luminaries of the Fourth Estate, the *Graphic* and the *Mirror*) presents the news in the luscious form in which it is discussed over our best dinner tables by the people who read the *Times*.

J. S. McCULLOH—Who, although he is the president of the New York Telephone Company, is not, careful investigation has proved, personally responsible for the weekly changing of everybody's telephone number. A big printer of business and personal stationery is thought to be at the bottom of it.

CAPTAIN ROALD AMUNDSEN— Who has arrived in New York with the purpose of touring the country to raise funds for the purchase of a dirigible airship in which he intends to fly across the North Pole. The Navy Department would probably be glad to present the Captain, who seems to love combating difficulties, with one free of charge.

P. G. WODEHOUSE—Who, despite the vigilance of General Smedley Butler and Commissioner Enright, has been stolen, in a daring daylight robbery, from the *Saturday Evening Post*, by *Liberty*, the Weekly for Everybody but George Horace Lorimer.

Figure 1.1. Ralph Barton, 'Heroes of the Week', *The New Yorker*, 24 October 1925, p. 8. © The New Yorker Collection.

Alongside the 'Heroes of the Week' cartoon of Frank Hause was a drawing of an English author who spent much of his life in America: P. G. Wodehouse. The caption says that Wodehouse 'has been stolen, in a daring daylight robbery, from the *Saturday Evening Post*, by *Liberty*, the Weekly for Everybody but George Horace Lorimer'. Lorimer was editor of the long-established *Saturday Evening Post*, while *Liberty*, its new competitor, had been launched in 1924 and was already highly popular. The citation of *Liberty*'s subtitle, 'A Weekly for Everybody', works to differentiate it from *The New Yorker*, which was a weekly with a deliberately restricted target audience. Yet the distinctions which Barton's caption sets up are difficult to maintain. Some writers published in both the mass market and the smarter magazines: Morris Markey, for instance, wrote for *Liberty* as well as for *The New Yorker*, and Wodehouse himself had been publishing regularly in *Vanity Fair*.[11] Although Barton designates Wodehouse as a 'hero of the week', the caption presents him not as an autonomous artist but as a passive, though commercially valuable, property, rather like a football player who is being transferred. This cartoon feature is slippery and difficult to interpret, yet it clearly shows *The New Yorker*'s simultaneous fascination with, and disdain for, gossipy tabloids and mass circulation weeklies.

The question of periodicity is important here. The rhythms of reporting, writing, and production were, of course, different for dailies, weeklies, and monthlies, and a different conception of news governed each type of publication. For monthly magazines, the new was the fashionable; in daily papers, news was about events. The weeklies combined these two modes of novelty, slowing down the pace of current affairs by providing more space for comment and analysis, but speeding up the cycles of fashion by focusing on cultural and social events rather than lifestyles and seasonal trends. In this system, magazines were dependent on newspapers for updates on the daily life of the cities and regions they served. Yet since the amount, and significance, of each day's news could not be predicted, newspapers also borrowed the strategies of magazines, imitating their repeating, formulaic features such as advice columns and serial stories. As well as participating in this media ecology, *The New Yorker* also reflected on it. In October 1925, Morris Markey – himself a former newspaper man – offered the following analysis, in a long article on 'The Current Press':

> Driven by that necessity which hangs at the heels of all great commercial enterprises wherein huge sums of money are invested, the newspapers of to-day have cunningly fortified themselves against that bugaboo of other

times, a dull day in the news. So shrewdly have they fashioned their daily produce that the ebb and flow of spectacular events is no longer able to create a parallel rise and fall in circulation. The newspaper reading public has been taught to take sensation in its stride – and also to take in its stride slack times, when the happenings recorded on the front pages are trivial and unamusing.

This condition [. . .] was wrought by developing a backbone which depends not in the least upon the rise and fall of news: in short, the high perfection of comics, daily essays, verse, commuters' wit, women's pages, fiction pages – all the invariables which we group under the name of features.

These features, generally speaking, are terribly bad.[12]

Markey presents the modern newspaper as a commercial product. Its purpose, he suggests, is not to inform the public, nor to interpret current affairs, nor to build local or national communities, but purely to entertain, and thus to make money. In this account, a dramatic news item is a form of entertainment, and when none is available, distraction and amusement may be provided by stock journalistic contributions. The article also represents a defensive move, an attempt to locate *The New Yorker* itself in a very different territory, marked by a commitment to in-depth reporting, intellectual stimulation, originality, and high quality writing. The smart magazines often drew on this kind of exclusionary rhetoric, which was designed to separate their own subscribers from the undiscriminating reading public.

In his prospectus for the magazine, Harold Ross claimed 'it will print facts that it will have to go behind the scenes to get, but it will not deal in scandal for the sake of scandal nor sensation for the sake of sensation'.[13] *The New Yorker* not only castigated the sensationalism of the popular press, it also carried out extensive investigation into its operation: during the 1920s, Ross published numerous in-depth accounts of the underhand practices of editors, reporters, and financiers of various periodicals. *The New Yorker* also quoted copiously from a wide range of daily newspapers, with a variety of intentions and effects. Often, the papers' sycophancy, bias or crass reporting strategies came under fire. On 4 April 1925, the 'Talk of the Town' commented on the coverage of a splashy social event:

Mrs William Randolph Hearst, as all the world [. . .] should know, recently gave a party at the Hotel Ritz. [. . .] As was to be expected, the New York *American* and the New York *Mirror* scored beats on the occasion, both papers appearing on the streets early in the evening, before the party had begun, with full accounts of the night's festivities. [. . .]

'Under Joseph Urban's magic wand', the *American* had it, 'the famous Crystal Room was transformed into a gypsy camp, nestled away in a forest of pine trees. Gayly colored streamers were attached to the trees and an imitation gypsy fire added a picturesque touch. [. . .] [A]n organ-grinder and the inevitable monkey wandered among the guests, all of whom were in fancy dress.'

The name of the author of the *American*'s piece should be made public and broadcast. O! the bitter cynicism, and O! the glorious venom of the man! 'The inevitable monkey', he writes, and thereby he achieves in three words what lesser and cheaper authors could scarcely hint at in three thousand.[14]

This piece has great fun at the expense of the lowbrow papers because of their cliché style, their fawning over the rich, and their lack of objectivity – the two papers quoted were both owned by the media magnate William Randolph Hearst. The impression of the event as an orchestrated media spectacle is reinforced by the references to the fancy dress and imitation fire, and by the mention of the stage designer Joseph Urban. The article certainly doesn't encourage *New Yorker* subscribers to start taking the Hearst papers. But it *does* convey the substance of what they were reporting, so that its readers are kept up to date on tabloid gossip (or, what 'all the world should know') without having to soil their hands with the actual newspapers.

Morris Markey's 'Reporter at Large' column covered topics such as criminal cases, scandals, Prohibition, jails, baseball, royal visits, scientific evenings, concerts, spiritualism, prize fighters and preachers. But his accounts focus primarily on the way that these sensational events were reported in the press. Sometimes he even incorporates whole articles from other publications into his column, as he does in his piece on the murder of the boxer Battling Siki:

When the afternoon papers, a day or two since, announced with the customary excitement that Mr Battling Siki had been foully assassinated, notions of a gaudy obituary in his behalf to fill this present space came into my head. Most of our news these days is melodrama – but Mr Siki's passing differed from the rest in being superb melodrama, embellished with the touch of irony. Here was a giant out of Africa, a debonair and merry blackguard with the soul of a peacock, who had flipped his fingers at civilization [. . .]

Preparing for this piece of mine, I even went so far as to inspect Mr Siki's mortal remains. At the morgue, where his black body lay upon a white marble slab, I stared at his physical magnificence, at the leonine muscles of his flanks, the lean sculptured legs, the incredibly perfect biceps. And then, with deep chagrin, I discovered that there was no need for my piece to be written after all. Mr James M. Cain, on the editorial page of the *World*, had already done it.

But since Mr Cain said, in a brief flight of rich and gusty prose, most of the things which would have gotten, in some fashion, into this department anyway, I append forthwith the text of his composition. Mr Cain:

'What a monstrous fellow was this Battling Siki who has just been bumped off in so lamentable a fashion! Here was the brute primeval: musing on him, one could conceive him as the ancestor of the whole human race. [. . .] He had, it is true, the mentality of a backward toad [. . .] But he had the soul of a god.'[15]

This article plays up to the public fascination with violence and the exotic, and it shows the reporter 'reading' the city by visiting some of its less salubrious locations, such as the morgue.[16] But the main activity of the 'Reporter at Large' is actually reading the newspapers. The Cain obituary literally 'fills the space' where *The New Yorker*'s obituary might have been. There is a touch of humour here, at the expense of James Cain's rather grand style, but on the whole, the tone of the reprinted obituary is not dissimilar from that of Markey's own writing. The *New York World* was an entirely different kind of daily paper from the Hearst tabloids: a stylish and witty publication, it was edited by Herbert Bayard Swope with contributions from several members of the Algonquin Round Table. There was some exchange of staff between the *New York World* and *The New Yorker*: indeed, James Cain himself would at one point become *The New Yorker*'s managing editor. The extract from this paper, then, represents another form of position-taking in the media networks of the city, as Markey aligns the magazine with its closest equivalent in the newspaper world.

Throughout its history, *The New Yorker* has, of course, been influential in the construction of New York as a centre of elite culture and style. Yet in its early years the magazine was much more inclined to attack the poor taste and disappointing intellectual level of the city's inhabitants; its readers, therefore, were inevitably hailed as atypical, superior to the wider urban community. An article entitled 'Limitations of Intellectuals' was signed simply 'The Professor':

> New York is a most sophisticated city. It is fastidious, aesthetic. It is open to criticism, perhaps, as to its morals and its business methods, but you've got to hand it to the metropolis for its insistence upon good taste. It elects and re-elects John F. Hylan for Mayor. Its choice in literature is the illustrated *News*. Its favorite play is 'Abie's Irish Rose'. The explanation of all this is found in every Fifth Avenue bus. It is because we love nice things.[17]

Hylan's 1917 campaign to become mayor of New York was backed by Hearst, and *The New Yorker*'s antipathy to Hylan is connected to its contempt for Hearst's newspapers. *Abie's Irish Rose* was a highly popular and long-running Broadway show, but was widely panned by critics for its trite sentimentality. It was the play which Robert Benchley, in his capsule reviews of current theatre for *Life*, famously labelled with just these words: 'Hebrews 13:8'. The verse reads: 'Jesus Christ, the same yesterday, and today, and forever.' As to 'Because you love nice things', this was the company slogan of Van Raalte, a New York-based manufacturer of high-end silk, leather and hosiery products. This slogan has been chosen as a satiric target because of the specific resonances of the word 'nice' in the smart magazines. They used it disparagingly to designate a kind of unthinking, sentimental respectability, the exact opposite of the sophistication to which the magazines themselves aspired.[18] '*The New Yorker* was sophistication in the form of a weekly magazine', writes Ben Yagoda, 'it was knowing, a trifle world-weary, prone to self-consciousness and irony, scornful of conventional wisdom or morality, resistant to enthusiasm or wholehearted commitment of any kind, and incapable of being shocked'.[19] The sophisticated reading position which the magazine constructed for its subscribers also depended on their recognition of contemporary references and current humour. In my extract from the 'Limitations of Intellectuals' article – as in several of the other passages I quote in this chapter – the density of contemporary reference is considerable. I need to explain the references, in order to make the point of the extracts clear to a twenty-first-century reader. Yet these explanations inevitably impair the immediacy of the writing. We can never reconstruct the contemporary audience's sense of being part of a select group who share a certain cultural and local knowledge.

The New Yorker and its competitors

The second element of *The New Yorker*'s response to metropolitan print culture is its partly admiring, partly humorous commentary on its direct competitors. As Sharon Hamilton has persuasively argued, when *The New Yorker* was established, its primary model was *The Smart Set*, edited by George Jean Nathan and H. L. Mencken.[20] *The Smart Set* ceased publication in 1923, and the following year, Mencken founded *The American Mercury*. The light, yet highly literate tone of *The New Yorker* owes something to these models, and also to the other leading 'smart' monthly, *Vanity Fair* (1914–36), edited by Frank Crowninshield and published by Condé Nast. Some of *The New Yorker*'s regular features were comparable to those used by Mencken and Crowninshield: for instance, its 'Newsbreaks' feature was reminiscent of the 'Americana' column in the *Mercury*, while 'Heroes of the Week' is both an imitation and a parody of the Halls of Fame in the Condé Nast glossies. Yet *The New Yorker*'s visual style, its relationship to authors and advertisers, and its attitude to modernism are all markedly different from those of its competitors.[21]

Vanity Fair was much more interested in high culture than either of the others, and at the same time, it published far more advertising. It was also more internationally orientated. By contrast, the localised sphere of *The New Yorker*, and the information it offered on entertainment and cultural events in the city itself, was – and remains – one of its main selling points, both for readers and for advertisers. *The American Mercury* was different again: it was not illustrated, whereas pictures (though of different types) were crucial to the appeal of both the others. *Vanity Fair* commissioned work from most of the major photographers of the era, and was instrumental in the development of celebrity portraiture and modern fashion photography. It also published cartoon features.[22] *The New Yorker* did not use any photographs, and explicitly rejected superfluous illustration: a 'Talk' piece of May 1925 remarked contemptuously on 'the circulation value of pictures in a particularly illiterate city' and criticised several of the Sunday papers for hastily adding extra picture pages in order to boost sales.[23] However, *The New Yorker*'s cartoons and drawings have always been one of its most distinctive features, functioning as an important form of reporting or commentary in themselves. The *Mercury* and *Vanity Fair* also laid great emphasis on the individuality and high quality of their contributing authors, while, in contrast, *The New Yorker*'s articles, in its early years, were mainly written by staff or by employees of other periodicals writing under pseudonyms. Indeed, Ross tried to construct a sort of unified 'New Yorker' point of view and sense of humour, rather than emphasising diversity of opinion and individual styles.

The New Yorker's references to the smart magazines and their editors work both to reinforce its place in the sophisticated world of these magazines and to differentiate it from its rivals. The audiences for these periodicals certainly overlapped, and they advertised in one another's pages. *The New Yorker* accepted full-page ads for the *Mercury*, but at the same time, it ran cartoons of Mencken and Nathan, and irreverent paragraphs of gossip about them.[24] 'The Talk of the Town' noted in May 1925: 'Mr George Jean Nathan's plans still engage the attention of a portion of our citizenry, who seem to be taking sides.'[25] This was on the question of whether Nathan would leave the *Mercury*. The implication is that the 'portion of our citizenry' who are interested in Mencken and Nathan include many *New Yorker* readers. Indeed, these men were highly influential tastemakers, and they were also New York celebrities, whose career moves and personal lives were considered 'news'.[26] Another paragraph on Nathan appeared in 'The Talk of the Town' on 3 October:

Mr George Jean Nathan has issued his Fall denials. Not true, he says, that he has sold his interest in the *American Mercury*. Not true that he has severed relations with Mr Henry L. Mencken. Not true that he is going to Italy to write a novel. Not true that he is to write for screen. Not true that he is married. Not true that he is to do daily dramatic criticism – only once a week, Sundays, for the *Morning Telegraph*, on a one-year contract. Not true that he issues denials.[27]

This paragraph uses a strategy similar to that of Markey's 'Reporter at Large' column. Markey quotes from the tabloids, recirculating their sensational stories even as he abuses the papers themselves for their excessive sensationalism. The 'Talk of the Town' columnists likewise repeat rumours – in this instance, with the excuse that they are reporting on Nathan's denial of them. This is done self-consciously, and to comic effect, but it nevertheless functions to disseminate many of the stories taken from other papers, and to confirm some of the rumours – the one about *The Morning Telegraph*, for instance, was true, as might be guessed from the sudden increase in the level of detail for that item in the list.

In October of *The New Yorker*'s first year, a broadly admiring, though still flippant, 'Heroes of the Week' cartoon featured Frank Crowninshield:

> – Who, besides being the genius behind the practically perfect *Vanity Fair*, has always found time to do good turns to the most out-of-the-way people and to devote an enormous amount of energy to various projects for the advancement of this village among the civilized communities of the globe. His latest good deed is the memorial exhibition of the works of George Bellows, which opened at the Metropolitan Museum last Monday.[28]

George Bellows was an important American painter of urban scenes, associated with the Ashcan School. The cartoon caption evinces serious admiration for both painter and curator, even though Crowninshield is also humorously represented as a sort of boy scout figure, doing good turns. On the same page, Barton drew Franklin P. Adams, a frequenter of the Algonquin Round Table and columnist in the *New York Tribune* and *New York World* newspapers, being plugged for doing nothing-in-particular in a way which seems to take off his own repeated plugs for his friends in his 'Conning Tower' and 'Diary of our own Samuel Pepys' columns: 'Franklin P. Adams – Who, after having masqueraded for years as the ugly duckling of journalism, has blossomed forth in a dashing moustache.' Represented alongside Crowninshield and Adams is the novelist Sinclair Lewis:

> – Who in the current issue of the *American Mercury*, has hunted down and exposed to the light the Greenwich Villagers who have invaded and ruined

that once sweet refuge, the Café du Dome in Montparnasse. This will, of course, clear Montparnasse of the arty as much as Main Street has been cleared of Babbitts.

Analysing these light and witty passages too closely does, of course, tend to puncture their effect, and it may be too obvious to state that the joke in Barton's caption here is mainly at Lewis's expense. It suggests that his criticisms of expatriates will be ineffective, and perhaps also that his conception of what Montparnasse ought to be is idealistic. The mockery is quite genial, though, and in fact, Lewis was among the few novelists whom Harold Ross actually admired. H. L. Mencken also championed Midwestern regionalism.[29] In his last issue of *The Smart Set*, Mencken contrasted authors such as Lewis and Sherwood Anderson, whom he described as 'sophisticated, disillusioned, free from cant' with the 'posturing' groups of authors associated with *The Dial*, *Broom* and *The Little Review*.[30] In this respect, *The New Yorker* is aligned with Mencken's magazines, since they all tend to deride the expatriates in Paris (in spite of a certain fascination with them), and prefer a realist and/or comic aesthetic. Both Ross's and Mencken's magazines privilege, on the whole, literature with affinities to journalism.

The 'Hall of Fame' features which appeared in *Vanity Fair* and also in Condé Nast's *Vogue* often adopt a flippant tone, and provocatively juxtapose stars from the realms of high and low culture.[31] However, they only include celebrities who are being seriously proposed as worthy of admiration. The mixture is different in 'Heroes of the Week': Barton rather fiercely satirises some of the characters he depicts, while even those who might be counted among *The New Yorker*'s real heroes are gently mocked by the captions and the style of the drawings. The very title, 'Heroes of the Week', is suggestive of an ephemeral form of fame, depending precisely on media attention, rather than on long-term achievement. The substitution of cartoons for the attractive, posed photographs used in the Halls of Fame renders this difference visually. The difference is analogous to the divergent attitude to modernism exhibited by the two magazines in the interwar years.

Vanity Fair often printed parodies of modernist styles, but it also published modernists themselves, and gave serious and extensive consideration to their work. *The New Yorker*, on the other hand, did not print avant-garde writing, and was often – though not invariably – hostile to literary and artistic experiment.[32] It did, however, devote a certain amount of space to modernism, in the form of reviews, parodies, cartoons and news of the modernist scene. Over the course of the 1920s and early 1930s, *The New Yorker* began to take notice, occasionally, of modernist little magazines, such as *Poetry* in Chicago and *The Dial* and *The Little Review* in New York. Magazines published by American expatriates in Paris, such as the *transatlantic review* and *transition*, also received attention, usually in the 'Paris Letter' column, which Janet Flanner contributed for five decades, beginning in 1925.[33] This coverage ranged from passing remarks through gossip about editors to detailed discussion of the authors being published in the little magazines. *The New Yorker*'s audience could thus become familiar with the new publications and current debates of the modernist elite without going to the trouble of trying to decipher the work of Stein or Joyce.

This tendency was not, however, fully established in 1925, and there are only stray references during the magazine's first year. An extended comic series, 'The Making of a Magazine: A Tour Through the Vast Organization of *The New Yorker*' ran during 1925, and it pretends that the magazine has been established for decades and occupies an enormous, grand building. An episode entitled 'A Bird's Eye View of our Special Departments' claimed:

> On the forty-sixth floor, for example, is located the Initial Department, where proper nouns are sent to be capitalized. [. . .] These Capital Letters are used to begin every sentence in *The New Yorker*, a style which has since been copied by all the publications in the country, with the exception of certain vers libre magazines in Chicago.[34]

This slightly puzzling remark is an insider joke, since Harriet Monroe, editor of the Chicago-based *Poetry*, disliked lines of verse which started with lower-case letters, and wrote on copy submitted to her, 'begin all lines with Caps'.[35] Daniel Tracy notes in his comparative discussion of *The New Yorker* and *Vanity Fair* that their jokes about, and parodies of, modernism signal 'a genre of middlebrow mastery and playful display of expertise in a variety of forms. It communicates the sense of a circle of well-informed friends.'[36] This might explain the remark about *Poetry*. The only other reference to an American little magazine which I have found in any of the 1925 issues is in the 'Talk of the Town' column for 4 April. It mentions 'a woman from St Louis, who comes to New York about every other year, like a copy of the *Dial*'.[37] This reference, again, benefits from unpacking: *The Dial*, in its 1920s incarnation, actually had a larger circulation than any of the other modernist magazines: it reached 14,000 in 1922.[38] At the same time, it was expensively priced at 50 cents a copy, and presented itself as a collectors' item, durable and beautiful like an art book.[39] It may, therefore, have struck the *New Yorker* columnists as a product which deliberately made itself scarce. This, as numerous recent critics have argued, is one of the primary strategies by which modernist artworks accrue cultural prestige.[40]

Conclusion: *The New Yorker* and the middlebrow

In its earliest issues, through references to other magazines and papers, *The New Yorker* negotiates its position and status in the urban periodical marketplace. Ranging freely from high to lowbrow publications, it effectively mediates the whole range of the city's press for its readers. Its attitude to contemporary print culture positions *The New Yorker* as a distinctly middlebrow institution, although this is unlikely to have been a word its inner circle would have favoured. Ben Yagoda describes the magazine as follows:

> It was rarely receptive to elliptical, experimental, gritty, or subversive artists, or to work that came from the margins of society. [. . .] Yet *The New Yorker* at its best [. . .] had a unique quality in our literary culture. It was mindful of readers, aiming to amuse them, delight them, instruct them, or transport them; it always respected their intelligence and never pandered.[41]

What is this but a definition of middlebrow? The combination of entertainment with instruction is typical of the institutions of middlebrow culture, and often goes along with a resistance to challenging or experimental art forms. Yet Yagoda does not apply the label 'middlebrow' to the magazine.[42] The word appears only twice in his book, once in reference to the type of fiction which Edmund Wilson disparaged in his reviews for the magazine during the 1940s, and once to describe the dominant opinion of *The New Yorker* among academics in the postwar years ('a pablum for the middlebrow masses').[43] The word 'sophistication', by contrast, is used a great many times; indeed, a whole chapter is devoted to this topic. Yagoda's approving use of 'sophisticated' and careful avoidance of 'middlebrow' suggests that he thinks these two terms are not compatible. I would argue, by contrast, that early twentieth-century middlebrow culture was partly defined by a fascination with sophistication. Nina Miller in her chapter on the Algonquin Round Table in *Making Love Modern*, writes:

> The periodical forms of popular modernism – cartoons, newspaper columns, farcical sketches, short fiction, and the glossy magazines of urban life – comprised the most prominent area in the 1920s for the negotiation of modern selfhood, a selfhood that came to be (and in many ways, still is) defined by irony, urbanity, and humor. More than any other discursive project of the time, middle-brow culture made modern selfhood its explicit and relentless

business. Meeting modernity head-on, it answered the crisis of value and dislocation with the heartbreakingly (and deceptively) simple panacea of style.[44]

Periodicals which participated in the interwar middlebrow project often achieved a delicate blending of such apparently incompatible ingredients as sentiment and sophistication, optimism and disillusionment, frivolity and engagement, conservatism and subversion. This blend was maintained by *The New Yorker* in later decades, and while it partly accounted for the magazine's continued success, its perceived lightness of tone would infuriate some midcentury commentators. Media theorist Marshall McLuhan wrote in his polemic *Counterblast* (1954): 'BLAST ... THE NEW YORKER whimsical sycophant of CREAM PUFF culture.'[45] His view of *The New Yorker* as a flattering tribute to an American culture which is in fact hollow, light and fluffy chimes with John Guillory's description of it as 'lodged just at the interface of the middlebrow and a non-existent high culture'.[46] Yet McLuhan's word 'whimsical' is actually key to understanding *The New Yorker*'s careful construction of a detached urbanity, a tone which resists analysis, categorisation, and even parody.[47] Indeed, the commodification of taste and sophistication, an important aspect of middlebrow culture, was crucial to the sense of verbal privilege on which magazines such as *The New Yorker* depended. Harold Ross commented, 'my theory was that the more local humour is, the better it is within its limited circle'.[48] This notion of the limited circle, the in-crowd of *New Yorker* readers, is crucial to the magazine's pose of sophistication, and one of the ways in which it appealed to this localised community was through extensive reference to the print culture of the city. Engaging with, evaluating, and mocking the other periodicals of 1920s New York, Ross's magazine addressed a readership of broad interests yet discerning tastes, positioning itself, in the process, as a tastemaker and a cultural arbiter.

Notes

1. 'The Talk of the Town', *The New Yorker*, 14 November 1925, pp. 1–5 (p. 1).
2. See the Virtual Newsstand for the summer of 1925, created by David Earle and his students, for an overview of the variety of titles appearing on an American newsstand <http://uwf.edu/dearle/enewsstand/enewsstand_files/Page333.htm> (accessed 1 May 2014).
3. Trysh Travis, 'What We Talk About When We Talk About *The New Yorker*', *Book History*, 3 (2000), 253–85 (p. 254).
4. Daniel Tracy, 'Investing in "Modernism": Smart Magazines, Parody, and Middlebrow Professional Judgment', *Journal of Modern Periodical*

Studies, 1.1 (2010), 38–63 (p. 40). Janet Carey Eldred claims similarly that 'the *New Yorker*, well into the 1960s, was solidly middlebrow'. See *Literate Zeal: Gender and the Making of a 'New Yorker' Ethos* (Pittsburgh: University of Pittsburgh Press, 2012), p. 47.

5. John Guillory, 'The Ordeal of Middlebrow Culture', Review of *The Western Canon* by Harold Bloom, *Transition*, 67 (1995), 82–92 (p. 90).

6. Ibid., pp. 83, 90.

7. Sean Latham and Robert Scholes, 'The Rise of Periodical Studies', *PMLA*, 121.2 (2006), 517–31 (p. 529).

8. 'Of All Things', *The New Yorker*, 21 February 1925, pp. 1–2 (p. 1).

9. Latham and Scholes, 'The Rise of Periodical Studies', p. 529.

10. 'Pulps' were pulp paper monthlies publishing genre fiction and confessions, consisting of densely packed type with few illustrations, and intended for a wide audience. 'Slicks' were so-named because of their glossy paperstock; in a larger page size with different departments and lots of images, they positioned themselves as aspirational. At different times, mass circulation popular magazines, and also medium circulation 'smart' magazines, have adopted this format. Little magazines used diverse print formats, published the avant-garde and experimental, and appealed to intellectually elite audiences. *The New Yorker* was closest to the slick format, though it was never a luxury production like, for instance, *Vanity Fair*.

11. Markey's best-known article in *Liberty*, 'Alcoholics and God', appeared on 10 September 1939.

12. Morris Markey, 'The Current Press', *The New Yorker*, 24 October 1925, pp. 15–16 (p. 15).

13. Harold Ross, 'Announcing a New Weekly Magazine' (1924), repr. in Thomas Kunkel, *Genius in Disguise: Harold Ross of 'The New Yorker'* (New York: Random House, 1995), Appendix I, p. 440.

14. 'The Talk of the Town', *The New Yorker*, 4 April 1925, pp. 1–5 (p. 1).

15. Morris Markey, 'A Reporter at Large', *The New Yorker*, 26 December 1925, pp. 13–14 (p. 13).

16. At the same time, the representation of Battling Siki accords with contemporary animalistic and primitive stereotypes. Ben Yagoda notes, 'to say that the *New Yorker* traditionally held itself at a remove from racial matters would be a significant understatement. [. . .] In the early days, black people were stereotypically depicted in short stories, cartoons, and advertisements as servants, Pullman porters, and comic figures.' See *About Town: 'The New Yorker' and the World it Made* (New York: Scribner, 2000), p. 316. Siki's death was both violent and scandalous: he was murdered when drunk, probably following brawls in a bar. For a discussion of the journalistic rendering of scandal in interwar New York, and of the prominence of expressive bodies in urban print culture, see Will Straw, 'Squawkies and Talkies', *Parallax*, 14.2 (2008), 20–30.

17. The Professor, 'Limitations of Intellectuals', *The New Yorker*, 11 April 1925, p. 19.

18. On the smart magazines' aspiration to sophistication, see Yagoda, *About Town*, p. 57; on niceness see Faye Hammill, *Sophistication: A Literary and Cultural History* (Liverpool: Liverpool University Press, 2010), pp. 132, 136.

19. Yagoda, *About Town*, p. 57.
20. Sharon Hamilton, 'The First *New Yorker*? *The Smart Set* Magazine, 1900–1924', *The Serials Librarian*, 37.2 (1999), 89–104.
21. Tracy proposes that 'in 1925, Harold Ross would fashion *The New Yorker* [...] after *Vanity Fair* and the more persistently humorous smart magazine *Life*' ('Investing in "Modernism"', p. 44). This seems doubtful. My reading of these magazines is more in accordance with Yagoda's. He comments: '*Life* and especially *Judge* were suffused with an old-fashioned, heavy strain that stood out in the airy twenties like a mahogany secretary in an art deco penthouse' (*About Town*, p. 35), adding that 'Ross would never have thought of starting a publication in any significant way modeled on *Vanity Fair*. [...] He never developed the slightest interest in or appreciation of music, fine art, or highbrow literature, and *Vanity Fair* was steeped in all three' (p. 37).
22. On *Vanity Fair* and fashion photography, see Tobia Bezzola, 'Lights Going All Over the Place', in *Edward Steichen: In High Fashion. The Condé Nast Years: 1923–1937*, ed. William A. Ewing and Todd Brandow (London: Thames and Hudson, 2008), pp. 187–97; on celebrity portraiture, see Terence Pepper, 'The Portrait Photograph in the Modern Age', *Vanity Fair Portraits: Photographs 1913–2008*, ed. David Friend, Christopher Hitchens and Terence Pepper (London: National Portrait Gallery, 2008); on cartoon features, especially those by Anne Harriet Fish, see Faye Hammill, *Women, Celebrity, and Literary Culture Between the Wars* (Austin: University of Texas Press, 2007), pp. 35–8.
23. 'The Talk of the Town', *The New Yorker*, 2 May 1925, pp. 1–6 (p. 2).
24. See, for example, *The New Yorker*, 26 December 1925, p. 1.
25. 'The Talk of the Town', *The New Yorker*, 2 May 1925, pp. 1–6 (p. 3).
26. On Mencken and Nathan as tastemakers, see Sharon Hamilton, 'American Manners: *The Smart Set* (1900–29); *American Parade* (1926)', in *The Oxford Critical and Cultural History of Modernist Magazines*, ed. Peter Brooker and Andrew Thacker, 3 vols (Oxford: Oxford University Press, 2009–13), vol. II: North America 1894–1960 (2012), pp. 224–48.
27. 'The Talk of the Town', *The New Yorker*, 3 October 1925, pp. 1–5 (p. 4).
28. Ralph Barton, 'Heroes of the Week', *The New Yorker*, 17 October 1925, p. 6.
29. M. K. Singleton, *H. L. Mencken and the 'American Mercury' Adventure* (Durham, NC: Duke University Press, 1962), pp. 73–7.
30. H. L. Mencken, *H. L. Mencken's Smart Set Criticism*, ed. William H. Nolte (Washington, DC: Gateway Editions, 1987), p. 331.
31. For discussion see Hammill, *Sophistication*, pp. 154–63, and Michael Murphy, 'One Hundred Percent Bohemia: Pop Decadence and the Aestheticization of the Commodity in the Rise of the Slicks', in *Marketing Modernisms: Self-Promotion, Canonization, Rereading*, ed. Kevin J. H. Dettmar and Steven Watt (Ann Arbor: University of Michigan Press, 1996), pp. 61–89.
32. For an overview of *The New Yorker*'s relationship with modernism, see Faye Hammill and Karen Leick, 'Modernism and the Quality Magazines: *Vanity Fair* (1914–36); *American Mercury* (1924–81); *New Yorker* (1925–); *Esquire* (1933–)', in Brooker and Thacker, ed., *Oxford History*,

vol. II, pp. 176–96 (pp. 185–90). For an in-depth account, see Tracy, 'Investing in "Modernism"'. I would, however, dispute Tracy's claim that Ross's magazine 'from its earliest issues, championed modernist experimentation' (p. 39). Although *The New Yorker* certainly published some art and book reviews which protest against old-fashioned, conventional styles and praise innovation, there are very few wholly favourable reviews of high modernist works. Even those columnists who do acknowledge the greatness of modernist novels still dissuade subscribers from attempting to read them.

33. In her first letter, Flanner commented on a new English magazine, *The Calendar of Modern Letters*, in connection with its attempted publication of the 'Anna Livia Plurabelle' section of Joyce's 'Work in Progress'. Genêt [Janet Flanner], 'Paris Letter', *The New Yorker*, 10 October 1925, pp. 26–7 (p. 27).

34. 'A Bird's Eye View of our Special Departments', *The New Yorker*, 14 November 1925, inside front cover.

35. Helen Carr, '*Poetry: A Magazine of Verse* (1912–36), "Biggest of Little Magazines"', in Brooker and Thacker, ed., *Oxford History*, vol. II, pp. 40–60 (p. 56).

36. Tracy, 'Investing in "Modernism"', p. 56.

37. 'The Talk of the Town', *The New Yorker*, 4 April 1925, pp. 1–5 (p. 5).

38. Christina Britzolakis, 'Making Modernism Safe for Democracy', in Brooker and Thacker, ed., *Oxford History*, vol. II, pp. 85–102 (p. 86).

39. Ibid., pp. 93, 100–1.

40. For a particularly incisive account of this process, see Aaron Jaffe, *Modernism and the Culture of Celebrity* (Cambridge: Cambridge University Press, 2005). Jaffe draws on Lawrence Rainey's foundational study, *Institutions of Modernism: Literary Elites and Public Culture* (New Haven: Yale University Press, 1998), as well as on recent work on modernism's relationship to the marketplace and to the celebrity system.

41. Yagoda, *About Town*, p. 21.

42. Nor does Mary F. Corey, *The World Through a Monocle: 'The New Yorker' at Midcentury* (Cambridge, MA: Harvard University Press, 1999), which avoids the word altogether.

43. Yagoda, *About Town*, pp. 216, 239. There is an entry on *The New Yorker* 'as a middlebrow publication' in Yagoda's index. It gives two further page references, directing the reader to the following quotations (neither of which use the word): a 1937 comment by Dwight Macdonald on the 'amiability' of *New Yorker* criticism (p. 108), and a 1947 account by Cyril Connolly, in which he identified *The New Yorker*, as well as *Time* and *Life*, as magazines that 'only just miss out being [. . .] highbrow' (p. 214).

44. Nina Miller, *Making Love Modern: The Intimate Public Worlds of New York's Literary Women* (New York and Oxford: Oxford University Press, 1998), p. 88.

45. Marshall McLuhan, *Counterblast* (Berkeley: Ginko Press, 2011 [1954]), n.p.

46. Guillory, 'The Ordeal of Middlebrow Culture', p. 90.

47. Catherine Keyser notes in her discussion of the New York smart magazines, 'Urbanity, supposedly achieved by way of Manhattan, was a major uniting

pose for the middle-class readers all over the country who subscribed to these periodicals.' See *Playing Smart: New York Women Writers and Modern Magazine Culture* (New Brunswick, NJ: Rutgers University Press, 2010), p. 15.

48. Yagoda, *About Town*, p. 37. Ross made the comment in 1949, in a letter to Margaret Case Harriman, daughter of Frank Harriman, who owned the Algonquin Hotel during the era of the Round Table. He was replying to her questions about his concept of the magazine at the time of its founding.

Chapter 2

'We Stand Corrected': *New Yorker* Fact-checking and the Business of American Accuracy

Sarah Cain

In 2003, the writer John D'Agata finished a long article on the 2002 suicide of a young Las Vegas boy, Levi Presley. The magazine editor who had originally commissioned it turned it down, on the suspicion that it contained 'factual inaccuracies': it was eventually published seven years later in *The Believer*.[1] In 2012, it reappeared as part of *The Lifespan of a Fact*, a book co-authored with *The Believer*'s fact-checker Jim Fingal: the book version reprinted D'Agata's essay in central blocks on each page, surrounded by what appear to be the notes made by Fingal in the process of fact-checking the essay. With two epigraphs purporting to be by Lao-tzu ('True words are not beautiful', 'Beautiful words are not true'), the book juxtaposes D'Agata's original essay text with a meta-text of Fingal's notes and the authors' subsequent conversational commentary on its content, context and afterlife.

An extended meditation on the nature of journalistic fact-writing, *The Lifespan of a Fact* aims to lay bare on the page the process by which modern journalistic writing is fact-checked for publication. Reviewing the book in 2012 in a blog post for *The New Yorker* online, Hannah Goldfield, a *New Yorker* fact-checker herself, puzzles over what she calls the 'hostile and delusional' nature of D'Agata's tricksy responses to Fingal's checking queries, his insistence on the essentially provisional and shifting quality of the essay's facts:

> The conceit that one must choose facts *or* beauty – even if it's beauty in the name of 'Truth' or a true 'idea' – is preposterous. A good writer – with the help of a fact-checker and an editor, perhaps – should be able to marry the two, and a writer who refuses to even try is, simply, a hack.[2]

Supported by what is perhaps the most famous department of fact-checking in publishing history, *New Yorker* editorial philosophy is founded precisely in a sense that 'the challenge, and the art, lies in confronting the facts – all of them, whether you like them or not – and shaping them into something beautiful'; this philosophy runs, Goldfield suggests, throughout all the departments of the magazine: 'it should be noted that, at *The New Yorker*, when a fictional world intersects with the real world, or when comedic exaggeration seems poised to do damage, the details are fact-checked. Even in cartoons.'[3] (Robert Mankoff, in a *New Yorker* blog post from 1 February 2012, recounts some specific occasions when cartoons have been turned down for factual inaccuracy, including a canine barfly with buttons on the 'wrong' side of his suit, and a cartoon that wrongly placed Interstate 95 between Connecticut and New York.[4]) In March 2010, at an international conference in Germany on fact-checking – quite possibly the first ever conference devoted solely to the topic – Peter Canby, senior editor at *The New Yorker*, similarly described the magazine's famous emphasis on factual accuracy as an integral part of its ethos of ironic sophistication: 'We do things as crazy as check cartoons, and covers, and fiction, and poetry; [. . .] we want humour, fiction and poetry to be *knowing* in its departures from the fact-world, rather than accidental.'[5]

The New Yorker's dedication to the pursuit of the 'fact-world' dates from its earliest decade. The fact-checking department was reportedly established in 1927 as a response to a particularly error-ridden profile of Edna St. Vincent Millay, whose mother threatened to sue if the magazine did not print a correction: Harold Ross made it clear in a memo to his staff that 'A SPECIAL EFFORT SHOULD BE MADE TO AVOID MISTAKES IN THE NEW YORKER.'[6] Magazine competitor *Time* apparently had a department of female researchers acting as checkers as early as 1924, echoing Joseph Pulitzer's famous call for 'Accuracy, accuracy, accuracy!'[7] By midcentury, however, it was *The New Yorker*, above all mainstream American publications, that had become synonymous with an editorial commitment to scrupulous accuracy and fact-checking – and not only in its non-fiction 'Department of Fact' but also in fiction and poetry: 'This magazine', editor Peter De Vries apparently explained to the young Richard Wilbur in 1948, 'is notoriously fastidious about points of fact, and we feel the same way about poetry, either rightly or wrongly.'[8]

The magazine's reputation for fastidiousness over 'points of fact' continues to this day: Canby, in conversation with Deborah Treisman, *The New Yorker*'s fiction editor, similarly suggested in 2013 that the magazine's fact-checking of poetry and fiction reflects a long 'tradition we have of paying attention to the factual underpinnings of things'.[9] Notably time-consuming, labour-intensive and expensive, fact-checking departments are largely unknown outside the United States and Germany, and for the most part restricted to large or well-established print media publications. Fact-checkers are integral to the editorial process: their purpose is not only to prevent errors from appearing in the magazine, but also to mediate between writer, editor, copy editor and lawyers. Since *The New Yorker* does not tend to have assistant or associate editors, checkers fill an essential gap in the editorial machinery: 'the checking department attempts to ask really critical questions, to look at logic, at the flaws in arguments, and to try to get these things addressed so that what ultimately appears in the magazine does have this texture of freshness and originality and accuracy'.[10]

The best evidence of good fact-checking, of course, should be that traces of it appear nowhere within the magazine itself. A perfectly checked publication should never need to print a correction, for everything, pre-corrected and perfected before publication, should be true. Ideally, like its emblem Eustace Tilley's monocle, *The New Yorker* should reveal accuracy in every detail at any level of magnification, but without mention of the process that has gone into creating it; and, true to form, *The New Yorker* rarely mentions its own fact-checking processes directly (though 'Checkpoints', a lengthy article by long-standing non-fiction writer John McPhee, is an exception; and in recent years several *New Yorker* fact-checkers or editors have written about the process in blogposts for the magazine's website).[11] Former staff writer Renata Adler once noted the existence of a long-standing *New Yorker* prohibition on publishing 'pieces that referred to themselves or to the process by which they were written'.[12] Whilst a favourite device of the magazine's staple filler 'Newsbreaks' was to hold up errors in other publications for ridicule, *The New Yorker* itself fought rather shy of printing serious corrections of its own content. The occasional appearance of the variously titled Departments of 'Amplification', 'Correction' and 'Abuse' pointing out the magazine's own errors tended to be either tongue-in-cheek, or, at the very least, delivered in characteristic *New Yorker* ironic tone – as were the more obviously ironically titled 'Go Climb a Tree Department' and the (largely pre-war) 'Pshaw Department'.

Both the ideal of editorial perfection, and the famous tenacity of the fact-checking department, have become central to *New Yorker* mythology, but if obvious traces of or reflections on fact-checking are scarce – and intentionally so – within the magazine itself, the aesthetic of facts and fact-checking nevertheless makes itself felt throughout *The New Yorker*. Harold Ross's preoccupation with facts came to dominate the early editorial ethos of the magazine, and often appeared as part of a concern with the relationship between the magazine's material organisation and production, and the magazine as material product. From its inception in 1925, the magazine has run features echoing, often humorously, a curious interest in the connections between editorial process and content, and self-mythologising *The New Yorker* as unusually concerned with perfection, accuracy and organisation. By midcentury, *The New Yorker*'s famous commitment to accuracy also acted as a powerful marketing strategy, implying (and flattering) an audience who aspired to aesthetic, as well as social and moral, correctness. In this context, what was and is a genuine editorial commitment to the synthesis of truth and beauty, detail and particular, fact-world and aesthetic value, also became a shrewd way of appealing to an elite and educated readership: an emphasis on factual accuracy assumed a certain kind of knowing *readerly* work and efficiency, in which the reader's eye for truth and detail was implicitly aligned with that of the magazine.

'The vast history of *The New Yorker*': the organisation of facts

Julian Barnes opens his collection of reprinted *New Yorker* London letters with an introduction meditating on the magazine's editorial process:

> After your article has been clipped and styled [. . .] it is delivered to *The New Yorker*'s fact-checking department. The operatives here are young, unsleeping, scrupulously polite and astoundingly pertinacious. They bug you to hell and then they save your ass. They are also suspicious of generalization and rhetorical exaggeration, and would prefer that last sentence to read: 'They bug you a quarter of the way to hell and on 17.34 per cent of occasions save your ass.' Making a statement on oath before a judge is as nothing compared with making a statement before a *New Yorker* fact-checker. They don't mind who they call in their lust for verification. They check with you, with your informants, with their computerized information system, with objective authorities; they check to your face and they check behind your back.[13]

The *New Yorker* fact-checker's tyranny over the writing and editing process is easy to satirise. A comic short film in 2008 for the Sundance Festival even spawned a series of NBC web shorts titled 'FCU: Fact Checkers Unit', a satirical portrait of life at the fictional magazine *Dictum*, whose checkers heroically address such thorny problems as whether the actor Bill Murray drinks warm milk at bedtime. Aside from the potential for journalistic scandal should a libellous error creep into the magazine, fact-checking seems ripe for comic portrayal precisely because of the combination of triviality and importance it embodies. Reviewing 'FCU: Fact Checkers Unit' for a *New Yorker* blog post, Meredith Blake calls fact-checkers 'the hidden heroes of journalism, multi-talented polymaths who toil in relative anonymity, both at this publication and others'.[14] Despite this portrayal of the checker as lowly functionary, the prestige of *The New Yorker*'s checking department is borne out in not only the high respect it is afforded within professional journalism, but also the coveted nature of jobs as *New Yorker* checkers, which may lead to more senior editorial positions within the magazine or elsewhere. A job traditionally for the young, smart and well-educated college graduate on the way to somewhere important in the media world, *New Yorker* fact-checking confers a covertly elite status in professional print journalism. Legends of successful novelists and writers who worked as *New Yorker* checkers – or nearly so – lend the department an additional literary glamour (Philip Roth was apparently offered a job as a *New Yorker* checker in 1957, turning it down to take up a position teaching at the University of Chicago; Thomas Meehan, humorist, writer of Broadway musicals, librettist and screenwriter, was a *New Yorker* fact-checker and 'Talk of the Town' contributor early in his career; William Gaddis, Susan Choi and Jay McInerney all spent time working in the checking department.)[15]

From early on in *The New Yorker*'s history, Ross's desire for the magazine to be consistently both elite and well-informed generated an organisational preoccupation with accuracy versus error. After running the disastrous profile of Millay, the magazine printed a scathing and lengthy letter of complaint from her mother, Cora Millay, in the edition of 23 April 1927, under the heading 'We Stand Corrected':

> The Editors of *The New Yorker*, Dear Sirs:
> In the issue of your magazine of February 12, last, under the heading *Profiles*, I read Griffin Barry's article called 'Vincent', supposed to be a sketch of my daughter, Edna St. Vincent Millay.
> It would seem that more reliable sources might have been found for the statements concerning the parents of Edna St. Vincent Millay and her sisters, since both of these parents are living, and in possession of their faculties.[16]

Cora Millay's letter was embarrassing enough to the magazine to substantiate Ross's existing preoccupation with facts in the creation of a specific department devoted to fact-checking. Ben Yagoda suggests that Katharine Angell oversaw the first few years of the checking department, before Ralph Ingersoll received a memo from Ross in 1930 to 'Add Fact Checking to your list of chores'.[17] Despite the new emphasis on fact-checking, an occasional series of features under the 'We Stand Corrected' heading followed during the late 1920s and early 1930s, including a letter from Leo Stein complaining about having been wrongly reported as saying he hated his sister: 'all our friends know that her writings whether autobiographic or other find from me no commendation but it is monstrously false that I have ever expressed personal hatred'.[18] Printed as stand-alone entries in this way, 'We Stand Corrected' items looked rather less like genuine admissions of editorial error, and more like the magazine's staple features of gossipy, potentially ironic or satirical sketches of the preoccupations of the literary and social elite, picking up on the knowing tone of the usual *New Yorker* content such as the tongue-in-cheek voice of the 'Newsbreaks'.

Rogers Whitaker, in charge of the fledgling checking department between 1931 and 1936, was succeeded by Frederick Packard, who turned the department into a formidable professional operation between the 1930s and the 1950s: notably, 'We Stand Corrected' disappeared during these years. A professionalisation of the checking process also coincided with the reorganisation of the fact and fiction departments in the late '30s, and the simultaneous establishment, under the new fiction editor William Maxwell, of a stable of *New Yorker* writers who would develop long-standing relationships with the magazine throughout the midcentury. The gradual formalisation of the checking department suited Harold Ross, who was notoriously addicted to annotating writers' proofs with endless questions and drafting up his own 'query sheets' with comments on factual matters (some of his favourite annotations, according to Brendan Gill, being 'Who he?' and 'Given facts will fix').[19] Ross, Gill reminisced, 'clung to facts as a shipwrecked man clings to a spar'.[20] James Thurber noted:

> And how, in those years, he loved a fact – a great big glittering exclusive fact! When the King of Siam was operated on for cataract in 1933, Ross wanted to know if I could find out how much he had paid the great surgeon who performed the operation. [. . .] It wasn't until about seven years later that I brought him this particular fact, and laid it on his desk. [. . .] The fact fascinated Ross, but the story was cold and seven years old, and he wouldn't use it.[21]

Ross's interest in facts, and his insistence on 'pegging' – pinning the opening of a story, whether fiction or non-fiction, to orientating details of time and place – helped create a specific kind of detail-heavy, easily recognisable (and easy to satirise) *New Yorker* style, one which remained essentially unchanged throughout the following decades. This was supported and facilitated by what Gill called 'the machinery of benign skepticism [. . .] of editors, copy editors, and checkers' – detailed procedures and processes for editing and sub-editing involving lengthy passing of annotated galley proofs back and forth between writer, editors and checkers before finally going to print – and also by the new *material* infrastructures that made it possible to carry out extensive editing, proof-setting and checking, from the number of dedicated fact-checkers to the use of the telephone, telegram, public libraries, carbon copies, filing systems and reference books and archives, and, in the late twentieth century into the twenty-first, computerised databases and other kinds of new media.[22] Ross's facts had to be substantiated; and his devotion to facts was equally supported by his dedication to filing systems, collections of non-fiction books and reference books of all kinds. Thurber recalled Ross as 'surrounded by dictionaries, which he constantly consulted, along with one of his favorite books, Fowler's *Modern English Usage*':

> He read the *Oxford English Dictionary* the way other men read fiction, and he sometimes delved into a volume of the *Britannica* at random. One of the funniest moments in Wolcott Gibbs's *Season in the Sun* showed the actor who played Ross calmly looking up the word '*hurricane*' in *Webster's Unabridged* while the advance gales of a real hurricane swept toward him like a cavalry charge.[23]

It is unsurprising that *The New Yorker* and its staff generated a great number of (occasionally facetious) style guides, reflections on, and rules for, house style, including, of course, E. B. White's bestselling 1959 revision of William Strunk Jr., *The Elements of Style*.[24] As well as Ross's delight in reference books (and the establishment of a *New Yorker* staff library), he had a weakness for the newest ideas in business and organisation management, and was prey to the belief that the magazine's fortunes would be transformed by a series of managing editors or 'geniuses' (soon corrupted to 'jesuses').[25] Thurber, briefly in 1927 hired as one of the 'geniuses' himself, recalled that despite Ross's scorn for American big business, he 'talked constantly of "running this place like any other business office"', and was prone to an 'obsessive reverence for Order and Organization', constantly reordering and reorganising both editorial process and physical office in search of the perfect formulation of workflow and work space.[26]

Beset by a preoccupation with systems, spaces and processes, Ross's organisational fantasies reflected a backdrop, in twentieth-century America, of more widespread contemporary interest in new sciences of management theory, information storage and retrieval, and industrial and commercial psychology – including library science, advertising and business studies. In 1934 Ross hired a librarian, Ebba Jonsson, to bring some order to *The New Yorker*'s own library and archive; she arrived 'to find the files in much the same shape as a house in which only men had been living for years. In one small dusty room there was an old couch loaded down with carbons of letters, documents, and papers of all kinds. It must have taken her a year to get the files in order.'[27] Despite all efforts, the various working spaces of *The New Yorker* were from the outset notoriously cluttered, disorganised and crammed with unfiled papers, which no 'genius' quite managed to address. Thurber thought that Ross was looking for 'two separate kinds of Miracle Men':

> (1) the administrative genius who would sit at a Central Desk, push buttons, and produce Instant Perfection of organization, and (2) a literary wizard who would wave a magic wand over writers and artists and conjure up Instant Perfection in prose, drawings, and all other contents of the magazine.[28]

Ross's desire for someone who would perfect and unify the content of the magazine through organisation reflects a more deep-rooted and persistent desire, throughout *New Yorker* history, to collapse the material processes of textual editing and production into the content of the magazine itself. The August–December issues in 1925, for example, included Corey Ford's series of charming imaginary sketches titled 'The Making of a Magazine: A Tour Through the Vast Organization of *The New Yorker*'. Ford's 'A Bird's Eye View of Our Special Departments' parodies the professionalisation of editing and publishing, with the Proof Reading Department 'located on the top floor, since so perfect is the system on this paper that typographical errors never occur in its ifficient organization'.[29] In 'Operating the Pneumatic Air-Tubes' the magazine is rendered nothing *but* material system, an 'intricate network of pneumatic tubes which circulate constantly the various parts of the magazine from one department to another, up and down the seventy-four floors of the structure, until they finally join together to form the weekly issue of *The New Yorker*'.[30]

Ford's running conceit of a Swiftian fable about the magazine's construction shows how from the outset *The New Yorker* made its own processes of textual production part of the magazine's content; and also that the emphasis on fact, accuracy and error already formed part, as early as 1925, of the self-mythologisation of *The New Yorker* as a commodity. In 'The Anniversary of a Great Magazine: Looking Back Over the Vast History of *The New Yorker* With Mr. Eustace Tilley', printed in the first anniversary issue in February 1926, Ford suggests that:

> As New York has increased, so has *The New Yorker* grown from that first modest issue – stamped crudely on the back of any old scrap of paper that happened to be blowing about the office, printed by someone sitting down hard on the press; and delivered by the editor on his own bicycle.[31]

This fictional history, like so much about *The New Yorker*'s combination of light humour and self-irony, encapsulates the paradoxical nature of the commerce between the magazine's content and its tone: the 'factual underpinnings' of the magazine's world are simultaneously ironised or undermined by the lightness of its voice.

'The factual underpinnings of things': information management

The New Yorker's knowing self-parody is nowhere more visible than in its rare explicit references to the ways in which the magazine's own material and editorial organisation might shape its content. 'Documented', Mark Singer's 1991 'Talk of the Town' piece, which gently pokes fun at the organisation of the magazine's notoriously untidy offices, imagines curators from the Smithsonian arriving to catalogue the offices of *The New Yorker*. (Around this time, the *New Yorker* archives were donated to the New York Public Library, and the magazine moved offices for the first time in decades.)[32] The Smithsonian curators express 'enthusiasm for several artefacts they discovered in the Makeup Department, the busy room on the nineteenth floor where each week's issue of the magazine was put together and laid out':

> In the early days of the magazine, each member of the Makeup Department was issued a shovel and a piece of coal and a kerosene lamp. More recently, computers were introduced. But most of the equipment was original, so the Smithsonian requested and received several bulletin boards and tables and file cabinets and a pneumatic tube.[33]

Curiously reminiscent of Ford's 1925 conceits of magazine-making, 'Documented' satirises all at once the fact-laden style of *New Yorker* writing, the (lack of) organisation of the magazine's offices, databases, files, archives and artefacts ('he had a shelf filled with book-mailing envelopes in which he kept notes for articles he'd written'), and *The New Yorker*'s obsession with self-memorialising and self-mythologising. The magazine's interest in facts and accuracy repeatedly surfaces in the imagined work of organising or 'documenting' the magazine's material and textual surroundings ('we carefully documented everything photographically').

Fact-checking is itself a form of information management and manipulation, and relies upon rapid storage, searching, retrieval and communication of information, such as index-card catalogues and filing systems, a public library system, the telephone, commercial cuttings services, microfilm, archives and records management, the database (in both its material and electronic forms), and, eventually, the internet.

These are all technologies or systems which were either invented or professionalised primarily during the twentieth century, at a time when *The New Yorker* was consolidating its market share, as Mary Corey suggests, as 'the voice of an intellectual community – a kind of *New Yorker* village – in which readers' most compelling urges – to know about and possess elite goods and services and to be citizens of a truly progressive society – could coexist peacefully'.[34] By the middle of the twentieth century, *The New Yorker* had successfully established itself as the most socially sophisticated and elite of mainstream American print publications, and it had done so by appealing precisely to a demographic of readers who saw themselves as technologically and educationally progressive (if, however, perhaps socially or politically conservative). By the time Ross's editorship had given way to William Shawn's, *The New Yorker*'s readership would itself have been very familiar with the new discourses of business organisation and information management: in 1949, according to one of the magazine's own marketing surveys,

> three quarters of the magazine's subscribers had an annual family income of over $5,000 a year, at a time when the national average family income hovered around $1,900. Nearly half of subscribers were employed in 'business or industry,' whilst 21% were 'owners, partners, managers, or major executives'.[35]

This readership saw itself as sophisticated in commercial terms, and as interested in the technological and commercial aspects of modernity as much as the conservation of cultural and intellectual civilisation. A background discourse of the professionalisation and technologisation of knowledge, information, and commerce also appeared around the edges of *New Yorker* content, in its adverts and the ephemera of book reviews, Newsbreaks, cartoons, and other textual paraphernalia. An issue from 22 March 1958, for example, advertises a large, partly ornamental edition of *Webster's New International Dictionary* as 'The World's Greatest Information Center in your own home . . . for only $39.50' (Fig. 2.1). 'An "information center" so informative and intriguing that someone in the family turns to it every day', the book is exhaustively comprehensive: 'As your family', the advert promises, 'develops the "look it up" habit, their daily questions will be answered accurately.' In one of those uncanny synchronies of *New Yorker* advertising and content, the Webster's Dictionary ad runs alongside a review by Winthrop Sargeant of Max Lerner's *America as a Civilization*, 'a massive attempt to describe the main characteristics and currents of American life and thought': 'a colossal job of organization and scholarship, [. . .] a small encyclopedia of the literature of American history,

THE NEW YORKER   153

ner's, and if its point of view is not over-
whelmingly original, it is nevertheless
the product of a mind of striking assimi-
lative powers and a work whose details
provide no end of interesting reading.
It considers dispassionately nearly every
generalization ever made about the subject, from de Tocqueville and Bryce to
William H. Whyte's "The Organization Man," and its bibliography—including critical notes by the author—is a
small encyclopedia of the literature of
American history, social habits, folk-
ways, technology, art, politics, and economics. Mr. Lerner ponders America's
European psychological and cultural
heritage, its national and racial makeup,
its regional differences, its dominant
myths, its dominant religious beliefs, its
practical political attitudes, its industrial
structure, its changing class concepts,
its minority problems, its ideals of social
behavior, its cultural peculiarities, and
its place in the modern world. Whether
what he is describing is a "civilization"
is a matter of definition. He acts as a
detached and unprejudiced social scien-
tist examining an organism. His conclu-
sions, if it is possible to boil them down,
are that America is big, dynamic, "plu-
ralistic" (a word he likes), obsessed with
"the metaphysic of promise," capable
of indefinite growth, and, in general,
good. And though he deplores its in-
termittent and isolated failures and fol-
lies, he has an unshakable faith (this
will be old stuff for the readers of *Time*
and *Fortune*) that its dynamism, prac-
ticality, bigness, and capacity to assimi-
late and reconcile the conflicting elements in its society will, in the long run,
save it. These ideas, as has just been
said, are not particularly new; they
constitute a summary of widely held
belief.

The less blandly optimistic reader
will detect in Mr. Lerner's huge assemblage an absence of moral perspective
and a tendency to regard vitality, diversity, size, and capacity for survival as
the most positive of virtues. Though he
demolishes the prophecies of Karl Marx
that concern America, he is inclined,
like Marx, to consider man the creature
of the great demi-urge known vaguely
as "social forces," and this attitude
entails a weedy, pagan mystique that
avoids the problem of ultimate values.
Mr. Lerner is aware of this difficulty.
Having celebrated America's conquest
of scarcity and noted that we have tran-
scended the plight of "economic man"
in the primitive sense (i.e., man struggling against his environment), he asks,
"Where do we go from prosperity?"—
a pertinent question, which he cannot

THE WORLD'S GREATEST
INFORMATION CENTER
in your own home...for only $39.50

Thousands of families like yours value
Webster's New International Dictionary,
Second Edition, as the great question
answerer, an "information center" so
informative and intriguing that someone
in the family turns to it every day. In
this one volume, there is accurate information on literally every subject
known to man. It equals in printed
material an 18-volume encyclopedia —
always open and inviting use, rather
than buried in a bookcase.

As your family develops the "look it up"
habit, their daily questions will be
answered accurately, for the New International is relied on by schools and

libraries as "the Supreme Authority" of
the English-speaking world.

Examine this famous Merriam-Webster
at your department, book, or stationery
store. Its 3,350 pages (more than 600,-
000 entries!) will convince you that
here is a wonderful investment for your
family and yourself.

WARNING: Webster's New International Dictionary is never available as
a premium in any "free" offers. Always
look for the *Merriam-Webster* trademark to protect yourself from inferior
substitutes. G. & C. Merriam Co., Spring-
field 2, Mass.

INSIST ON

MERRIAM-
WEBSTER

Webster's New Collegiate Dictionary
($5 and up) is the only desk dictionary
based on the New International. It is the
dictionary required or recommended by
nearly all schools and colleges.

Figure 2.1. Advertisement, Merriam-Webster, *The New Yorker*, 22
March 1958, p. 153. By permission, Merriam-Webster Inc. (www.
Merriam-Webster.com).

social habits, folk-ways, technology, art, politics, and economics'. Alongside de Tocqueville, the review name-drops *The Organization Man* (1956), William Whyte's non-fiction bestseller on the increasing dominance of business management in the organisation of American life.[36] Sargeant's review sits amidst *The New Yorker*'s usual mix of ads offering luxury commodities from Chevrolets, nylons, and stockbroking firms, to John Cheever's latest novel, the Bell Telephone System (which readers can invest in by owning AT&T stock), and other magazines such as *Holiday* ('with incomes nearly triple the national average, these Holiday families can afford the things they want to buy. More and more advertisers are reaching this rewarding market in Holiday. Are you?')[37] If the *New Yorker* reader, too, is encouraged to develop a 'look it up' habit, then this eye for the 'knowledgeable' consumption of facts is also implicitly aligned with the purchase of luxury objects, so that a focus on fact appears as a form of elite luxury. During this period in particular, Mary Corey suggests, *The New Yorker*'s 'unapologetic conflation of high commerce with high-mindedness did allow the perquisites of privilege to be presented as integral to the socially conscious civilized world'.[38] If the twin discourses of aspirationally highbrow content and up-to-the-minute consumer product found their expression on the pages of *The New Yorker*, both coalesced around information, organisation, and knowledge, especially factual knowledge ('Knowledgeable people', another advertisement for whiskey suggests, 'buy <u>Imperial</u> because they have an educated taste.')[39] The Ross-era enthusiasm for the 'great big glittering fact' was thus reconfigured, in the midcentury magazine, as a mastery of the technological world that is explicitly available for consumption, so that *The New Yorker*'s reputation for accuracy became, from this point onwards, a powerful advertisement for its elite and 'knowledgeable' status. For a magazine famous for its apparent refusal, for much of its history, to allow economic and commercial considerations to dictate its content, *New Yorker* fact-checking proved to be one of its best-known selling points, subtly advertising to readers its commitment to factual, literary and aesthetic truth against commercial value, and positioning accuracy itself as a form of luxury commodity.

'We carefully documented everything': truth and beauty

During the second half of the twentieth century the fact-checking department went from strength to strength: by the end of his editorship, William Shawn (once referred to in 1936 by Wolcott Gibbs as *The New Yorker*'s 'information man')[40] reportedly, and perhaps only in slight exaggeration, claimed that the magazine would 'send a fact checker by the Concorde to London to check on a fact'.[41] Shawn argued in a 1985 piece that his famous insistence on editorial independence from the magazine's commercial constraints embodied a commitment to 'substance', 'coherence', 'clarity', 'principles and standards', 'worth', 'beauty' and 'truth':

> if *The New Yorker* could be everything we want it to be it would unfailingly combine thorough, accurate, fresh, inspired reporting with fiction that runs deep and says something that hasn't been said before. [. . .] We believe that the truth can turn up in a cartoon, in one of the magazine's covers, in a poem, in a short story, in an essay, in an editorial comment, in a humor piece, in a critical piece, in a reporting piece. And if any single principle transcends all the others and informs all the others it is to try to tell the truth.[42]

Whilst this somewhat disingenuous aspiration towards idealised truth is, as the midcentury *New Yorker* advertisements suggest, not as disconnected from commercial values and business concerns as it might appear, Shawn did nevertheless see the evolution of *The New Yorker* in primarily intellectual and moral terms. The Ross-era interest in facts as the building-blocks of journalistic and organisational 'Perfection' gradually became overlaid by an altogether loftier notion of the fact as an index to transcendent, even Platonic, ideals of aesthetic and stylistic perfection. This was reflected in an increasingly luxurious and unhurried editorial process: Canby recounts that during the Shawn era,

> writers would work on pieces for as long as they felt was useful and necessary, and that often meant years. Once the pieces were accepted, they were edited, copyedited, and fact-checked on a schedule that typically stretched out for weeks and sometimes for months.[43]

This process was extremely expensive, as well as time-consuming and idiosyncratic: Renata Adler recalled the 'great luxury', in the Shawn era, of

> fresh galley proofs, almost every day, from the time the editing process began to the day the story or article appeared in print. [. . .] One drawback of this luxury was that it permitted the inclusion, in each day's galleys, of the many queries and suggested revisions of all the editors, copy editors, and checkers who read the piece before it went to press.[44]

Supported by Shawn's insistence on the separation between the magazine's editorial content and the commercial concerns of the finance and advertising departments, such 'luxury' might appear to embody a defiance of a magazine culture of profit, mercantile values and the bottom line. In reality, though, what appeared to be an anti-commercial concern for accuracy and aesthetics over profit often worked subtly to the magazine's advantage: an apparent disregard for the immediately or nakedly commercial motive was, paradoxically, a strong selling point for the magazine's audience.[45] The fact-checking of fiction, critical pieces, poetry, captions, art, cartoons, Newsbreaks, 'Talk of the Town' columns and even the table of contents, all helped create this impression of *The New Yorker* as a stylistic unity of detail and whole, in which any particular might act as a wider lens onto an aesthetically pleasing, and beautifully constructed, social panorama. This sense was reflected back in the magazine's willingness to shape its content to generate a sense of holistic unity with the social and factual world outside. The magazine's famous practice of changing fictional details to synchronise with the dates of publication represented one kind of attempt to align *The New Yorker*'s world with the 'fact-world'; the other side of an attention to the factual underpinnings of literary pieces could involve a rather disastrous sense-of-humour failure: Adler recounts that a checker, 'once reading a poem by Ogden Nash, which began "Today I am thirty," had noted Mr Nash's birthdate in the margin, and added, "He is thirty-one"'.[46]

Despite its obvious openness to ridicule, a dogged insistence on the fact as an anchor for aesthetic or even philosophical 'truth' underlay *The New Yorker*'s unique intellectual style during this era; and it was by no means the case that contemporary critics of the magazine accepted that its lofty ambitions were as removed from commercial taint as they seemed. During the 1960s, *New Yorker* fact-checking increasingly came to stand, for some critics of the magazine, as symbolic of its overweening pretensions to cultural and intellectual superiority. In a 1962 essay for the *Village Voice* Seymour Krim suggested that:

> even during the heyday of intellectual snobbery as canonized by the *Partisan* and *Kenyon* reviews during the 40s, the *New Yorker* felt eminently protected, sure of itself, because the underlying axis of the magazine was always journalistic, concrete, and it excelled with the tangible as did no competitor. Harold Ross or his heir William Shawn might not understand or enjoy James Joyce or even Picasso, being expert newsmen first and artistic dilettantes second, but their roots in the American experience were unquestioned, ruggedly sustained by the journalist's reliance on facts and the exciting job of putting out a tough-minded but lightly handled organism every week.[47]

Krim argues, however, that despite this reliance on the 'tangible', the 'new wave' of American writing of the 1960s coincided with a decline in the magazine's aesthetic standards:

As the world shoves its genuine leering face into the pages of the magazine, not in the editorial niceties but in the encroachingly covetous advertisements, the *New Yorker*'s conspiracy against reality suddenly takes on the willed perversity of a porcelain thumb stubbornly thrust in the bloodshot eye of the truth.[48]

This countercultural scepticism regarding *The New Yorker*'s social and stylistic aspirations to a perfected marriage of truth and beauty was picked up by Tom Wolfe's famous, similarly excoriating 1965 essays on the ossification of the magazine under Shawn's editorship. 'Tiny Mummies! The True Story of the Ruler of 43rd Street's Land of the Walking Dead!' read like an acidly tongue-in-cheek but strangely fond piece of character assassination of Shawn and his editors.[49] 'Lost in the Whichy Thicket' caricatured *The New Yorker*'s famously luxurious editing system as 'more completely *group journalism*, or *org-edit*, as it is called at *Novy Mir*, than anything *Time* magazine ever even contemplated'.[50] Wolfe's description of *The New Yorker*'s editing process followed its proofs as they circulated several times around editors, checking department, writer, copy editors, researchers and query editors, and ended up in the 'Transferring Room', where:

a small group of people is hunched over tables, pulling all these sheets together, copying everybody's scrawls and queries onto a set of master galleys. [. . .] The author then is given a glimpse of what an . . . interesting . . . mutation his story has undergone if somebody calls him in at that point to answer queries about facts and do the needed rewriting. And finally, as the culmination of this great . . . evolution, the homogenized production is disgorged to the printers – in Chicago, via electronic impulses – and the *New Yorker* Style is achieved.[51]

Despite Wolfe's tongue-in-cheek tone, Shawn and his editors at the magazine responded to his essays with what looks in hindsight to have been something of an excessive reaction: Shawn apparently tried to block publication of Wolfe's pieces, and Adler recounts that the *New Yorker* staff's response to them was to compile a ('funny and well-framed') list of fact-checks on Wolfe's essays, which ran as a letter in the *Columbia Journalism Review* and as part of an article by Dwight Macdonald in the *New York Review of Books*.[52] However funny or well-framed (or, as Tom Perrin argues in Chapter 11 of this book, 'shot through with envy'), it seems particularly apposite that *The New Yorker*'s response to the ironised, slippery relationship between journalistic fact and fictional licence practised in Wolfe's New Journalism was to reassert its own sense of the importance of the facts as validated by the very fact-checking systems Wolfe had decried.

That was by no means the only fact-checking scandal to arise at *The New Yorker* towards the end of the century. In the increasingly litigation-heavy culture of the 1960s, 1970s and 1980s (arguably, especially post-Watergate, the heyday of American investigative journalism), the cultural prestige of the long-form non-fiction essay, as exemplified in *The New Yorker, Vanity Fair, Mother Jones, Time* magazine, and others, meant that the verifiability of writers' factual claims was more important than ever. Lengthy legal wrangling was generated by a negative profile of psychoanalyst Jeffrey Masson by *New Yorker* writer Janet Malcolm (eventually cleared of libel in 1994), whom Masson had accused of fabricating quotes. As a result the fact-checking department began to demand from writers not just evidence of their print sources, but their notes, tapes, and where possible audio transcripts, as well as calling sources to confirm the gist (if not the exact wording) of their quotations.[53] In another incident, a restaurant review by writer John McPhee included a quote from an anonymous source accusing the well-known French restaurant Lutèce of serving frozen turbot: this turned out not to be the case, obliging McPhee to write a 'Department of Amplification and Correction' acknowledging the error. As always, such *New Yorker* self-corrections managed enough of a tongue-in-cheek tone to render the correction itself something of a delight:

> Attention has been called to a slice of turbot that I mentioned on page 88 of the February 19th issue of this magazine, in a Profile of a chef called Otto. Referring to a slice of turbot he consumed at the restaurant Lutèce, Otto was quoted as follows: 'The turbot is delicious, very fresh, perfectly cooked. My guess is it was frozen.' Otto guessed wrong.[54]

The *New Yorker* tone rescues such mishaps by implying that its seriousness about facts might not *really* be that serious after all: the pleasing mundanity of the turbot scandal flags up again the combination of triviality and importance, seriousness and irony inherent in *The New Yorker*'s emphasis on factual detail. The 'fact' can be as much an amusing irrelevance as index to a Platonic truth, and the magazine's knowing voice lends such 'corrections' a lightness that undercuts their apparent severity. If the flip-side of the reverence for the fact is the ironic nod to the occasional unavoidable error, *The New Yorker*'s facts always run the risk of ending up as occasions for satire; and the fact-checking scandals of the '60s, '70s and '80s allowed other print publications their own chance to see *The New Yorker* hoist with its own petard for factual errors that would have gone unnoticed elsewhere. Paradoxically, however, the magazine's reputation for fact-checking seemed bolstered, not undermined, by such publicity, to the point of being immortalised in Jay McInerney's *Bright Lights, Big City*, in which the protagonist is fired from his checking post in the Department for Factual Verification for having deliberately failed to check a prominent story. In the period following Shawn's editorship the checking department grew, rather than declined, in prominence. In 2013 the magazine employed sixteen fact-checkers, overseen by Peter Canby; the number had doubled from the previous eight under Tina Brown's editorship, when publication lead times shortened dramatically, requiring more checkers to cope with a much faster timescale for editing.[55] Today, the expense of maintaining a dedicated checking department is increased by the cost of the technological infrastructure required to perform the checking: Canby notes that the checking is heavily reliant on access to databases such as the 'incredibly expensive, but kind of indispensable' LexisNexis, the successor to Ross's reference books.[56] More recently, this apparatus has been augmented by the digitisation of *The New Yorker*'s entire archive, itself a testament to the magazine's continuing aesthetic of exhaustive perfectionism in the material technologies of editing and reading.

'Everyone wants *The New Yorker* to get things wrong', fiction editor Deborah Treisman suggests, and certainly the magazine's enjoyment of its own cultural dominance lays it open to attack if and when its commitment to perfection misfires.[57] Despite the partly performative nature of this commitment to the pursuit of truth and perfection, in an electronic age the value of fact-checking is potentially more crucial than ever, for the writer as much as the reader: 'I felt like I was in the middle of an ancient ritual', the Chinese writer Qian Gang recalled in a piece titled 'I was Fact-checked by *The New Yorker*'.[58] The writer's experience of the checking process, when it goes well, is captured in John McPhee's 2009 reflection 'Checkpoints', in part a retrospective account of the fact-checking of a paragraph in one of his own non-fiction series, 'The Curve of Binding Energy', in 1973. A 60,000-word examination of 'weapons-grade nuclear material in private industry and what terrorists might or might not do with it', the 1973 articles dealt not just with highly technical information, but also with the murkiness of personal anecdotes released from wartime secrecy: the challenges of checking the pieces were very great.[59] McPhee recounts how dependent the process was on the detailed and complex reading of his text, the extensive use of telephone and reference sources, and the extraordinary efforts of his fact-checker, Sara Lippincott, to substantiate the anecdotal claim that a Japanese incendiary balloon had once landed on the secret American reactor in Washington that was making the plutonium destined to destroy Nagasaki.[60] Subtitled 'Where Accuracy Meets Flair' in that issue's table of contents, 'Checkpoints' recounts so many amusing and just-in-time accounts of fact-checking heroics that the piece itself reads like a tall tale of the unverifiable activity behind the scenes of the checking process. Facts, here, slip between the anecdotal, provisional and potentially fictional, and the relative certainty of numbers, dates and objects. To work, it seems as if both kinds of 'fact' must be in concert: if accuracy seems pointless without the 'flair' of writerly invention and tone, flair must be grounded in some kind of belief in objective truth for *The New Yorker*'s readers and editors to feel comfortable accepting its marriage of truth and beauty. McPhee recounts:

> After an error gets into *The New Yorker*, heat-seeking missiles rise off the earth and home in on the author, the fact-checker, the editor, and even the shade of the founder. As the checking department summarises it, 'No mistakes go unnoticed by readers.' In the waning days of 2005, Rebecca Curtis's fine short story 'Twenty Grand' appeared in *The New Yorker*. Its characters, in 1979, go into a McDonald's for Chicken McNuggets. McNuggets appeared in *The New Yorker*'s Christmas mail. McDonald's had introduced them in 1983.[61]

A further irony, typical of *The New Yorker* in its subtlety, underlies McPhee's comments. Curtis's story itself maps out the very tensions implicit within the magazine's obsessive return to the fact and factuality. Recounting the loss of an 'old Armenian coin' given to the protagonist by her grandmother, Curtis's tale rests on our inability to determine the coin's true status, aesthetic, financial or personal.[62] When the narrator's mother, in desperation, uses the coin to pay a one-dollar toll on the road to visit her husband, the coin appears as a token of authentic personal history, linked as it is with the death of the narrator's 'mother's mother'.[63] Yet in the central twist of Curtis's story, the coin's value is shown to lie in its *financial* value: after its loss to the unsmiling toll attendant, the narrator's father reveals its value was 'twenty grand'. The inflation of the coin's value 20,000-fold paradoxically displaces its authentic personal value with its ability to purchase a section of beach or at least 'a lifetime of unshared Happy Meals'.[64] Reconfiguring Henry James's obsession with the connection between truth, beauty and monetary value for the McNugget era, Curtis inadvertently embodies the tensions at the heart of the magazine's obsession with the fact. If Curtis's coin shifts unstably between the fields of truth, beauty and commerce, then so does the fact; and *The New Yorker*'s insistence on fact-checking is perhaps the most eloquent acknowledgement that the fact is always tricksy, never one thing pure and simple, but an uneasy interaction between the competing economies of truth, commerce and aesthetic perfection.

'What are facts?' the historian Mary Poovey has asked. 'Are they incontrovertible data that simply demonstrate what is true? Or are they bits of evidence marshaled to persuade others of the theory one sets out with? Do facts somehow exist in the world like pebbles, waiting to be picked up?'[65] For *The New Yorker*, the fact has always been part of an interest in overall system, whether in 'organisation', 'style', 'truth', or in a sense of the correspondence of part and whole: the relationship between material or objective detail and holistic system is part of the magazine's guiding philosophy of the marriage of fact with beauty and truth. Moreover, whilst *The New Yorker* has always imagined the fact to be the particular in service to the whole, it has itself managed to synthesise these into a recognisable system, both a material organisation of what Mary Corey calls 'the magazine's lavish discursive detritus', and a mode of being which aspires to offer its readers a way to manage their relationships with the social world.[66] If, as Poovey argues, an interest in what we have come to call the factual is one of the hallmarks of capitalist modernity, *The New Yorker*'s obsession with fact-checking 'truth' acts as a shorthand for the rightness of a certain set of guiding social, moral and aesthetic principles embodied in the magazine's commercial project. Because the fact is balanced between 'the phenomenal world and systematic knowledge', Poovey argues, 'the epistemological unit of the fact has registered the tension between the richness and variety embodied in concrete phenomena and the uniform, rule-governed order of humanly contrived systems'.[67] In *The New Yorker*, as in the history of modernity in general, the fact thus becomes an emblem of both the conceptual and the material processes by which truth and beauty are sutured into an intellectually and commercially valuable whole.

Notes

1. John D'Agata and Jim Fingal, *The Lifespan of a Fact* (New York and London: W. W. Norton, 2012), front and end matter.
2. Hannah Goldfield, 'The Art of Fact-Checking', available at <http://www.newyorker.com/online/blogs/books/2012/02/the-art-of-fact-checking.html> (accessed 1 May 2014).
3. Ibid.
4. Robert Mankoff, 'Cartoon Fact-Checking', available at <http://www.newyorker.com/online/blogs/cartoonists/2012/02/the-new-yorker-is-known-1.html> (accessed 1 May 2014).
5. Peter Canby, video footage <http://vimeo.com/10783265> (accessed 1 May 2014).
6. Ben Yagoda, *About Town: 'The New Yorker' and the World it Made* (New York: Scribner, 2000), p. 203.

7. Ibid., p. 202.
8. Ibid., p. 203.
9. Deborah Triesman, Peter Canby, Nicholas Thompson et al., 'Our Failure in Afghanistan', <http://downloads.newyorker.com/mp3/outloud/120709_outloud_afghanistan.mp3> (podcast, accessed 1 May 2014).
10. Peter Canby, 'Fact-Checking at *The New Yorker*', in *The Art of Making Magazines: On Being an Editor and Other Views from the Industry* (New York and Chichester: Columbia University Press, 2012), pp. 73–84 (pp. 74–5).
11. John McPhee, 'Personal History: Checkpoints', *The New Yorker*, 9 February 2009, pp. 56–63. For blogposts, see, for instance, Blake Eskin's piece on the best pencils for fact-checking, available at <http://www.newyorker.com/online/blogs/newsdesk/2011/09/back-in-blackwing.html> (accessed 1 May 2014); and, more recently, Katia Bachko's remarks on the delights of the checkers' library: 'What We're Reading', available at <http://www.newyorker.com/online/blogs/books/2014/01/what-were-reading-debretts-peerage-and-baronetage-rachel-kushner-henry-adams.html> (accessed 1 May 2014).
12. Renata Adler, *Gone: The Last Days of 'The New Yorker'* (New York: Simon & Schuster, 1999), p. 67.
13. Julian Barnes, *Letters from London: 1990–1995* (London and Basingstoke: Picador, 1995), pp. xiii–xiv.
14. Meredith Blake, 'Fact-Checkers: Our Heroes', available at <http://www.newyorker.com/online/blogs/books/2010/08/fact-checkers-our-heroes.html> (accessed 1 May 2014).
15. See, for example, Yagoda, *About Town*, p. 296; Adler, *Gone*, pp. 50–2.
16. Cora B. Millay, 'We Stand Corrected', *The New Yorker*, 23 April 1927, pp. 89–90.
17. Yagoda, *About Town*, p. 203.
18. Leo Stein, 'We Stand Corrected', *The New Yorker*, 18 May 1935, p. 91.
19. Brendan Gill, *Here at 'The New Yorker'* (New York: Random House, 1975), pp. 10–11.
20. Ibid., p. 14.
21. James Thurber, *The Years with Ross* (Boston: Little, Brown, 1959), pp. 93–4.
22. Gill, *Here at 'The New Yorker'*, p. 7.
23. Thurber, *The Years with Ross*, p. 71.
24. See, for example, Yagoda, *About Town*, pp. 200–1, 205–11.
25. Ibid., pp. 44–5.
26. Thurber, *The Years with Ross*, p. 121.
27. Ibid., p. 137.
28. Ibid., pp. 99–100.
29. Corey Ford, 'A Bird's Eye View of Our Special Departments', *The New Yorker*, 14 November 1925, p. 1.
30. Corey Ford, 'Operating the Pneumatic Air-Tubes', *The New Yorker*, 21 November 1925, p. 1.
31. Corey Ford, 'The Anniversary of a Great Magazine', *The New Yorker*, 20 February 1926, pp. 28–9 (p. 28).
32. Yagoda, *About Town*, p. 419.

33. Mark Singer, 'Documented', *The New Yorker*, 29 April 1991, pp. 28–9 (p. 29).
34. Mary F. Corey, *The World Through a Monocle: 'The New Yorker' at Midcentury* (Cambridge, MA: Harvard University Press, 1999), p. 2.
35. Ibid., p. 11.
36. Winthrop Sargeant, 'The Humanist and the Dynamist', *The New Yorker*, 22 March 1958, pp. 151–4 (pp. 152–3).
37. Ibid., pp. 64–5.
38. Corey, *The World Through a Monocle*, p. 39.
39. *The New Yorker*, 22 March 1958, p. 53.
40. Wolcott Gibbs to Rea Irvin, 22 April 1936, quoted in Yagoda, *About Town*, p. 243.
41. Reportedly said in discussions with Si Newhouse over the purchase of the magazine in 1984–85. See Carol Felsenthal, *Citizen Newhouse: Portrait of a Media Merchant* (London and Toronto: Seven Stories Press, 1998), p. 259; see also Yagoda, *About Town*, p. 409.
42. William Shawn, 'The Talk of the Town', *The New Yorker*, 22 April 1985, pp. 35–9 (p. 36).
43. Canby, 'Fact-Checking', p. 76.
44. Adler, *Gone*, p. 64; Ved Mehta provides a similar account of the exhaustive workflow for editing galley proofs in the Shawn era in *Remembering Mr. Shawn's 'New Yorker': The Invisible Art of Editing* (New York: Overlook Press, 1998), passim, and especially pp. 132–5.
45. See Corey, *The World Through a Monocle*, pp. 11–13.
46. Adler, *Gone*, p. 160.
47. Seymour Krim, 'Who's Afraid of *The New Yorker* Now?', *Village Voice*, 8 November 1962, repr. in *Shake it for the World* (London: Allen & Busby, 1971), p. 173.
48. Ibid., p. 185.
49. Tom Wolfe, 'Tiny Mummies! The True Story of the Ruler of 43rd Street's Land of the Walking Dead!', *New York Herald Tribune*, 11 April 1965, repr. in *Hooking Up* (London: Jonathan Cape, 2000).
50. Tom Wolfe, 'Lost in the Whichy Thicket: *The New Yorker – II*', *New York Herald Tribune*, 18 April 1965, repr. as 'Lost in the Whichy Thickets: *The New Yorker*', in Wolfe, *Hooking Up*, p. 270.
51. Ibid., p. 276.
52. Adler, *Gone*, pp. 84–90; Adler and Gerald Jonas, 'The Letter', *Columbia Journalism Review*, 4.4 (1966), 32; Dwight Macdonald, 'Parajournalism II: Wolfe and *The New Yorker*', *New York Review of Books*, 3 February 1966, available at <http://www.nybooks.com/articles/archives/1966/feb/03> (accessed 1 May 2014), following his earlier 'Parajournalism, or Tom Wolfe & his Magic Writing Machine', *New York Review of Books*, 26 August 1965, available at <http://www.nybooks.com/articles/archives/1965/aug/26> (accessed 12 June 2014).
53. Canby, 'Fact-Checking', pp. 81–2.
54. John McPhee, 'Dept. of Amplification and Correction', *The New Yorker*, 12 March 1979, p. 147.
55. Canby, 'Fact-Checking', pp. 76, 79.
56. Ibid., p. 80.

57. Treisman, Canby, Thompson et al., podcast.
58. Evan Osnos, '"I was Fact-Checked by *The New Yorker*"', available at <http://www.newyorker.com/online/blogs/evanosnos/2009/09/i-was-fact-checked-by-the-new-yorker.html> (accessed 26 September 2013).
59. McPhee, 'Checkpoints', p. 56.
60. Ibid., p. 57.
61. Ibid., p. 59.
62. Rebecca Curtis, 'Twenty Grand', *The New Yorker*, 19 December 2005, pp. 78–85 (p. 79).
63. Ibid., p. 82.
64. Ibid.
65. Mary Poovey, *A History of the Modern Fact* (Chicago: Chicago University Press, 1998), p. 1.
66. Corey, *The World Through a Monocle*, p. 209.
67. Poovey, *A History of the Modern Fact*, p. 1.

Chapter 3

Marianne Moore and the Hidden Persuaders

Fiona Green

'You don't like tail fins and maybe I don't like tail fins, but can you imagine what would happen to the American economy if <u>nobody</u> liked tail fins?' This 1957 *New Yorker* cartoon offers a sharp angle on postwar prosperity.[1] Following its debut on the 1949 Cadillac, the tail fin loomed large in the designs of American automobiles for the next decade, and came to stand for the manufacturing of consumer desire by means of styling. It signals the shift in power at the Big Three auto manufacturers – General Motors, Chrysler, and Ford – from engineers to 'styling centres', and so signifies an era in which automotive form visibly took leave of function. The tail fin brings no aerodynamic advantage; it is simply a marker of prestige, a means, once every American has a car, of selling 'more car per car' in an annual cycle of planned obsolescence that speeds up turnover in a buyer's market.[2] It's clear from Barney Tobey's cartoon that automotive design was by 1957 teetering on the verge of self-parody, at least in the eyes of a certain kind of consumer, the kind of reader who could see the tail fin for what it was: a marketing ploy designed not so much to speed up your car as to accelerate the economy (Fig. 3.1). Five months on, E. B. White made passing mention of tail fins in a 'Letter from the East', which fondly recalled a textbook he had used as a student at Cornell, the so-called 'little book', by William Strunk, Jr.:

> 'The little book' has long since passed into disuse. Will died in 1946, and he had retired from teaching several years before that. Longer, lower textbooks are in use in English classes nowadays, I daresay – books with upswept tail fins and automatic verbs. I hope some of them manage to compress as much wisdom into as small a space, manage to come to the point as quickly and illuminate it as amusingly.[3]

Here automotive gadgetry tropes written forms – modern textbooks, and by implication the kinds of writing they promote – in which length supplants concision, cliché stands in for thought, and 'lower', less valuable things might be upswept, by sleight of styling, into speciously high performing vehicles of expression. White's *New Yorker* piece caught the eye of an editor at Macmillan who persuaded him to collaborate in reissuing the retired 'little book', and so to put back into circulation a text that has, along with White himself, long been considered the prototype of *New Yorker* style, according to which plainness, compression, and precisely geared syntax deliver sense with neither visible labour nor mere automated smoothness.[4] More than a practical manual, *The Elements of Style* also includes, in the final chapter White wrote for the 1959 reissue, a treatise on the relation between style and person – on the transparent revelation of self in the writing that has emerged from it. For E. B. White and the little book, you could say, the mysterious heart of style was anything but a midcentury styling centre.

Tobey's cartoon and White's 'Letter from the East' are typical of *The New Yorker* in holding up for wry scrutiny a marketing device that readers will see through, but which they might nonetheless fall for. The magazine also features plenty of ads for cars with tail fins – one of them, as it happens, turns up part way through White's 'Letter'.[5] This prompts the thought that a knowing attitude towards advertisements needn't make you any less susceptible to them, and so instantiates the often noted self-ironies of *The New Yorker*, which invite readers to desire the things the magazine advertises at the very moment those desires are being spoofed, cartooned, and otherwise lampooned.[6] But a close-up on the local habitat of the tail fin cartoon yields a more intriguing double act. The joke shared its page in *The New Yorker* with a profile of Marianne Moore, a poet then circulating in the mass media, so profiler Winthrop Sargeant claimed, in the form of 'a literary monument handily labeled for ready reference, a quaint and rather stylish spinster who, at the age of sixty-nine, lives in a cluttered apartment in Brooklyn and writes poems about animals'.[7] In the column that lies alongside the tail fin picture, Sargeant describes the kinds of creature to which Moore's verse is most often devoted. She does not write much about 'her fellow man', he reports, but,

> her love is expended instead on a still-life or a landscape world inhabited by plants and animals that are usually small and very self-sufficient. Yet she is apt to regard this world pessimistically; the environment in which her little animals play out their dramas is nearly always a threatening one. The odds are against them, even though, often covered with protective armor, they make their dwellings in snug holes and have admirable qualities of adaptability and strong powers of survival. They appear as symbols of virtues that Miss Moore repeatedly extols – courage, patience, firmness, loyalty, integrity, good sense, modesty, persistence, and independence.[8]

"You don't like tail fins and maybe I don't like tail fins, but can you imagine what would happen to the American economy if nobody liked tail fins?"

Figure 3.1. Barney Tobey, Cartoon, *The New Yorker*, 16 February 1957, p. 40. © The New Yorker Collection.

There is something strangely prescient about the way those virtues – integrity, good sense, modesty – stack up next to an icon of hubris and excess, the way the survival modes of Moore's little animals, the snug fit of creature to dwelling place, consorts in this page space with its opposite, an absurdly exaggerated form, not so much adapted to its environment as standing crudely out from it. It was perhaps by chance too that the column inches left vacant at the end of the Moore profile were taken up with a filler quoting a preposterous advertisement from the *Los Angeles Times*: 'What is a '57 Cadillac? It is speed made subject to human will. It gives mankind dominion over distance. It opens the avenues of all the world to humanity [. . .] It is the most capable and constant servant in the homes of men. It bears the sick swiftly and gently out to nature. It . . .' to which *The New Yorker* drily replied 'You're getting warm.'[9] Whether these juxtapositions in the February 1957 *New Yorker* between Marianne Moore and the extravagances of the auto industry were matters of accident or design, they do make for sharp contrasts: the spinster poet and the automotive business, you would think, were worlds apart. Except, of course, that they would shortly emerge in partnership in the form of the Ford Motor Correspondence, also published in *The New Yorker*, which is perhaps the most widely circulated and the least valued thing that Marianne Moore was ever to write.

On reading Winthrop Sargeant's profile of Marianne Moore, Clarence Brown of the University of Michigan was moved to send *The New Yorker* a sheaf of letters exchanged eighteen months previously between Moore and David Wallace, of Ford's Special Products Division, concerning a name for a new line of cars. The correspondence had been initiated by Wallace and subsequently lent to Brown 'by an official of the Ford Company as the sort of thing that should interest a university English department'.[10] *The New Yorker* published the letters, with their authors' permission, as a 'Department of Amplification' piece in April 1957. This addendum, run towards the back of the magazine, has enjoyed a more various afterlife and a much wider readership than the profile it supplemented. Moore chose to reprint *Letters From and To the Ford Motor Company* as a limited edition book in 1958, and again in *A Marianne Moore Reader* in 1961. Yet despite – or more likely because of – its popular appeal, the correspondence has not so far proved the sort of thing to interest university English departments. The most dismissive remark on the Ford letters came in 1978 from Helen Vendler, writing also for *The New Yorker*: 'it is a pity that Moore's own struggle culminated in things like the weaker poems and the preposterous exchange with the Ford Motor Company over the naming of the Edsel', Vendler opined, and thereby set the tone for other critics who have assimilated the Ford letters to the cartoonish figure Moore cut for herself in later life, with celebrity appearances at baseball games, in *Life* magazine, and on the cover of *Esquire*.[11]

If Moore's correspondence with Ford has so far had a peripheral place in critical readings of her poetic oeuvre, it comes in for yet briefer mention in histories of the marketing catastrophe that the Edsel notoriously became. Having invested $350m dollars in its new line of cars, Ford was forced by poor sales to withdraw the Edsel from production within two years of its launch. Moore's part in this story features parenthetically, if at all, in histories of the campaign. James L. Baughman's fascinating and detailed account of the Edsel debacle is typical in this respect: 'Ford ignored exhaustive research on the car's name. Company officials rejected [ad agency] FCB's recommendations (Corsair, Citation,

Pacer, or Ranger) – and several from the poet Marianne Moore – in favour of Edsel, for young Henry's late father.'[12] In putting the Ford Motor Correspondence at the centre of this chapter I mean in part to answer a question posed by Moore's biographer Linda Leavell: 'is the poet as hilariously remote from the modern world as the letters indicate? Or is she the savvy performer of a Chaplinesque dance through the cog wheels of mid-century consumerism?'[13] My argument leans towards Moore as savvy performer, but I want also to say more than this. In bringing out certain continuities between modernist Moore – sometime contributor to and editor of *The Dial* – and 'preposterous' Moore – one-time naming consultant at Ford marketing, as featured in *The New Yorker* – this chapter offers a close-up on the complex relations between modernist poetry, the commercial sphere, and periodical culture in the first half of the twentieth century. One suggestion will be that the Ford letters, as published in *The New Yorker* in the lead up to the launch of the ill-fated Edsel, were readily recruitable to Ford's advertising campaign, which played, as Moore's letters knowingly do, on the simultaneous visibility and covertness of 1950s marketing techniques. This paradox of explicitly hidden persuasion brings the Ford letters into correspondence with the elements of style that are everywhere felt, yet nowhere seen, in *The New Yorker*, and which serve as the magazine's own most enduring self-promotional device.

The perfect setting

Winthrop Sargeant's *New Yorker* profile pictures Marianne Moore at ease in various habitats. At sixty-nine she belongs both in 'big-circulation family magazines', and in her local neighbourhood, 'the fairly nondescript area' of Brooklyn in which 'armed with a shopping basket [. . .] she passes the time of day with her grocer or her vegetable man'. Her apartment, and by implication her poetry, is 'the apotheosis of snugness', a 'thoroughly self-sufficient refuge – [. . .] its occupant, when hidden away in it, is as independent of the world at large as a barnacle in its shell.'[14] Eccentrically at home in all these milieux, Moore comes across as spryly adaptable, yet fully self-integrated. Sargeant has Moore recall with particular nostalgia the period in the 1920s when her home ground was the centre of poetic experiment now known as modernism. Borrowing from the poet's own memoir of her time at *The Dial*, he lists the contributors to that little magazine: 'Thomas Mann, Ortega y Gasset, Paul Morand, Maxim Gorky, Ezra Pound, T. S. Eliot, D. H. Lawrence, W. B. Yeats, Roger Fry, Robert Morss Lovett, Paul Valéry,

Ford Madox Ford, Gilbert Seldes, William Carlos Williams, Wallace Stevens and Kenneth Burke among them.'[15] He goes on,

> in the middle of all this intellectual ferment sat Miss Moore, fastidiously reading and editing manuscripts. The offices of the *Dial* were in a three-story brick building on West Thirteenth Street that had brownstone steps leading up to the front door, carpeted staircases, and rooms with fireplaces and white mantelpieces. 'There was the recurrent flower-crier in the summer, with his slowly moving wagon of pansies, fuchsias, geraniums, petunias, ageratum,' Miss Moore recalled in her memoir. 'Or a man with straw*berries* for sale; or a certain fishman with his pushcart-scales, and staccato refrain so unvaryingly imperative, summer or winter, that Kenneth Burke's bit of parenthetic humour comes back to me almost as an epic, "I think if he stopped to sell a fish my heart would skip a beat."' As an editor in these pleasant surroundings, Miss Moore is reputed to have worked with tact, taste, and vast enthusiasm.[16]

From 'intellectual ferment' to 'pleasant surroundings', this casts the *Dial* offices, and so implicitly *The Dial* itself, as highbrow yet comfortable, a well appointed refuge that is also a centre of business, with the suggestion that the rhythms of commerce in the world outside are allowed to drift in – albeit that an actual sale would have produced an alarming hiatus in the fastidious work of that rarefied interior. In Moore's memoir, the Thirteenth Street offices have 'in gold-leaf block letters, THE DIAL, on the windows', as though the building has turned itself out in luxury bindings, and what comes in through its windows also finds a place in the magazine itself: the pansies marketed by the 'recurrent flower-crier' crop up again in the 'start of pleasure' with which, as Moore relates in her memoir, she came on D. H. Lawrence's '*Pansies*: "Pensées, like pansies, have their roots in the earth, and in the perfume there stirs still the faint grim scent of under-earth."'[17] This openness to the imperatives and odours of the market, along with the conflation of high quality fittings in the *Dial* offices and those of *The Dial* itself – Sargeant notes the magazine's 'beautifully printed pages' – underlines the degree to which lavish patronage and competitive business manoeuvres came together at *The Dial*.[18]

That Marianne Moore was wise to this convergence of elite aesthetic production and commercial enterprise becomes clear, I want to suggest, not only in the retrospective descriptions of *The Dial*'s 'pleasant surroundings' that Winthrop Sargeant was to reproduce in the 1957 *New Yorker*, but also in 'People's Surroundings', a poem *The Dial* had published in 1922. The constituents of that poem – the materials from which it was made, and the environment in which it was printed – serve in my argument as a certificate of Moore's apprenticeship, in the 1920s, to a mode of covert yet explicit styling that she would later employ in her correspondence with Ford, and which would subsequently bring into *The New Yorker* not so much a preposterous coda to a serious writing life, as a diagnostic playing out of those techniques of hidden persuasion practised by midcentury advertisers and shared, so it comes to seem in retrospect, in the making of modernism itself.

'People's Surroundings / they answer one's questions', Moore's 1922 poem begins, and it goes on to put in place a set of readerly puzzles, an arrangement of settings which tempt us to seek in them some trace of designing consciousness or previous occupancy.[19] It's a poem that thinks about the relation between style and personality, as in this plain opening stanza:

> a deal table compact with the wall;
> in this dried bone of arrangement,
> one's 'natural promptness' is compressed, not crowded out;
> one's style is not lost in such simplicity.

Whereas 'natural promptness' – something like the personal quick that Moore would later call 'gusto' – is allowed at first to hold its own, Moore proceeds in the poem to try on by means of pastiche the writing habits of contemporaries such as Wallace Stevens, and so to flirt with the possibility of disappearing 'like an obedient chameleon' into the surroundings she has confected from the styles of others.[20] Linda Leavell has suggested that the poem might also betray the presence of *Dial* editor Scofield Thayer, whose courtship of Moore (or at least of her poems) was in part responsible for drawing her into the scheme of *The Dial*.[21] Whether or not the poem's overstuffed interiors give an insider glimpse of Thayer's luxury penthouse, Moore's poem does do something very knowing with its prospective textual environs. 'People's Surroundings' was one of three poems Moore submitted in July 1921 for publication in *The Dial*, and she made significant revisions to it once it had been accepted – after, that is, the poem's own surroundings had been settled.[22] The most prominent of these was the Whitman-like catalogue of people and places at the poem's close; but for the purposes of my argument, a more telling late addition was of this line: '"a setting must not have the air of being one."' Moore came across the quoted phrase in the 1 August 1921 issue of *Vogue*. She could not have known at that point of the fraught negotiations that would shortly take place between Pound, *The Dial*, and *Vogue*'s sister journal *Vanity Fair*, over the publication of *The Waste Land*, nor that the transition of modernist poetry from coterie product to commercially valuable commodity would be indicated by Eliot's appearance in *Vogue*'s 'Hall of Fame' two years later.[23] But she did know, in 1921, that in lodging a snippet from *Vogue* in *The Dial* she was bringing under the covers of the little magazine a competitor for the 'select, restricted audience' that both Thayer's and Condé Nast's periodicals aimed to cultivate.[24] That the line Moore chose to quote was *about* the covert arrangement of '"a setting"', and that the quotation marks around it signalled that something was going on behind the poem's scenes, yet without revealing its source, further deepens the intrigue of 'People's Surroundings' in relation to its publishing context. It is this playful mode of concealment and display, I want to suggest, that anticipates Moore's canny involvement with Ford's 'peekaboo' style of mass marketing in the 1950s, and, more generally, with the impression of unlaboured transparency that *The New Yorker* has so consistently been at pains to construct.

The 1 August 1921 issue of *Vogue* exemplifies, at a number of points, the domestication of avant-garde experiment in mainstream culture: we read of 'the decorative possibilities of Picasso', and, in a feature on swimsuits, of a 'cubist foulard that makes [a] bodice'.[25] The issue is for the most part devoted to interior décor, with repeated emphasis on the importance of domestic interiors as the outward expression of personality, the medium whereby we advertise our tastes or risk having our settings betray faulty interior lives:

> What is nearer to us, more immediate in its influence on us, than the lines of our furniture, the decoration of our walls, the objects which surround us when we awake, or the furnishings which form the setting of our luncheons and dinners? [. . .] To many women, apparently, this means little, for much modern decoration is so impersonal that we find ourselves wondering what can be the use of this or that chair or what is the purpose of objects the form of which means nothing, while the colour amazes without pleasing. Anarchy, not order, reigns in such a room.[26]

It's unsurprising that this issue of *Vogue* should have caught the attention of Marianne Moore, then in the midst of revising a poem called 'People's Surroundings' which had already begun by saying 'they answer one's questions'. She added the following lines to her poem in September 1921:

> In these noncommittal, personal-impersonal expressions of appearance,
> the eye knows what to skip;
> the physiognomy of conduct must not reveal the skeleton;
> 'a setting must not have the air of being one'

That crucial quoted line comes from a *Vogue* article by French decadent novelist Francis de Miomandre called 'The Perfect Host in the

Perfect Setting', which takes the form of a letter to a young bachelor intent on winning over a certain young lady. The bachelor has finished furnishing his new apartment, and his mentor, Christine, outlines the degree of tact with which he should set his stage: 'I know that your excellent taste will add little by little, and with discernment, the small personal touches which will constitute, as it were, your signature, discreet, but recognizable, on these charming, and essentially modernist pages.'[27]

Marianne Moore might well have been wondering how to style the signature *she* was about to put on the essentially modernist pages of *The Dial*. This is the passage from *Vogue* which she copied into her reading diary and then added to the poem: Christine advises the bachelor,

> Here you are, installed in your handsome new apartment and eager to do honours to a little group of very special people – three or four intimate friends [including] the woman whom you most desire to please. She will come, I am very sure. But even if she does not come, if you have not even invited her, you must do everything as if she were coming. That is the only way to avoid being an awkward host in one's own home [. . .] *It is, in all truth, a prepared setting, and it must, of course, never have the air of being one.* The first of your guests to arrive must feel at the same time the impression of surprising you and of being waited for and expected. A négligée without negligence, that is the rule.

The maxim Moore chose to extract from *Vogue* and to publish in *The Dial* is about contriving the seamless impression of naturalness – about hiding the labour that has gone into the effect of transparency. When Moore published 'People's Surroundings' in *Observations* (1924), she supplied it, like other poems in that book, with notes crediting some of its sources. These reveal several borrowings from the commercial sphere, and especially from advertising copy. One long line, from the section of the poem concerned with business environments, for example, reads 'on "paper so thin that one thousand four hundred and twenty pages make one inch,"' and is annotated with a lengthy extract from a *New York Times* advertisement which ends, 'Warren's India is so thin that 1420 pages make only one inch.'[28] This plays with the compact and the prolix: 'one thousand four hundred and twenty pages' takes up more line space than '1420 pages', and yet the supplementary note is a twelve-line expansion on the very topic of compression. 'People's Surroundings', then, exemplifies Moore's fascination with the mechanisms of print culture, and with intersections between domestic, creative, and promotional activities, whether these are found in the mass media, or in a highbrow setting such as *The Dial*. It was a poetics developed in these surroundings, which was sharply aware of the degree to which it could expand on or thin out to the point of invisibility its own media of transmission, that equipped Marianne Moore especially well for the role of naming consultant to the Ford Motor Company, and which makes the publication of her letters in *The New Yorker* an event of particular interest to departments of English.

Association value

Marianne Moore was less than pleased with Winthrop Sargeant's *New Yorker* profile of her: 'I take it very hard', she wrote in a letter to her friend Chester Page.[29] What seems especially to have troubled her were Sargeant's remarks on the 'associative process of thought' that characterised both her poetry – 'not so much a matter of logic as it is of kaleidoscopic association' – and her conversation, which was, Sargeant knew from direct experience and on the authority of Moore's acquaintances, 'remarkable for its diversity, and for a certain recklessness that is likely to lead her, by a sequence of crowding and tumbling associations, into fields far removed from her starting point'.[30] On one occasion, Sargeant recalls,

> one of [Moore's] guests finally reached the point of exhaustion, and exclaimed, 'Marianne, don't jump around so in your conversation!'
> Miss Moore paused, turned pityingly toward the heretic, and replied with spirit, 'It isn't jumping around. It's all connected.' Then she was off again.[31]

You can see why Moore might have taken this hard, for its fondly belittling tone ('she was off again'), and its resort to easy caricature. Even so, that 'associative process of thought' is certainly recognisable in Moore's poems: they do, as her conversations reputedly did, lead to fields far removed from their starting points. At the same time, the poems are 'all connected', sometimes by argument or by substantive kinships between the diverse things, creatures, and sayings on which they alight, yet frequently also by the medium in which those arguments and objects are made and circulated – by lateral displacements across the syllabic surfaces of poetic language. To take some small examples: in 'Critics and Connoisseurs' (1916) the visual associations that bring together a piece of Chinese porcelain and 'a swan under the willows in Oxford' have added consistency if you notice that 'Certain *Ming* / products' and the swan's 'fla*ming*o colored, maple-/ leaflike feet' share a syllable.[32] Whether, as in the same poem, the logic connecting the title's '*Conn*oisseurs' to 'un*con*scious / fastidiousness' and the swan's ungainly 're*conno*iter[ ]' is quietly preserved in shared roots, or whether, as in the case of the later poem 'Four Quartz Crystal Clocks' (1940), the etymologies ('Jupiter or jour pater, the day god') and punning contrivances ('the bell-boy with the buoy-ball') are more explicitly hinged, the associative runs of thought in Moore's poems seem frequently to have been generated by the contingencies of their verbal medium.[33]

When David Wallace, one of the so-called 'whiskers', or university sociologists, at that time employed by Ford marketing, wrote to Marianne Moore in 1955 asking for her help in finding 'a name for a rather important new series of cars', a name that would 'convey, through association or other conjuration, some visceral feeling of elegance, fleetness, advanced features and design', he was asking the right person; and when Moore playfully made visible in her letters the threads of her associative thinking – 'Aeroterre Fée Rapide (Aérofée, Aéro Faire, Fée Aiglette, Magi-faire) Comme Il faire Tonnerre Alifère (winged thunder)' – she was not so much demonstrating the distance between 'the field of words and the fragile meaning of words [and] car-making' as Wallace had ventured, but proving their adjacency: the partnership between the modernist poet and the midcentury auto industry, I will suggest, lies precisely with their shared investment in the powers of association.[34]

The 1957 Ford Edsel was intended to capture the market in medium-priced cars for 'the younger executive or professional family on its way up'.[35] A prominent feature in the spectacular marketing failure that the Edsel eventually became was the high-profile role of 'motivation research' in the design and branding of the new Ford. Plans for the Edsel involved image profiles and 'personality objectives' in the course of which potential brand names were tested by word association surveys – though in eventually opting for 'Edsel', Ford seems to have ignored the most often reported associations of that name, with 'pretzel, diesel, and hard sell'.[36] The business of motivation research was no secret in 1957. The year that saw the launch of the Edsel was also the year that Vance Packard published *The Hidden Persuaders*, the bestselling book that revealed to American consumers how their unconscious desires were being manipulated by marketing men such as motivation research guru Ernest Dichter. Where would you advertise an exposé of advertising? *The New Yorker* offered one persuasive venue:

> when 'The Hidden Persuaders' pull the strings . . . you do as you're told! 'This Brisk, authoritative book is a funny and frightening report,' says *The New Yorker*, 'on how much such pressure groups as manufacturers, fundraisers, and politicians are attempting, with the help of advertising agencies and publicists, to turn the American mind into a kind of catatonic dough that will buy, give, or vote at their command.'[37]

This advertisement, which includes as a selling point a review from the magazine in which it also appears, chips away at the wall of separation between advertising and editorial that *The New Yorker* staunchly defended; and it hardly needs saying that the advertised product was designed to discredit the very medium in which it was being promoted. What people tend to remember about Packard's book is its case studies of the market research behind products such as Bisquick 'add an egg' cake mix, or, as highlighted by the *New Yorker* review, that 'a recent widespread slump in prune sales was partly the result of prunes' being associated with old maids and stinginess (the cure: bright-colored ads depicting prunes as a new "wonder fruit".)'[38] *The Hidden Persuaders* became a bestseller not – or not only – because readers took to heart its warnings about the infiltration of political institutions by the techniques of mass persuasion, but because they were intrigued by the inside view it offered of their own shopping habits, of their own susceptibility to persuasion by means of unconscious association.

Ford's marketing campaign for the Edsel played on this same fascination, on the interest midcentury consumers had *in* marketing. Rather than mounting a campaign of hidden persuasion, the Special Products division at Ford offered potential customers an insider glimpse of its publicity machine, inviting them to become spectators on their own manipulation. A three-page advertisement in *The New Yorker* shortly after 'Edsel Day' (the car was officially launched, after much anticipatory fanfare, on 4 September 1957) exemplifies this strategy. Before you see the car, its makers tell you what they think about what you think:

> Just remember that every hour of every day, we are called upon to make decisions based on OUR opinion of YOUR opinion. A new line to the rear deck, for instance. How will it look to *You*? A new kind of transmission control? How will it appeal to *You*?
>
> *Why* did we decide to bring out the Edsel? Again, there is a one-word answer. *YOU*.[39]

So the long and costly process of motivation research that has fed into the styling of Ford's new line of cars is laid bare (we've invested time and money in market research, we know who you are and what you want, and we've produced a commodity you'll want to buy), and a moment later that same machinery disappears: it's as if the purchaser has magically brought into being exactly what he desires, and the costly labour of research, production, and press mediation collapses into 'a one-word answer. *YOU*.' Alongside this kind of vanishing trick, what we see played out in the pages of *The New Yorker*, as elsewhere in the national press in 1957, is a game of now you see it, now you don't, centred on the car itself. During the protracted lead-up to the launch (almost a year elapsed between the announcement of the name, and 'Edsel Day'), Ford staged a game of 'peekaboo', a so-called automotive striptease, so that among all the promotional material, the newspaper ads and travelling shows, the Edsel was never seen as a whole.[40] A 1957 *New Yorker* 'Talk' piece reports on a sneak preview hosted by a Manhattan Edsel dealer: '"when the final veil drops"', says the unfortunately named Charles Kreisler, '"it's got to drop with a bang!"', yet he is permitted to show his *New Yorker* visitors, and they to pass on to readers, a long list of the Edsel's interior features, or as he puts it, with special emphasis, the car's '"*inside* gimmicks."'[41]

Marianne Moore's correspondence with Ford about the naming of the new car was conducted over three months in 1955, but it was published in April 1957, half way through the year-long lead up to Edsel day, and two weeks after the publication of *The Hidden Persuaders*.[42] In the context of *The New Yorker*, the letters click into gear with the game of hide and seek taking place in the mass media. In his first letter to Moore, David Wallace writes, 'we should like [. . .] a name, in short, that flashes a dramatically desirable picture in people's minds'. But a picture of what? The most advertised aspect of the car at this point was that no-one had seen it. 'Perhaps you could give me a sketch of its general appearance', Moore asks, 'or hint as to some of its exciting potentialities – though my brother reminds me that such information is highly confidential'.[43] Wallace writes back, 'now we on this end must help you by sending some tangible representation of what we are talking about. Perhaps the enclosed sketches will serve the purpose. They are not IT, but they convey the feeling'. When Moore received the drawings she replied as follows:

> The sketches. They are indeed exciting; they have quality, and the toucan tones lend tremendous allure – confirmed by the wheels. Half the magic, – sustaining effects of this kind. Looked at upside down, furthermore, there is a sense of fish buoyancy. Immediately your word impeccable sprang to mind. Might it be a possibility? The Impeccable. In any case, the baguette lapidary glamour you have achieved certainly spurs the imagination. Car innovation is like launching a ship – 'drama'.[44]

This epistolary version of automotive striptease allows an alluring glimpse of a glamorous form, some flashes of colour, quality, and tone, yet includes almost nothing of substance. The letter hints at the secrets to which Moore has been privy, and at the same time reproduces the kind of research that's gone into the product – because Moore is surely parodying exactly those 'depth' techniques in which the hidden persuaders, the motivation researchers, specialise: 'looked at upside down. . .' she says, turning the sketches as she might have an inkblot test, and up floats 'fish buoyancy', with its inevitable teasing association with fins (the Edsel, it was later revealed, had none), followed by a stagey slippage from buoyancy to 'launching a ship'. This is indeed '"drama"'. Reading this letter in *The New Yorker* five months before the Edsel was unveiled means, as with the peekaboo advertisements, almost but not quite getting to see 'IT', or rather, seeing a poet's response to some confidential sketches, not of 'IT' but conveying the feeling of 'IT', cast in a knowing parody of the market research that has gone into styling the mysterious 'IT' that will meet your deepest desires. It might be flattering, after all, to think that you were being persuaded not by some slick advertiser, but by a poet and a sociologist, and that they were sharing something of their craft with you.

A symptom of Moore's supposed unworldliness that is very much on show in the letters is her refusal to be paid for consultancy work. 'My fancy would be inhibited' she says, 'by acknowledgment in advance of performance.'[45] This is consistent with the carefully managed distinctions between payment and patronage according to the modernist institutions with which Moore was familiar. When she writes to Wallace 'under contract, esprit could not flower', we might even recall the 'Bel Esprit', the patronage scheme proposed in 1922 by Ezra Pound to free T. S. Eliot from waged work, and whose future recipients, Pound suggested, might have included Moore herself.[46] The Bel Esprit plan came to nothing, but even so, Moore's insistence that 'etymological hits' will come only when her associative machinery runs free of obligation is continuous with that modernist insistence on the difference between creative work and contracted industry.[47] Ford, for its part, allowed Moore her freedom from payment – though they did send her flowers; yet just when it appears that the naming project is not really work – 'I'm not working day and night for you', says Moore – the letters publicise the considerable labour that went into producing potential 'hits'. A typical passage reads, 'Turcotinga (turquoise cotinga – the cotinga being a South-American finch or sparrow) solid indigo. (I have a three-volume treatise on flowers that might produce something but the impression given should certainly be unlabored.)'[48] Documents later archived at the Pierpont Morgan Library show that Moore's automotive research included more conventional sources too. On a cutting from the *New York Times Magazine* advertising the Packard Clipper, she has underlined 'Torsion-level suspension' and noted such potentially Moore-ish details as 'coil and leaf springs'; another newspaper clipping features a new 'Mystery Car' that 'will work on the turbine principle'.[49] With her eye for syllables, Moore surely noted the typesetting accident that put a word break in 'tur-bine', of which the first syllable turns up in her suggestion to Wallace that Ford re-use 'Turbotorc (used elsewhere as an adjective by Plymouth)', again in 'Turcotinga'; and finally, 'tur-' is reintegrated in association with Moore's puzzle over 'the topknot of the peacock and topnotcher of speed' to emerge with a final flourish in 'Mr Wallace: May I submit Utopian Turtletop? Do not trouble to answer unless you like it.'[50] It's a preposterous name for a car, certainly; but the trains of thought and the letters in which they circulate amount to more than that. In turning upside down and inside out the mechanisms of poetic composition and, simultaneously, the workings of motivation research, the Ford letters published in *The New Yorker* find themselves participating in an overt display of hidden persuasion. This is not so much a selling out of poetic technique for the purposes of commercial enterprise as a playing out of their inseparable media.

Remodelling

In her 1978 article that ends by dismissing the Ford letters, Helen Vendler commends Moore's earlier poetry as follows:

> [Moore] placed herself in alliance with another American attitude toward words: our pragmatic, taxonomic, realistic conviction that words are useful, practical, and exact; that they can convey the specifications for a bridge, the identifying marks of an animal, the geographical directions for an explorer, and even, in our earliest literature, the path to salvation. To write so that no single word can be misunderstood is a mark of the American pride in accuracy, punctual speech, and laconic completeness.[51]

There's a good deal of truth to this characterisation of Moore's exacting and practical poetics, but Vendler also misses something in it. As we have seen, the poetry exploits misunderstanding as well as striving for precision, finding its material and impetus in the ways that one word can look or sound like another and so take a poem 'by a sequence of crowding and tumbling associations, into fields far removed from [its] starting point'.[52] Perhaps in her evident 'conviction that words are useful, practical, and exact; that they can convey the specifications for a bridge', Vendler was showing her own suitedness to *The New Yorker*: 'the American pride in accuracy, punctual speech, and laconic completeness' might have come straight from the desk of E. B. White.

White made no secret of his antipathy towards the ad men, alongside whom he had briefly worked as a young graduate, nor of his disdain for motivation research. A great admirer of 'valuable citizens' such as architects and engineers, he had no time for the interference of 'tipsters, pollsters, motivationalists and dream-mongers' in the vital work of design.[53] Not long after the Edsel was launched, White's 1958 'Letter from the North' tells of his frustrated attempts to purchase a new car. What he particularly objects to is the 'queer, corrupting conception of the automobile as a winged thing or a finny thing'.[54] Real style he says, doesn't come from styling centres or 'motivation research-monkeys or social psychologists'; it comes naturally:

> Purity of line, loveliness, symmetry – these arrive mysteriously whenever someone who knows or cares creates something that is perfectly fitted to its work, whether the object is a grain scoop, a suspension bridge, or a guillotine. Nobody styled the orb web of a spider, nobody styled the sixteen-foot canoe [. . .] A garbage scow carries a filthy cargo but it has clean lines – cleaner by far than the lines of the 1958 automobile.[55]

These sharp-edged distinctions clearly have their place also in White's writing about writing. In an important sense, nobody 'styles' the kind of clean written line that is perfectly fitted to its work of communication: though you could write a little book about the hard work that goes into crafting plain prose, *The Elements of Style* never employs its load-bearing term as a verb. The 'Approach to Style' that White added to Strunk's *Elements* is about the revelatory moment when writing shows itself as 'the Self escaping into the open'.[56] This is most likely to happen, paradoxically, when the writer places himself 'in the background', in other words, 'by [his] staying out of the act'.[57] Writing achieves the high mystery of self-revelation from a reserved centre of being, not from outward adaptation or gadgetry; in common with the kind of functional car E. B. White searched for in vain among the finny things of 1958, such revelatory style would serve as 'a vehicle requiring no wings'.[58]

The closest White came to finding the car of his dreams was 'the little Hillman', a British compact he took for a test drive. Among the various explanations for the failure of the Edsel – the downturn in the economy, the launch of the Soviet Sputnik, the mistaken reliance on motivation research – was the rising popularity of European compacts: as White ruefully notes early in 1958, 'only the foreign cars are enjoying an active market'.[59] While the Edsel still holds the front pages of *The New Yorker*, nearer the back of the magazine increasing numbers of low-key ads appear for Hillmans, MGs, and Fiats. Among them are the sleek modernist lines of the Citroën DS 19, the subject of brilliantly besotted critique in Roland Barthes' *Mythologies*.[60] It would take some years for

Mythologies to make its way into the notice of American readers, but Barthes' reading of the 'Déesse' would serve uncannily well as a diagnosis of another seamless product of 1958 whose immaculate surface belies the process of its assembly, that is the faultless style of *The New Yorker* itself. E. B. White mythologises the revelation of self in style as something very like 'a transformation of life into matter', and you might even say, as Barthes does of the material of the DS 19, that the magazine in which that style is everywhere felt yet nowhere seen 'promotes a taste for lightness in a magical sense'.[61] If White is the mythologiser of *New Yorker* style, perhaps Marianne Moore and David Wallace should be regarded as the mythologists, the demystifiers, of the ungainly product they were hired by Ford Motors to promote. In this sense the Ford Motor Correspondence turns the Edsel as well as itself inside out, showing us its jointed assembly, and putting the machinery of its coming into being on display.

Their efforts did not, of course, succeed in enchanting the public into buying the car, but the Ford Motor Correspondence, unlike the Edsel itself, remained in production, or reproduction, for some time to come. After their sojourn in *The New Yorker*, Marianne Moore and David Wallace donated their letters to the Pierpont Morgan Library and had them republished in a limited edition book, finely illustrated, not with pictures of the Edsel, but with a tissue-thin handprinted woodcut of the 'silver sword' plant, in homage to one of the names Moore had suggested.[62] There is yet another remake, however, that speaks volumes in retrospect as to the character and exchange value of the Ford Motor Correspondence. The Morgan Library holds some unpublished letters between Moore and Mr Wallace, from late 1957, when they were making arrangements for the limited edition. To one of these, Moore added a postscript:

> This is an (addendum,) enclosed with diffidence. Friends of mine – malapertly venturing such a suggestion even at dinner or a party, threaten to beg for me of you, a car! Since I have a license but no car – a license obtained before I attempted advertising. My relations with the Company were business and I would rather die than extort – seem to extort – any advantage of a commercial nature when I stipulated that I would not accept pay unless I was of service. They then say, 'the letters have represented hundreds of dollars of advertising. Success could not have succeeded better.' I do not weasel things in that manner. So – needing no answer – may I say that if you receive any irrelevant letters concerning my Fordless condition, do not give them another thought, I have answered them myself, now.[63]

In reply, David Wallace sent Moore the gift of a car: an eight-inch model of the 1958 Edsel Corsair. Moore replies:

An Edsel, turquoise like my armchair! Fins subordinated; I should say, no fins; inconspicuous bumpers, recessed wheels; 'in the moderate-priced field.' (You don't say anything about the fuel needed but the car goes quite a distance without extra gas on my oak entrance floor). Rhymed promotion – 'It's really new' paired with 'too' – whereas my 'sword' and 'Ford' would not have been quite so direct a compliment to Mr Edsel. I <u>may</u> consider one change, with your permission. I so admire that sword-plant which grows in the House of the Sun, I might wilfully substitute for the circular radiator-device a little white gold sword; – or a small silver turtle, though the rear top of my car has not quite the slope of the top at the front.[64]

In toying with this two-tone turquoise vehicle, Moore and her correspondent put the Edsel through one final phase of reproduction. Inconspicuous, recessed, subordinated, moderate, economical, the Edsel is thus remodelled as a compact. That Moore went back to her own devices and turned the little Edsel into a turtletop is a fittingly small act of esprit. More suitable still is the line with which she signed off: 'My deepest thanks, Mr. Wallace. I love machinery, and association value is not lost on me!'

Notes

1. Barney Tobey, cartoon, *The New Yorker*, 16 February 1957, p. 40.
2. My take on tail fins is much indebted to David Gartman's excellent *Auto Opium: A Social History of American Automobile Design* (London: Routledge, 1994), chapter 6.
3. E. B. White, 'Letter from the East', *The New Yorker*, 27 July 1957, pp. 35–45 (p. 43).
4. William Strunk, Jr., *The Elements of Style*, with revisions, an Introduction, and a New Chapter on Writing by E. B. White (New York: Macmillan, 1959). For a fascinating account of the publication history of 'the little book', see Mark Garvey, *Stylized: A Slightly Obsessive History of Strunk & White's 'The Elements of Style'* (New York: Touchstone 2009).
5. Cadillac advertisement, *The New Yorker*, 27 July 1957, p. 37.
6. Mary F. Corey discusses *The New Yorker*'s mixed messages in *The World Through a Monocle: 'The New Yorker' at Midcentury* (Cambridge, MA: Harvard University Press, 1999), pp. xi, 17. On *New Yorker* double talk in postwar travel advertisements and cartoons, see Fiona Green, 'Elizabeth Bishop in Brazil and the *New Yorker*', *Journal of American Studies*, 46.4 (November 2012), 803–29 (pp. 805–8).
7. Winthrop Sargeant, 'Humility, Concentration, And Gusto', *The New Yorker*, 16 February 1957, pp. 38–77 (p. 38).
8. Ibid., p. 40.
9. *The New Yorker*, 16 February 1957, p. 77.
10. 'Department of Amplification', *The New Yorker*, 13 April 1957, pp. 140–6 (p. 140).
11. Helen Vendler, 'Books: On Marianne Moore', *The New Yorker*, 16

October 1978, pp. 168–94 (p. 194). John Slatin, for example, says of Moore's late poems that 'they get buried, as things so often do in *Vogue* and *Harper's Bazaar* and even the *New Yorker*, between feature articles and glossy photographs and the advertisements she had once been able to transform into the stuff of art.' *The Savage's Romance* (University Park: Pennsylvania State University Press, 1986), p. 15. An exception to the tendency to dismiss Moore's later poetry in this way is Elizabeth Gregory, '"Combat Cultural": Marianne Moore and the Mixed Brow', in *Critics and Poets of Marianne Moore: 'A Right Good Salvo of Barks'*, ed. Linda Leavell, Cristanne Miller and Robin G. Schulze (Lewisburg: Bucknell University Press, 2005), pp. 208–21. The present chapter shares ground with Gregory's excellent essay, whose focus is the poetry Moore published in, and, arguably, wrote for *The New Yorker*, from 1955. Gregory does not discuss the Ford letters.

12. James L. Baugham, 'The Frustrated Persuader: Fairfax M. Cone and the Edsel Advertising Campaign, 1957–59', *The Other Fifties: Interrogating Midcentury American Icons*, ed. Joel Foreman (Urbana and Chicago: University of Illinois Press, 1997), p. 34. My account of the campaign is indebted to Baugham, and to John Brooks, 'Annals of Business: The Edsel I', *The New Yorker*, 26 November 1960, pp. 57–102; 'The Edsel II', *The New Yorker*, 3 December 1960, pp. 199–224.

13. Linda Leavell, *Holding on Upside Down: The Life and Work of Marianne Moore* (New York: Faber, 2013), p. 360.

14. Sargeant, 'Humility', pp. 38, 42, 47.

15. Ibid., p. 67. That these serve as 'names that guaranteed the quality of which Miss Moore wrote in her memoir' shows the afterlife of what Aaron Jaffe has called the 'trafficking in various authorial names like so many emergent currencies' of the 1920s and '30s, each name by 1957 a more or less stable token of value whose listing credits readers with the expertise to know what it stands for. See Jaffe, 'Adjectives and the Work of Modernism in an Age of Celebrity', *Yale Journal of Criticism*, 16.1 (2003), 1–37 (p. 4).

16. Sargeant, 'Humility', p. 67. The profile quotes from Moore's '*The Dial*: A Retrospect' (1940), in *The Complete Prose of Marianne Moore*, ed. Patricia C. Willis (London: Faber, 1987), pp. 357–64 (p. 357).

17. Moore, '*The Dial*: A Retrospect', pp. 357, 358.

18. Sargeant, 'Humility', p. 64. Lawrence Rainey describes 'the sensibility epitomized by the *Dial*' as 'a form of production supported by massive and unprecedented patronage that facilitated modernism's transition from a literature of an exiguous elite to a position of prestigious dominance'. He goes on to position the magazine as a compromise between the 'intransigent aestheticism' of *The Little Review*, and the much more commercial *Vanity Fair*. See *Institutions of Modernism: Literary Elites and Public Culture* (New Haven: Yale University Press, 1998), pp. 86, 95.

19. Marianne Moore, 'People's Surroundings', *The Dial*, 72 (June 1922), 588–90, facsimile reprint, *Becoming Marianne Moore: The Early Poems 1907–1924*, ed. Robin G. Schulze (Berkeley: University of California Press, 2002), p. 269.

20. For Moore's pastiche of Stevens in the Bluebeard's Tower section of the poem, see Slatin, *The Savage's Romance*, pp. 129–30, and Robin G.

Schulze, *The Web of Friendship: Marianne Moore and Wallace Stevens* (Ann Arbor: University of Michigan Press, 1995), pp. 29–32.

21. Leavell, *Holding on Upside Down*, p. 189.
22. See *Becoming Marianne Moore*, p. 274.
23. Pound's negotiations over the publication of *The Waste Land*, and the *Dial* editors' eventual decision to buy the poem with *The Dial* Award, forms the centre of Rainey's argument about 'The Price of Modernism' (*Institutions of Modernism*, chapter 3). Jaffe discusses Eliot's celebrity appearance in *Vogue*'s 'Hall of Fame' in 'Adjectives and the Work of Modernism', p. 14.
24. Rainey, *Institutions of Modernism*, p. 96.
25. *Vogue*, 1 August 1921, pp. 43, 38. *Vogue* also reviews 'the new spectacles presented by M. Diaghileff', including 'a series of Spanish dances' whose costumes illustrate 'the genius which Picasso can show when he is not jesting with his public' (p. 39). I am very grateful to Hannah Crawforth for having located a copy of this issue of *Vogue*.
26. Ibid., p. 43.
27. Francis de Miomandre, 'The Perfect Host in the Perfect Setting', *Vogue*, 1 August 1921, pp. 62–3 (p. 62).
28. Marianne Moore, *Observations* (New York: Dial Press, 1924), pp. 66, 100, facsimile reprint, *Becoming Marianne Moore*, pp. 108, 142.
29. Leavell, *Holding on Upside Down*, p. 359.
30. Sargeant, 'Humility', pp. 40, 39, 48.
31. Ibid., p. 49.
32. *Becoming Marianne Moore*, p. 77.
33. 'Four Quartz Crystal Clocks', *The Complete Poems of Marianne Moore* (New York: Viking, 1967), p. 115.
34. 'Department of Amplification', pp. 140, 145. That these threads run through verbal associations in French as well as English is surely a result of Moore's lengthy labours – 1945–54 – on her translation of La Fontaine's *Fables*.
35. Brooks, 'Annals of Business: The Edsel I', p. 76
36. Ibid., pp. 76, 82.
37. Advertisement, *The New Yorker*, 22 June 1957, p. 102.
38. Vance Packard, *The Hidden Persuaders* (London: Penguin, 1960 [1957]), pp. 71, 117–18; review, *The New Yorker*, 18 May 1957, pp. 167–8 (p. 168).
39. Advertisement, *The New Yorker*, 7 September 1957, pp. 55–7.
40. Brooks, 'Annals of Business: The Edsel I', p. 90.
41. 'The Talk of the Town: Moment in History', *The New Yorker*, 24 August 1957, pp. 24–7 (pp. 23, 25).
42. If suspicion arises that Ford somehow engineered the submission of the letters to *The New Yorker*, or that David Wallace had initiated the correspondence with future publication in mind, nothing I have so far found in the archives corroborates it.
43. 'Department of Amplification', p. 142.
44. Ibid., pp. 143–4.
45. Ibid., p. 142.
46. Ibid., p. 144. For the Bel Esprit plan, see *Selected Letters of Ezra Pound to John Quinn 1915–1924*, ed. Timothy Materer (Durham, NC: Duke

University Press, 1991), pp. 10–12. Pound publicised the Bel Esprit – much to Eliot's embarrassment – in his 'Paris Letter' in the *Waste Land* issue of *The Dial*, 73.5 (November 1922), 549–54 (pp. 550–2).

47. 'Department of Amplification', p. 144.
48. Ibid., p. 146.
49. Packard Clipper Advertisement, *New York Times Magazine*, 27 November 1955, p. 79; 'Mystery Car Tied to Turbine Drive', *New York Times*, 23 November 1955, p. 25; clippings, Pierpont Morgan Library, folder MA 1909.
50. 'Department of Amplification', pp. 145, 146.
51. 'Books: On Marianne Moore', p. 170.
52. Sargeant, 'Humility', p. 48.
53. E. B. White, 'Letter from the North', *The New Yorker*, 5 April 1958, pp. 34–8 (p. 38).
54. Ibid., p. 34.
55. Ibid., p. 34.
56. Strunk and White, *Elements of Style*, p. 53.
57. Ibid., pp. 56, 60.
58. White, 'Letter from the North', p. 34.
59. Ibid., p. 38. For the various explanations offered for the failure of the Edsel, see Brooks, 'Annals of Business: The Edsel II', pp. 207, 210, 215–18.
60. *The New Yorker* issue of 7 September 1957, the week the Edsel was launched, carried ads for the MG, 'this pretty gay little car, clean of line, happy in spirit' (p. 73), and the Hillman Minx convertible (p.107), as well as for the Ford Edsel. The 'Chic Parisienne elegance' of the new Citroën features in black and white two-column advertisements in issues from 31 March 1956, p. 59, through to 23 April 1960, p. 157, by which point compact American models are increasingly on show in the front pages: see, for example, the colour Chevrolet advertisement, reading 'thrift (a wonderful virtue) is compulsory in the compact Corvair', *The New Yorker*, 23 April 1960, p. 10.
61. Roland Barthes, 'The New Citroën', *Mythologies* (1957), trans. Richard Howard, Annette Lavers (New York: Hill and Wang, 2012), pp. 169–170.
62. Marianne Moore and David Wallace, *Letters From and To the Ford Motor Company* (New York: Pierpont Morgan Library, 1958), n.p. The woodcut is by Leonard Baskin.
63. Marianne Moore, letter to David Wallace, 17 December 1957, Pierpont Morgan Library, folder MA 1909.
64. Marianne Moore, letter to David Wallace, 7 February 1958, Pierpont Morgan Library, folder MA 1909. The model Edsel is also held at the Morgan Library.

II Self-Fashioning

Chapter 4

Philip Roth's Kinds of Writing

Bharat Tandon

> Above the cricket, towers that seemed like mountains of light rose up into the
> night sky. Even this late the neon signs were still blazing. Reds, blues, greens,
> and yellows flashed down on him.
>
> George Selden, *The Cricket in Times Square*[1]

> Staggering to see that face coming up at his. It was like kissing a billboard.
>
> Philip Roth, *Zuckerman Unbound*[2]

'. . . electrochemical pastels . . .'[3]

It should not, perhaps, come as much of a surprise to find that one of
twentieth-century New York's major public cultural and commercial
spaces, Times Square, should have been such a recurring source of
fascination for another major cultural and commercial space, *The New
Yorker*. After all, they both testify, in their different modes, to an emerg-
ing and defining quality of twentieth-century urban phenomenology,
one particularly manifest in Manhattan itself: the experience of the
cityscape as a hybrid environment of solid and textual material, with the
practical result that writing such a city is, by definition, an exercise in
intertextuality. Almost from the beginning of its modern life, the idea of
Times Square has been tied in with the presence of its distinctive signage,
the first electric sign having gone up within weeks of Longacre Square's
official renaming in April 1904.

Michel de Certeau famously suggested that to move around a city at
all is to write a text:

> The ordinary practitioners of the city live 'down below,' below the thresholds
> at which visibility begins. They walk – an elementary form of this experience
> of the city; they are walkers, *Wandersmänner*, whose bodies follow the thicks
> and thins of an urban 'text' they write without being able to read it [. . .] The

networks of these moving, intersecting writings compose a manifold story that has neither author nor spectator, shaped out of fragments of trajectories and alterations of spaces.[4]

And if this is true to some extent of any city, then how much more will that be the case when that city is one so full of giant texts as twentieth-century Manhattan? Of course, the textual, specular city is not a phenomenon that began in the twentieth century; as critics have noted, Victorian London often presented its inhabitants with a barrage of handbills, billboards and other textual material in their lines of sight. Lynda Nead, for example, has offered an excellent analysis of how nineteenth-century urban advertising worked:

> Advertisements not only covered the walls and temporary hoardings of the city, they also circulated on the roads and pavements. Businesses and shops sent out their sandwich-board men and advertising vans; even advertisements had to be on the move within the metropolitan ethic of unceasing mobility [. . .] The advertisement is the ultimate synthesis of the central themes of the modern metropolis: movement, exchange and the image. It is part of the visual fabric of the city; it speaks to the eye and sustains the exchange of money and goods. Walked round the streets and pulled on carts, the advertisement creates an alternative mapping of the city, tracing the contours of commodity capitalism.[5]

However, there remains an important difference between such textual cityscapes and Times Square in the middle of the twentieth century. Reading a nineteenth-century poster or a handbill may have been fascinating or disorientating to a passer-by, but for the most part, the implicit power-relationship of conventional reading would not have been challenged; in contrast, a different set of anxieties might arise to a twentieth-century Manhattan flâneur, wandering into Times Square and measuring his or her relationship to the sights – not least because the simple act of reading a bit of text that is so patently larger than oneself questions a hierarchical relationship between 'big' humans and the 'little' bits of text that they read. Selden's Chester the cricket is overwhelmed by the gigantism of the Square's lights; but part of the irony of his description comes from the fact that it only exaggerates, through an insect's perspective, the kind of response that a typical human might feel on experiencing the scene: a feeling that the manufactured iconography of human commerce has somehow become unmoored from the conventions of human scale, that the visible (and, importantly, legible) signs of commerce have come to define the judgements and transactions in which they once only played subordinate parts. In this chapter, I shall explore *The New Yorker*'s distinctive relationship with the Manhattan cityscape within which it was conceived and produced, and shall suggest ways in which both the magazine's treatments of the value of readable social indicators, and the larger cultural cachet of the magazine itself in the 1950s and 1960s, offered the young Philip Roth an early engagement with ideas that were to become defining imaginative preoccupations across his fictional and critical oeuvre, from *Goodbye, Columbus* to *Nemesis* – in particular, the question of how far individuals can control and manage their own self-images in the face of others' accidental or wilful misconstructions. In his famous interview from 1974, Roth responded to Joyce Carol Oates's questions (*'Have you come to know more* because *of your fame? Or has the experience of enduring the bizarre projections of others been at times more than you can reasonably handle?'*) in words that describe brilliantly the tragi-comic double-binds with which his fiction has repeatedly dealt:

> 'Enduring the bizarre projections of others' isn't just something that famous novelists have to contend with, of course. Defying a multitude of bizarre projections, or submitting to them, would seem to me at the heart of everyday living in America, with its ongoing demand to be something palpable and identifiable. Everyone is invited to imitate in conduct and appearance the grossest simplifications of self that are mercilessly projected upon them by the mass media and advertising, while they must, of course, also contend with the myriad expectations that they arouse in those with whom they have personal and intimate associations.[6]

Roth's commentators, however, have not for the most part paid much attention to the fact that, at the beginning of his fictional career, *The New Yorker* presented Roth with both a prestigious opportunity for publication, and subject matter for his ongoing dramas of merciless projections and 'myriad expectations'.

Manhattan and the material page in *The New Yorker*

From the earliest days of *The New Yorker*, then, Times Square figured large in the magazine's cultural geography, as witnessed, for example, by the number of times it crops up as a subject, not only in short 'Talk of the Town' pieces, but in some of the longer pieces of reportage by Morris Markey, Harold Ross's original 'Reporter at Large'. For example, Markey's 'The Village Green' from 5 March 1927 muses sardonically on the metonymic resonances which the Square clearly already has for out-of-towners:

> For ourselves, who remember Times Square now and again as the place where the traffic is bad, the attitude toward it held by the sturdy yeomen of this far-flung Republic is almost inconceivable. To them, it *is* New York. It is the throbbing heart, the mystery, the romance of our fantastic town, this acre of land with its snarled currents of packed humanity, its looming buildings, its muffled roar, and its shifting, brilliant lights.[7]

For all its Manhattan-*mondain* humour (staying wise to the prosaic reality of the city, and, by implication, staying wiser than those visitors from the sticks), Markey's sentence nevertheless recognises and accommodates the allure of what the square represents, as the existential bluntness of '*is* New York' gives way, via 'is the throbbing heart', to the blurred, figurative 'muffled roar', and the seemingly inevitable 'shifting, brilliant lights' – as if even the hard-bitten *New Yorker* observer were not wholly immune to Times Square's influence, and to what it has come to symbolise. It is notable how prominently those lights feature in Markey's often quite tart assessments of the Square and its significance. 'The Village Green' opens with a joke about the out-of-towners: 'Down in Toccoa, Georgia, they are wondering these days what New York can possibly be like, now that the Wrigley sign is gone', and concludes by noting that 'twenty-four more hours are in sight during which the world will be safe for Maxwell House Coffee and Arrow Collars'.[8] The signs are still very much in evidence in a comparably sardonic piece that Markey wrote about 'Small Hours in Times Square' for the 2 June 1934 number. Following the lead of chronologically structured nineteenth-century journalistic works such as G. A. Sala's *Twice Round the Clock; or the Hours of the Day and Night in London* (1859), Markey concludes his after-hours survey of the Square by remarking that 'the flamboyant names of the movies stood up in vast letters, more preposterously inane than ever'.[9] Discussing Markey as an antecedent of the 'New Journalism' of Mailer, Wolfe, and Hunter S. Thompson, Ben Yagoda has suggested that his innovations were due to the fact that he 'didn't only display his emotions in his stories, he displayed himself, habitually structuring them around the act of reporting. This near-revolutionary unveiling of the traditionally invisible reporter prefigured the "new journalists" of forty years hence.'[10] An innovatively 'visible' reporter surveying the sometimes aggressively visible cityscape of Times Square: this typifies much of *The New Yorker*'s imaginative relationship to the physical being of Manhattan in general, and the Square in particular. Compare Markey's 'Reporter' articles, for instance, with the 'Talk of the Town' piece from 9 August 1930, which features an account of Mr Glenn H. Phillips, 'the man who walks around the Times Square district on stilts, advertising things'.[11] Time and again in early twentieth-century metropolitan spaces, walking advertisements, whether stilt-walkers or sandwich men, offered a suggestive figure for the intersections of bodies, text, and commerce on which those cities relied – although they could also highlight the potential comic unravellings of city life, as when the Hely's sandwich-men in *Ulysses* repeatedly threaten to move out of meaningful sequence ('At Ponsonby's corner a jaded white flagon H. halted and four tallhatted white flagons halted behind him, E. L. Y'S, while outriders pranced past and carriages'[12]). In this light, the fact that the Georgia residents in Markey's account are so agitated about the disappearance of the Wrigley sign is telling: for them, Times Square represents New York because it is a place in which the relation between culture and commerce is, literally, 'writ large', as spectators are confronted directly with the signs of commodity-based aspiration.

I am taking this circumstance as my starting point because, from its foundation to the present, *The New Yorker* has existed as a textual counterpart to that aspirational city. Read Markey's 1930 piece about the giant billboards in its original format, for example, and one finds oneself moving through a textual cityscape in which large signs and advertisements force themselves repeatedly upon one's attention. The page-range for 'Small Hours in Times Square' runs from p. 58 to p. 66, but that includes full-page advertisements for Lion Beer, French Line cruises, La Corona cigars and Haig & Haig whisky, as well as a very large one for 'Sportocasin' golf-shoes; not only that, but Markey's piece is immediately followed by a full-page ad for Bromo-Seltzer sickness tablets – as if anticipating that a reader might have been rendered dyspeptic by the experience of so much conspicuous consumption. Although a case like this one – in which the writing appears at times to be 'illustrating' the ads, rather than the other way around – is an extreme case, it still points to a particular quality of *The New Yorker*'s cultural performance, one in which the idea of the magazine as physical object, a textual space with its own identifiable mise-en-page and spatial logic, plays a central role. If, as Sean Latham and Robert Scholes suggest, 'magazines and newspapers [. . .] create often surprising and even bewildering points of contact between disparate areas of human activity',[13] then *The New Yorker*, especially after the beginning of the 1930s, embodies this synthesis, setting up a populated textual and imaginative space, in which print and visual material combine to form a *Gestalt* of aspirational signifiers. Of course, one could argue against this that a miscellany such as *The New Yorker*, a magazine as often dipped into as read cover to cover, cannot dictate or wholly anticipate what its readers read, in what order, and with what degree of attention or inattention: at the very same moment in 1940s Manhattan, for example, an aspiring comic writer might have been devouring the latest issue from beginning to end, while elsewhere in the same building, a dentist's next patient would be cherry-picking the cartoons from the same issue in the waiting room. Then again, this may in fact be another way in which the magazine and its home city resemble one another, in that whatever route an individual plots through either space, the billboards seem inescapable.

By the mid-1950s, the early years of Shawn's editorship, the magazine had become identified, as I shall examine, with a notion of the 'smart' – not just the 'smartness' of the writing, but also the smart lifestyle trappings with which that writing was surrounded on the page. Both overtly and covertly, *The New Yorker* constructed and appealed to its implied reader, its model consumer – which is one reason why it might have figured so creatively in the imagination of the twenty-something Roth, at the beginning of his fictional career. With this, though, came the possibility of writing's hardening into an orthodoxy, a cultural house style or party line that could be identified both in the articles' words and values, and in the material spaces in which they were set. Seymour Krim's famous broadside against *The New Yorker*'s values (and its recent assessment of Edward Albee) in the *Village Voice* captures well what the 'establishment' magazine had come to represent in the Beat/counterculture circles of New York by the early 1960s, and it bears careful examination:

> McCarten – following in the footsteps of the finest *New Yorker* staff writers – uses a combination of the spoken and written language with that deceptive ease which comes from an admiration and imitation of *informal style*. That, I think, will be the *New Yorker*'s greatest contribution to sophistication and the country's style at large [. . .] As we read it now, there is more crass life and inventiveness in the advertising than in the body copy; from the middle of the magazine to the end you will come upon pages with 5½ inches' width of advertising to three of writing, and the painful thing to anyone in the business is the fact that the writing wastes even the petty amount of space it can still command because of the echo of the old colloquial style, using its now trivial diction and informalities to fill up precious space instead of revolutionizing the style to fit the reality.[14]

Krim's withering attack is valuable both as a critique of the cultural standing of *The New Yorker* at an important point in its (and American vernacular literature's) history, and for what it reveals, perhaps despite itself, about the magazine's fundamental modes of expression. On one level, it is understandable that a writer of Krim's stamp might have felt an increasing disaffection towards what he saw as an unthinking reproduction of a once vital style of reporting ('its now trivial diction and informalities'). After all, the history of periodical writing is littered with examples where house style has slipped from being a badge of collective identity to being a potentially oppressive tic – as witnessed, for example, by Dickens's periodicals of the 1850s and '60s, where an aggressive editorial policy produced the ironic spectacle of a staff of younger writers often trying to imitate 'The Inimitable'. That said, Krim's attack also clearly implies that the state of affairs that he observed in *The New Yorker* of 1962 was the result of modern editorial weakness (with the buck, presumably, stopping at Shawn), whereas, as I have been exploring, the historical truth is rather more complicated. 'Just recall the stories of Ross not allowing the advertising people even to walk on the editorial floor', Krim argues, but the evidence of the magazine's mise-en-page, even in the prelapsarian heyday of Ross's stewardship, suggests that he had a harder time keeping them off the magazine's pages.[15] Indeed, Krim's nostalgic vision of the old *New Yorker* rather underplays that defining quality of its larger 'style' – the fact that, from its earliest incarnations, the magazine has invited readers to consume it as what one might now term a 'mixed-media installation', to interpret verbal wit and sophistication as somehow of a piece with the visual appeals of cartoons and advertising. And it is this aspect of *The New Yorker*, as a publication vitally dependent on the legibility of its verbal and visual signs, that, as I shall explore in the rest of this chapter, suggests itself to the young Roth as both display space and fictional subject. From *Goodbye, Columbus*, through the Zuckerman novels, to *Nemesis*, a recurring and defining concern in Roth's writing has been the tragicomic irony of selfhood and self-fashioning, in which characters' desire to be themselves is repeatedly trammelled by others' constructions and misconstructions of them, and their first-person aspirations can become indistinguishable from the third-person ideals of fashion, consumerism, or ideological conformity. Taking some examples from the late 1950s and early 1960s, I shall explore Roth's uses of the idea and reality of *The New Yorker*, and consider in turn what they might tell critics and historians about the status of American 'smart magazines' in the period.

'The kind of person I am': 'as sociological as hell'

There is a telling moment of mis-recognition in *Zuckerman Unbound* (1981), Roth's most comic, and most disturbing, treatment of the phenomenon of literary celebrity. Nathan Zuckerman, thrust into a whole new kind of fame after the *succès de scandale* of his 'dirty' novel *Carnovsky* (not unlike what happened to Roth himself after he published

Portnoy's Complaint in 1969), is travelling down Fifth Avenue on a bus, only to find his reputation catching up with him:

> 'Hey. *Hey.*' Zuckerman's excited neighbor was trying again to distract the man in the aisle from his *Times*. 'See this guy next to me?'
>
> 'I do now,' came the stern, affronted reply.
>
> 'He's the guy who wrote *Carnovsky*. Didn't you read about it in the papers? He just made a million bucks and he's taking a bus.'
>
> Upon hearing that a millionaire was on board, two girls in identical gray uniforms – two frail, sweet-looking children, undoubtedly well-bred little sisters on their way downtown to convent school – turned to look at him.
>
> 'Veronica,' said the smaller of the two, 'it's the man who wrote the book that Mummy's reading. It's Carnovsky.'
>
> The children kneeled on their seats so as to face him. A middle-aged couple in the row across from the children also turned to get a look.[16]

Part of the comic profundity of this sequence springs from the skill with which Roth stages and juxtaposes different acts and senses of 'reading'. At the broadest level, there's the typically Rothian glissade between art and life, as 'He's the guy who wrote *Carnovsky*' swiftly and ominously turns into 'It's Carnovsky'. Over and above this, though, Roth arranges the scene to emphasise how much the characters' sense of each other depends on the way in which they read their surfaces. If, on the one hand, Zuckerman the celebrity author is rapidly turned into a hybrid of devotional icon and sideshow freak ('kneeled . . . so as to face him', 'turned to get a look'), it is not as if he is above judging according to type himself ('undoubtedly well-bred little sisters on their way downtown to convent school'). Eliding author with character, 'bizarre projections' with authentic essence, this scene of social embarrassment chimes with *Zuckerman Unbound*'s larger anxiety about art's ability to turn creators into creatures ('would Zuckerman's imagination beget still other Peplers conjuring up novels out of his – novels disguising themselves as actuality itself, as nothing less than real?'[17]). It is also an anxiety which has its roots in the world of 1950s smart-magazine culture, the world of Shawn's *New Yorker*.

Roth's first contribution to *The New Yorker*, published in the issue of 29 November 1958, is entitled 'The Kind of Person I Am'. It's a strange, playful performance, one of those occasional Roth pieces, shorter relations to books such as *The Facts* and *Patrimony*, that work at once as sketches, critical essays and forms of self-reflexive fiction (compare his 1994 piece 'Juice or Gravy?', published in the *New York Times Book Review*). From the beginning, this piece flirts self-consciously with the associations of the kind of informed, but essentially mainstream lifestyle that *The New Yorker* had come to typify by the end of the 1950s, the culture against which the Village counterculture, with its *Village Voice*, was to define itself. Roth's story's central conceit revolves around the various forms of social bunco that people practise on each other, beginning with the Roth character's memories of being genteelly tricked as a child, by his father's friend Harry Kirsch: 'Mr. Kirsch would look up at the sky, close his eyes, and place his fingertips lightly on the lids. A moment later, looking at me again, he'd say, "You're ten years old." And, of course, I was.'[18] A version of this recurs many years later, where the narrator now finds himself being 'read' by a woman he meets at a University of Chicago cocktail party, in what initially appears to be a consumerist twist on Sherlock Holmes's methods:

> She looked at my shoes, and I waited for them to inform her about my eating habits.
> 'And the *Reporter*,' she said. 'You read that?'
> 'Yes.'
> 'And the London *Times Literary Supplement*?'
> 'Yes.'
> 'Subscriber to *that*, aren't you?'
> 'No!' I said triumphantly. 'I buy it at the bookstore.'
> 'Of course!' she said. 'That way, you have to *carry* it home. With the cover page out.'[19]

On the surface, this may not be all that different from some other humorous *New Yorker* pieces of the period that gently poke fun at the world in which the magazine participates, such as Howard Moss's 'Small Elegy' from 16 June 1956, which muses on the death of the archetypal Fifth Avenue man:

> Damn it, he had good taste! That's all he had.
> He knew the nearly-good from the not-quite-bad.
> Lennie wore the first vest made of plaid.
> Lennie gave it up when it became a fad.[20]

However, 'The Kind of Person I Am' engages with this idea in rather different ways, anticipating so many later instances from the novels where comic social embarrassment suddenly shades into existential crisis. For one thing, while the method by which the narrator gets 'read' is seemingly revealed as a sly, bet-hedging kind of cocktail confidence-trick, this fact does not appear to undo the anxieties that it has created. On the one hand, Roth's narrator claims confidently to have perfected what he jokingly ennobles as a 'methodology':

> The way to approach a stranger, I had learned, was not head on but from the side. Instead of telling him he did a certain sort of work ('You're in

advertising,' for instance), I would say, 'So – you're the sort of person who works in advertising, eh?' Then, whether his answer was yes or no, I would still sound as sociological as hell.[21]

On the other hand, the very end of the story sees the narrator realising that the judging-by-type that the woman visited on him at the cocktail party may in fact be an inescapable condition of existence, and succumbing despite himself to her original reading of him ('I started to phone the repairman, but then I thought, Why not be the kind of person who drops by the shop to talk it over on the way to the bookstore to buy the *Times Literary Supplement*? I could carry it home with the cover out'[22]).

What makes 'The Kind of Person I Am' so much more than just a skit about late-1950s cultural commodities is the way in which it sets rolling what was to become central to Roth's fiction in later years, in particular the sobering realisation that the choices and actions that a character might imagine would mark him out as an individual serve only to mark him out as a type, a genre, a 'kind of person'. Time and again, the piece plays off not just explicit textual markers such as 'kind' and 'type', but also more fundamental worries about the interchangeability of modern selves, creating a mode of Heideggerian slapstick out of the fear of 'falling into the "They"': 'It seemed that there must be dozens and dozens of young men just like myself [. . .] And what was I? A faddist. A copycat. A member of the cultural élite! How could I deny it?'[23] Hand in hand with this goes a self-referential, metaphorical emphasis on the idea of character-types as 'readable'; for example, Roth's narrator originally encounters the woman at the cocktail party standing by the bookcase. 'She'd been thumbing through our host's books', he tells us,

> and when I bumped into her, she turned and looked at me expressionlessly, as she might have gazed at the cover of a volume the title of which was unknown to her. But we talked, and as our conversation progressed, her gaze changed; by the time it was over, she had examined me as though she knew not only my title but the quality of the glue that kept me bound together.[24]

Anticipating *Zuckerman Unbound*'s staging of the famous author as the object of the public's merciless gaze, and the schoolgirls' conflating Zuckerman with Carnovsky, 'The Kind of Person I Am', with its relentless emphasis on interpreting visual signs, including visual aids ('she wore tortoise-shell glasses. You know the kind who wear *them*'[25]), explores brilliantly the interplay between identity and 'projection' at a particular time in American cultural history, and in doing so, draws a great deal of ironic energy from the very physical and textual surroundings in which the story unfolds.

Over the years, pieces in *The New Yorker*, especially editorial and commentary pieces, have not been shy about writing the magazine itself and its connotations into their subject matter, whether comic, deadly serious, or somewhere in between: for instance, just two days before Hiroshima (not that Ross could have known that at the time), the 'Talk of the Town' piece for that week's issue opened with a joke about an old *New Yorker* that had supposedly been discovered in the cellar of the Berghof:

> One rather obvious thing in the issue was a cartoon, by Carl Rose, showing a group of foreign statesmen seated around a conference table, one of the statesmen remarking, 'Oh, let's declare war and get the whole damn thing over with!' It seems possible that Hitler's rat-nosed assistant spotted that one and sent it along marked 'For your information,' or 'What d'ya make of this?'[26]

The particular historical stage on which *The New Yorker* plays a walk-on part may be a large and momentous one here, but the basic idea remains the same: the magazine is seen to participate obliquely in the world outside its pages, with the result that it grafts itself onto the very cultural anthropology that it is observing. At first glance, something altogether different would appear to be going on in 'The Kind of Person I Am'; for one thing, the main action of the narrative is clearly located in and around Chicago, where Roth was teaching; moreover, the story's significant cultural references are either transatlantic (the *Times Literary Supplement*), or connote a different section of Manhattan's cultural life from that represented by *The New Yorker*. The woman at the cocktail party deduces from the Roth-narrator's clothes that he reads *Partisan Review*; in his failed attempt to 'read' someone at the next party, he conjures up bohemian Manhattan ('the Village, publishing. Probably she liked Samuel Beckett'[27]); and one of his rewards for finally perfecting his soi-disant 'methodology' is the discovery that a 'young couple from Evanston' not only 'had linoleum on the floor of their children's bedroom' but also 'subscribed to *Dissent*'.[28] The *TLS*, the Village, intellectuals like Philip Rahv and Irving Howe, 'little-magazine affiliations': even when he does refer to New York, Roth seems to be conjuring up a less well-heeled (and noticeably more left-wing) version of the city than that of *The New Yorker*.

However, that is not to take into account the manner in which Roth's words perform in the specific material context in which they appear, so as to conjure up *The New Yorker* as an unnamed presence in the story, a smart-clad elephant in the room. Looking at 'The Kind of Person I Am' in the light of Krim's attack, one can see that it exists in exactly the phenomenological environment that he had so come to deplore, since the text of Roth's story only ever takes up one column's width of text on the page, the other two-thirds being occupied by the likes of Botany 500 sportscoats, Guerlain perfume and the Haiti tourist board. That said, Roth would have had a good idea that a piece of that length, and of that type, would have ended up, if it were published in *The New Yorker* at all, in precisely that part of the magazine where, as Krim was to lament, the articles were there to illustrate the advertisements. Indeed, the suggestions that Rachel MacKenzie made to Roth about revisions themselves revolve around the credible role that lifestyle accoutrements play in the plot: she suggested that 'giving the hi-fi-set away puts a strain on credulity', to which Roth replied 'to tell you the truth [. . .] I don't even know what stereo *is*'.[29] Thus, the combination of a story which explicitly foregrounds the social cachet of legible signs, with a material text so inset and bordered with commercial images of 'lifestyle', creates a reading experience in which *The New Yorker* becomes both an oblique subject of, and the performative medium for, Roth's earliest satire on commodified life. His protagonist's exasperation underpins the situations of so many of Roth's subsequent characters: 'There simply was no escape from being *some* kind of person, damn it!'[30] As Roth's early relationship with *The New Yorker* went on, though, the magazine's form and socioeconomic associations were to play an altogether more serious part, since both those factors influenced how readers responded to Roth's first 'scandalous' story, 'Defender of the Faith'.

'Defender of the Faith' and beyond: *The New Yorker* and identity

In *The Facts*, Roth (or, more properly, 'Roth', since this version of the autobiographical narrator doesn't share all of his namesake's history), recounts his journalistic endeavours while a student at Bucknell in 1952, endeavours shaped by the example of *The New Yorker*: 'Our own "Talk of the Town" was a two-page miscellany of putatively witty reportage, called "Transit Lines," a heading we thought nicely appropriate on a campus where an engineering student was always out on one of the walkways sighting through a telescope.'[31] However, by the time his first major *New Yorker* story appeared, seven years later, the magazine and what some took it to represent had come to take on much graver resonances, ones which were to shape both the manner and the matter of his subsequent writing career:

That the *New Yorker*, like *Partisan Review* and *Commentary*, had a Jewish editor, William Shawn, Jewish contributors – like S. J. Perelman, Irwin Shaw, Arthur Kober, and J. D. Salinger – and a sizeable Jewish readership would only have suggested, to those I'd incensed, that identifying with the *New Yorker*'s privileged, unequivocally non-Jewish aura furnished those Jews (as it undoubtedly did Roth himself) with far more sustenance than they derived from their Jewish status. I soon understood self-hatred to mean an internalized, though not necessarily conscious, loathing of one's recognizable group markings that culminates either in quasi-pathological efforts to expunge them or in the vicious disparagement of those who don't even know enough to try.[32]

Note in particular how Roth appropriates the voice of collective, implacable, third-person judgement ('furnished those Jews [as it undoubtedly did Roth himself]'), as he does much later in rendering the anonymous note written to Coleman Silk in *The Human Stain* ('Everyone knows you're / sexually exploiting an / abused, illiterate / woman half your / age'), and, most famously, in *The Ghost Writer*'s fictional recasting of these very events as Judge Wapter's 'TEN QUESTIONS FOR NATHAN ZUCKERMAN' ('Can you honestly say that there is anything in your short story that would not warm the heart of a Julius Streicher or a Joseph Goebbels?').[33] A decade before *Portnoy*, 'Defender of the Faith' was to be Roth's first major encounter with what he describes in the Zuckerman novels as 'the unforeseen consequences of art';[34] and it was an encounter especially pertinent to my argument here, since its place of publication, and the association which it carried for at least some of its readers, were central to the unexpected controversy that it generated.

As well as 'The Kind of Person I Am', Roth submitted versions of two of the stories that were later to be collected in *Goodbye, Columbus* to *The New Yorker* in 1958: 'Eli, the Fanatic', and 'Defender of the Faith'. The first was rejected, apparently for being too overtly 'fabulist', with MacKenzie suggesting that it 'keeps sliding off into caricature and farce and [. . .] in the end it falls between realism and didactic modern fable'.[35] However, 'Defender of the Faith' found a much more sympathetic hearing at the magazine, and MacKenzie seems to have taken a proprietorial attitude towards it. 'I shall be grieved and distressed if it doesn't go through', she wrote to Roth on 6 October; 'I felt, reading it, that special excitement you feel when you come on a first-rate, perfectly controlled story',[36] and the story itself duly appeared in the 14 March issue the following year, with 'Eli, the Fanatic', having found an alternative home in the interim, coming out in the April number of *Commentary*. However, whereas in his first *New Yorker* piece, Roth could, as I have discussed, play on the connotations of 'smartness' carried by magazines such as the *TLS*, *Dissent*, and *Partisan Review* (and, by association, *The*

New Yorker itself), the extreme responses to 'Defender of the Faith' show that the material and cultural cachet of the magazine was capable of being interpreted in other, far more serious ways. For despite the magazine's Jewish editor and distinguished Jewish contributors, what so annoyed Roth's many detractors at the time was not simply that he had dared to portray such a character as the self-serving Sheldon Grossbart, but that he had dared to do so in the pages of *The New Yorker*. 'It's even possible', imagines 'Roth' in *The Facts*,

> that the ferment inspired a month later by the publication of *Goodbye, Columbus* [...] might never have reached troublesome proportions had 'Defender of the Faith' been certified as permissible Jewish discourse by appearing in *Commentary*. And had that happened – had there not been the inflammatory fanfare of the *New Yorker* exposure [...] it's likely that my alleged anti-Semitism might never have come to pervade discussions of my work.[37]

What stands out in this account of the story's reception, as it does in some of the original complaints made about it to B'nai B'rith, is the degree to which the content of 'Defender of the Faith' is seen to have an illocutionary force that is highly context-sensitive, the same words being acceptable in one publication, but offensive in another; and even the signifying material surfaces of *The New Yorker*'s pages are shown to have more than one effect.

In this light, it has to go down as an unfortunate contingency, an infelicitously meaningful accident of timing, that *The New Yorker* chose to run 'Defender of the Faith' when it did. For 14 March was two weeks before the Easter weekend of 1959, and as a result, the pages of that issue were replete with festive advertising, including '*Easter and Spring* NECKTIES' from Tripler & Co., 'The Easter Bunny Charm' from Olga Tritt, and the 'Dunhill Easter Classic' handbag. However, the grimmest circumstantial irony involves one of the story's central conversational scenes, in which sergeant Nathan Marx becomes the unwilling intermediary between the Jewish soldiers and the military brass, making representations on their behalf about dietary rules: '"Sir, Grossbart is strange –" Barrett greeted that with a mockingly indulgent smile. I altered my approach. "Captain, he's a very orthodox Jew, and so he's only allowed to eat certain foods."'[38]

To a reader in 1959, 'the unforeseen consequences of art' might have felt all too pertinent, given the accident that placed the page containing this conversation opposite a full-page ad for Campbell's frozen oyster stew – the 'lifestyle' quality of the magazine's material space here accidentally reproducing exactly the kind of cultural and theological misunderstanding that Roth's story is dramatising on the opposite page. At first sight, it might seem odd that it was the first of the two stories that caused such a furore, given that if one were to read them collected in *Goodbye, Columbus*, one might well consider 'Eli, the Fanatic' to be the more controversial story, being not only (as MacKenzie noted) part 'fable', but also dealing much more directly than 'Defender of the Faith' with debates about assimilation, since it is the Jewish residents who appear most anxious about the *yeshiva* in the neighbourhood ('The Jewish members of the community appointed me, Artie, and Harry to see what could be done. And we appointed you.'[39]) Then again, that is to downplay the meaning of medium, the fact that, as Roth discovered in 1959, there were sections of the reading public for whom *The New Yorker* didn't just connote 'smartness', but could also stand (even with Shawn at the helm) as a shorthand for a complex of suburban, assimilationist ambitions, whereas *Commentary* carried no such charge. Indeed, it may be that Roth's exceeding the comfortable requirements of 1950s *New Yorker* realism was not the only reason that 'Eli, the Fanatic' was rejected, since the story itself features a walk-on role for the magazine that is distinct from the parts it played in 'Talk of the Town' pieces over the years. Early on in the story, Eli Peck, Roth's troubled lawyer protagonist, has a late-night 'chat' with his unborn child, which lays bare a whole set of cultural and consumerist anxieties:

> Miriam pushed herself up in bed. 'Eli, please, baby, shouldn't you maybe stop in to see Dr Eckman, just for a little conversation?'
> 'I'm fine.'
> 'Oh, sweetie!' she said, and put her head back on the pillow.
> 'You know what your mother brought to this marriage – a sling chair and a goddam New School enthusiasm for Sigmund Freud.'
> Miriam feigned sleep, he could tell by the breathing.
> 'I'm telling the truth, aren't I, Miriam? A sling chair, three months to go on a *New Yorker* subscription, and *An Introduction to Psychoanalysis*. Isn't that right?'[40]

The clear implication of Roth's cultural synecdoche here is that Freud and *The New Yorker* represent not just a different kind of reading-matter from that studied in the *yeshiva* across town, but a radically different conception of Jewish identity.

Thus, the history of Roth's early engagements with *The New Yorker* came itself to furnish him with imaginative material for that ongoing exploration of selfhood and its discontents for which he has been famous and infamous ever since. In her 2004 critical study of Roth, *Countertexts, Counterlives*, Debra Shostak titles one of her chapters

'The Subject in/to History', which captures well the paradoxical situation in which Roth's characters, and his own works, have repeatedly found themselves: subjects 'in' history, active agents in and attempted self-fashioners of their own destinies; but, at the same time, subject 'to' history, the creatures of others' unpredictable misconstructions.[41] In *The Plot Against America*, the good American citizens of Newark suddenly find themselves redesignated as undesirable Jews by the Lindbergh administration; before that, in *The Human Stain*, the African-American Coleman Silk finds himself taken for a Jewish racist; before that, in *Zuckerman Unbound*, the respectable novelist suddenly finds himself remade by the popular imagination into a pornographer; and before all of these novels, the young Roth finds himself unexpectedly vilified as a self-hating Jew, peddling defamation to the smart set to which *The New Yorker* appeals. How true it is throughout Roth's fiction, that great line that he gives to Nathan Zuckerman, contemplating the ruin of Swede Levov's life in *American Pastoral*: 'The fact remains that getting people right is not what living is all about anyway. It's getting them wrong that is living, getting them wrong and wrong and wrong then, on careful consideration, getting them wrong again. That's how we know we're alive: we're wrong.'[42] In that regard, then, it is ironically fitting that, right at the beginning of that oeuvre, *The New Yorker*, as textual cityscape and cultural touchstone, should have furnished Roth with a performative space in which to stage his imaginative concerns, even as it furnished his critics with a label with which they could condemn him. With the notoriety of *Portnoy's Complaint*, Roth found himself commodified into a certain image against his will: as he complained in his 1981 interview with *Le Nouvel Observateur*, 'To become a celebrity is to become a brand name. There is Ivory soap, Rice Krispies, and Philip Roth. Ivory is the soap that floats; Rice Krispies the breakfast cereal that goes snap-crackle-pop; Philip Roth the Jew who masturbates with a piece of liver.'[43] However, the 'Brand Roth' that he identifies here began a decade before *Portnoy*, in Manhattan: for Roth to become, through trial, error and sheer chance, the magisterial analyst of projection and misprision that he became, one of the most important 'kinds of people' that he had to be was a *New Yorker* writer.

Notes

1. George Selden, *The Cricket in Times Square* (London: J. M. Dent & Sons, 1961), p. 32.
2. Philip Roth, *Zuckerman Unbound* (London: Jonathan Cape, 1981; repr. London: Vintage, 2005), p. 82.

3. This is Tom Wolfe's phrase for the neon signs of Las Vegas; see *The Kandy-Kolored Tangerine-Flake Streamline Baby* (London: Jonathan Cape, 1966; repr. London: Picador, 1981), p. 22.

4. Michel de Certeau, 'Walking in the City', *The Practice of Everyday Life*, trans. Steven Rendall (Berkeley: University of California Press, 1984), p. 93.

5. Lynda Nead, *Victorian Babylon: People, Streets, and Images in Nineteenth-century London* (New Haven & London: Yale University Press, 2000), p. 58.

6. Philip Roth, interviewed by Joyce Carol Oates, 'After Eight Books', *The Ontario Review*, Fall 1974; repr. in *Reading Myself and Others*, rev. edn (New York: Vintage, 2001), pp. 86–7.

7. Morris Markey, 'A Reporter at Large: The Village Green', *The New Yorker*, 5 March 1927, p. 36.

8. Ibid., pp. 36, 38.

9. Morris Markey, 'A Reporter at Large: Small Hours in Times Square', *The New Yorker*, 2 June 1934, p. 66.

10. Ben Yagoda, *About Town: 'The New Yorker' and the World It Made* (New York: Scribner, 2000), p. 76.

11. 'The Talk of the Town: Stiltwalker', *The New Yorker*, 9 August 1930, p. 11.

12. James Joyce, *Ulysses*, ed. H. W. Gabler (London: Penguin, 1986 [1922]), p. 208.

13. Sean Latham and Robert Scholes, 'The Rise of Periodical Studies', *PMLA*, 121.2 (March 2006), 528.

14. Seymour Krim, 'Who's Afraid of the *New Yorker* Now?', *Village Voice*, 8 November 1962, repr. in *Shake It for the World* (London: Allison & Busby, 1971), p. 174.

15. Ibid.

16. Roth, *Zuckerman Unbound*, p. 5.

17. Ibid., p. 198.

18. Philip Roth, 'The Kind of Person I Am', *The New Yorker*, 29 November 1958, p. 173.

19. Ibid., p. 174.

20. Howard Moss, 'Small Elegy', *The New Yorker*, 16 June 1956, p. 32.

21. Roth, 'The Kind of Person I Am', p. 177.

22. Ibid., p. 178.

23. Ibid., p. 175.

24. Ibid., p. 173.

25. Ibid., p. 176.

26. 'The Talk of the Town', *The New Yorker*, 4 August 1945, p. 11.

27. Roth, 'The Kind of Person I Am', p. 176.

28. Ibid., p. 177.

29. Rachel MacKenzie, letter to Philip Roth, 6 October 1958, New Yorker Records, box 763, folder 16; Philip Roth, letter to Rachel MacKenzie, 7 October 1958, ibid.

30. Roth, 'The Kind of Person I Am', p. 178.

31. Philip Roth, *The Facts: A Novelist's Autobiography* (New York: Farrar, Strauss & Giroux, 1988; repr. New York: Vintage, 1997), p. 62.

32. Ibid., p. 117.
33. Philip Roth, *The Human Stain* (London: Jonathan Cape, 2000; repr. London: Vintage, 2001), p. 38; Philip Roth, *The Ghost Writer* (London: Jonathan Cape, 1979; repr. London: Vintage, 2005), pp. 103–4.
34. Philip Roth, *The Prague Orgy* (New York: Farrar, Strauss & Giroux, 1985; repr. London: Vintage, 2006), p. 61.
35. Quoted in Yagoda, *About Town*, p. 300.
36. Rachel MacKenzie, letter to Philip Roth, 6 October 1958, New Yorker Records, box 763, folder 16.
37. Roth, *The Facts*, p. 116.
38. Philip Roth, 'Defender of the Faith', *The New Yorker*, 14 March 1959, p. 50.
39. Philip Roth, *Goodbye, Columbus and Five Short Stories* (Boston: Houghton Mifflin, 1959; repr. London: Vintage, 2006), p. 206.
40. Ibid., p. 194.
41. See Debra B. Shostak, *Philip Roth: Countertexts, Counterlives* (Columbia: University of South Carolina Press, 2004), *passim*.
42. Philip Roth, *American Pastoral* (New York: Houghton Mifflin, 1997; repr. New York, Vintage, 1998), p. 35.
43. Interview with Alain Finkielkraut in *Le Nouvel Observateur*, 1981, repr. in Roth, *Reading Myself and Others*, p. 98.

Chapter 5

Spark's Proofs

Deborah Bowman

1

In order that the value of the collected facts may be in no wise impaired by possibly erroneous correlation, speculative inferences have here been sharply differentiated from the data of observation. This arrangement of the subject is presented with the more confidence since it is believed that absolute progress in the science of ore-deposits will, in the future, be made largely, if not entirely, by inductive reasoning. [. . .] The correlation of the data obtained has for the present been considered of minor importance, and every effort has, on the other hand, been directed towards the presentation in readily accessible form of the salient facts of auriferous deposition.[1]

2

There's a sheet of bright yellow A4 lined paper in folder Acc: 10989/50 of the Muriel Spark Archive at the National Library of Scotland, and on it are two lines in Spark's handwriting:

Note Golden Fleece
  Alluvial gold in the stream

The folder also contains a typescript, on the first page of which the title 'PUTTING THE RECORD STRAIGHT' has been crossed out by hand and 'The Fifties: A Literary Life' written over the top, again in Spark's writing. The typescript was sent to Charles McGrath, at *The New Yorker*, on 16 February 1992. Its main content is a draft of Chapter Seven of *Curriculum Vitae: A Volume of Autobiography*, which Spark published later that year; the chapter begins:

After leaving the Poetry Society I became aware of the value of documentary evidence, both as a means of personal defence against inaccuracies and as an aid to one's own memory. Consequently, since 1949 onwards I have thrown away practically nothing on paper.[2]

The Muriel Spark Archive which is a product of that resolution was acquired by the National Library of Scotland in 1992 and is still being added to. It isn't yet fully sorted. Letters from the same year, to the same person, relating to the same publication, the galley proofs and the fax about those same galley proofs and the fax replying to that fax, are in different folders, series, accessions, both catalogued and uncatalogued. There's her passport, and there are her identity cards, and there are folders which open in unexpected blue flutters of three-inch-square note-lets. It makes you think of Carolyn Steedman's despairing in the dust of the record office that 'these people have left me *the lot*'; and of Richard Bentley writing of John Pearson that 'the very Dust of His Writings is Gold';[3] and it makes you think of Muriel Spark's golden goose:

> Myself, I killed the cackling thing and I ate it.
> Alas, many and many of the other recipients
> Died of gold-dust poisoning.[4]

It's a record but it isn't straight.

3

There's an odd moment in *Curriculum Vitae* when Spark singles out for praise an article she published in 1948 in *Argentor*, the official journal of the National Jewellers' Association:

> before I left *Argentor*, I had researched and written a long article on the Order of the Golden Fleece which adorns many famous and historical portraits. About this article I have a sense of great satisfaction. It bears no signs of immaturity and I would not hesitate to print it today.[5]

It's been reprinted in and lent its title to an edited volume of her non-fictional writing – Spark's *The Golden Fleece: Essays* came out in 2014 – but when you read it her fondness starts to look like sentimental valuation:[6]

> We are told with what joy and expectation Jason brought the golden fleece back to Thessaly. Instead, however, of regaining his kingdom, Jason fell foul of his uncle, who dispossessed and banished him. Such is the legend.
> It was Philip the Good, Duke of Burgundy, who founded the Order of the Golden Fleece on the day of his marriage (January 10) to Princess Isabella of

Portugal in 1429–30. History does not record the year with exactitude, nor is it known whether or not Philip was inspired by the ancient legend or whether he chose the name from some other motive.[7]

As the thorough redundant flatness of her prose and judgement here suggest ('researched and written', 'famous and historical', 'does not record the year with exactitude'; and can she really have thought that 'bearing no sign of immaturity' was a sufficient condition for publication?), it does read very much like a school project. The whole essay has this meticulous lukewarm consistency; it's difficult to fathom Spark's continuing 'satisfaction' with a piece of writing which, though perfectly well-constructed, is so dull that even her later description of it appears to glaze over in response.

But if you wanted to fathom it – if you wanted to bridge the gap between 1948/49, when Muriel Spark wrote a straight-laced article on the Golden Fleece and began to archive her documents in earnest and in defence, and 1992, when she published her autobiography 'to put the record straight' and then immediately sold her archived documents to the National Library of Scotland – you might use a stray sheet of yellow paper and the many and many typescripts she sent to *The New Yorker*.[8]

The note on the paper, 'Alluvial gold in the stream', refers to a fact sometimes offered speculatively as an explanation for the legend of the Golden Fleece: that fleeces can be stretched across river-beds to catch water-borne particles of gold, then hung up glittering to dry (Strabo recorded that in the Caucasus 'gold is carried down by the mountain-torrents, and that the barbarians obtain it by means of perforated troughs and fleecy skins, and that this is the origin of the myth of the golden fleece').[9] Spark's yellow note, then, looks like a free-floating fact which didn't make it into the *Argentor* article. It's no more speculative than the final contents, however, because the facts in this text aren't always quite facts, as the sentences in which they appear rush to explain right from their beginnings: 'We are told' things (but have no confirmation), 'Such is the legend', 'History does not record the year with exactitude, nor is it known. . .'. This anxious but stolid even-handedness, dealing so fairly with both knowledge and its absence, is one source of this essay's contagiously deadpan tone: *Curriculum Vitae*'s later pride that 'The Golden Fleece' 'bears no signs of immaturity' and that consequently its author 'would not hesitate to print' has caught a bad case of litotes.

As Freya Johnston remarks, litotes is a figure which can imply

a quality of determinedly hesitant, minutely enquiring, and intellectually rigorous perception that endeavours to arrive at the truth, but is equally conscious that it may have to conclude in uncertainty (in which case, to express its findings in a more overt or decisive form than that of litotes would be to exaggerate, or to produce a fiction).[10]

McGrath described *Curriculum Vitae* as 'a little masterwork of evasiveness and score-settling that reveals next to nothing about the woman who wrote it'.[11] For all these purposes the quality Johnston describes was ideal: litotes, in its evasive equivocation, can only be a 'little masterwork'; settles scores by pretending settled reason; in its attentive rubbing up against negatives is always 'next to nothing'. The figure's vicious modesty provides a counter-example to and provides for a counter-offensive against the inaccuracies, exaggerations and fictions from which Spark found herself most often in need of defence in both 1948/9 and 1992, because they had most skewed the record she wanted to straighten: those of Derek Stanford, her friend, lover, collaborator, biographer and enemy. The typescript in Acc: 10989/50 and Chapter Seven of *Curriculum Vitae* set out to displace Stanford completely with their superior 'endeavours to arrive at the truth': to overturn his biographical account of her by attacking particular examples of his 'sheer guesswork, mythomania, invention or what you will', and to discredit the methods by which it was produced by attacking his critical faculties:

> Derek Stanford's main fault as a critic was his inaccuracy. It brought in a great many complaints. [. . .] It was often small facts, dates and titles that Derek couldn't get right. [. . .] His later memory, untutored and unsupported by anything so trivial as evidence or documents, now flourished and ran wild. I give Derek Stanford full marks for bright colours. Some of his inventions are truly exotic.[12]

This reads like a school report made up of equal parts eye-rolling ('he's put us to so much trouble'), hand-wringing ('he simply can't manage it, what will he do next') and head-patting ('well, he's very . . . creative, isn't he'), and by the end of the account Stanford, D., has been put down a couple of forms at least.

Meanwhile Spark, M., was keen to draw attention to 'anything so trivial as evidence and documents'. Her 1991 *New Yorker* article 'Personal History: Visiting the Laureate' goes out of its way to label Spark's documentary evidence as documents and as evidence, emphasising the times of her remembering and writing down her encounters with John Masefield as much as the events remembered and written up. So, recounting her experience of the poet laureate reading his poems, she quotes from her own already-published account: 'I described that reading, years later, in a book'; arranging her visit, she mentions the exact date of her letter to him ('November 28, 1950') as well as that of the meeting at his house in Abingdon ('December 6th').[13] The visit itself is first relayed through her notes, presented as if directly cited:

> Here is the account of my meeting with Masefield which I wrote in my memorandum book.
>
> December 8, 1950: In bed with cold which was caught at Abingdon, and I can't help thinking that if Masefield were not so intemperately 'Temperant' I would not be snuffling and choking thus – i.e. if he had offered me a drink on frozen Wednesday last.[14]

The abbreviations of phrasing – 'i.e.' – and syntactical ellipsis – 'In bed with cold' – place it as a note, although this mode is soon dropped (she writes 'I can't help thinking' not 'can't help thinking'). Having related her visit to Abingdon, she revisits her notebook a day later:

> December 9th: Masefield also remarked [. . .] I have remembered, too, that Masefield said [. . .]
>
> December 9th (evening): I have just remembered more things about my visit to Masefield.[15]

The roughness of her ostentatiously drafted and redrafted story is displayed as a journalistic reality effect, an exaggerated attention to detail which, in respecting the jagged contours of Spark's rememberings, sanctions the irregularities of attention she apparently paid to her original experience. Instead of revising these 'notes' into a single coherent narrative, her final version of the encounter with Masefield seeks to preserve – or present – the integrity of her documentary record rather than that of the encounter itself. The impression is one of great delicacy in attending so to raw data in the difficult transition from collection to presentation, emphasised when Spark ends the piece by citing two further letters from Masefield as if neatly filing them in the archival folder relating to her visit, one in response to hers thanking him for the interview, the other in response to her treatment of him in her book. The latter begins, 'Please let me thank you for the patient care with which you have worked my things';[16] Spark, M., with her fine grasp of 'small facts, dates and titles' and her 'later memory' satisfyingly oversupplied with the 'evidence' in her own 'documents', can have a gold star.

4

There are three articles published by Spark in *The New Yorker* which were afterwards revised into sections of *Curriculum Vitae*.[17] '~~PUTTING THE RECORD STRAIGHT~~/The Fifties: A Literary Life' isn't one of them; they all predate it, relating periods of Spark's life before her 1949 archival watershed. The absence of an early record of her own obliged her to find other 'defence[s] against inaccuracies' than the 'personal'; as she explained:

> I determined to write nothing that cannot be supported by documentary evidence or by eyewitnesses; I have not relied on my memory alone [. . .] When a version of my childhood experiences first appeared in the *New Yorker* I was delighted by the number of people who wrote to me to confirm, modify and elaborate on what I had written.[18]

By the time she published the story of her first thirty-nine years and sold her papers, Spark's archive had provided the raw materials out of which she could create an autobiography, and her autobiography – Spark's need to assert the lines of her own life against the actual or possible distortions of others – had motivated the creation and maintenance of an archive. In between them she had discovered a defence against the 'inaccuracies' of even her own records, a place to 'confirm, modify and elaborate on what I had written', where she could muster ammunition as well as pan for the gold-dust of corroborated fact: a magazine.

The New Yorker was peculiarly effective for these purposes because it shared with Spark a famously exaggerated regard for factual accuracy, which it administered, as it still does, by means of its fact-checkers. Sara Lippincott, a *New Yorker* fact-checker between 1966 and 1982, explains that once a *New Yorker* article is in proof form, 'each word in the piece that has even a shred of fact clinging to it is scrutinized, and, if passed, given the checker's imprimatur, which consists of a tiny pencil tick'.[19] (Spark's gold stars. . .) The fact-checker's attention is devoted to nipping error in the bud, for once in print, it

> will live on and on in libraries carefully catalogued, scrupulously indexed . . . silicon-chipped, deceiving researcher after researcher down through the ages, all of whom will make new errors on the strength of the original errors, and so on and on into an exponential explosion of errata.[20]

Or in other words, as Spark puts it on the first page of *Curriculum Vitae*, 'the disturbing thing about false and erroneous statements is that well-meaning scholars tend to repeat each other. Lies are like fleas hopping from here to there, sucking the blood of the intellect.'[21] *The New Yorker* provided Spark with a defensive *garde d'honneur* against more than fleas, as 'with drawn sword, the fact-checker stands at the near end of this bridge';[22] its celebrated fact-checking department was the only means by which she could have retrospectively and emphatically endowed her early memoirs with the same protective 'value of documentary evidence' that she sought to preserve in the archive she had begun in 1949. This is because fact-checking – at least the part of it not dealing with the text's internal consistency – is a way of treating the entire possibly-knowable world as an archive, into which every part of the text in question must be filed or else rejected as invalid. Put simply, it extends proofreading – 'the reading of text in proof in order to find and mark errors for correction' (*OED*) – beyond print and into the realm of content.

In doing so, it ensures that all checked material is 'proofed' with a thoroughness which amalgamates the three main senses of 'proof' into Spark's desired 'defence against inaccuracies': proofs and proofings 'relating to the establishment or demonstration of truth or validity', those 'relating to the trying or testing of something', and those 'denoting something produced as a test, or which is a means of or instrument for testing'. Fact-checking takes a printer's proof – 'a trial or preliminary impression of a printed text, taken to be checked for errors and marked for correction before subsequent revision or final printing' – and attempts to find proof – 'something that proves a statement; evidence or argument establishing a fact or the truth of anything' – for all facts contained within it. This process is itself one of proof – an 'action, process, or fact of proving or establishing the truth or validity of a statement' and an 'action or an act of testing or making trial of something; the condition of being tested; examination, experiment; test, trial' – and, if successful, results in the article itself becoming proof – 'of tried or proven strength or quality; (originally *esp.* of armour) of tested power of resistance [. . .] impenetrable, impervious, invulnerable, resistant' (*OED*). A properly fact-checked article, then, no matter what its actual origins, has through this process been redeemed into and reconciled with the world of fact, and can be considered as 'documentary evidence'. All writing accepted for publication in *The New Yorker* passes through its fact-checking department; for Spark this meant seven articles, fourteen of her poems, twelve of her short stories, nearly the whole text of two novels (*The Prime of Miss Jean Brodie* and *The Driver's Seat*) and four substantial sections of another (*The Mandelbaum Gate*).[23]

In this way, *The New Yorker* wasn't just (although it was, also) a prestigious organ in which Spark was keen to publish; she experienced the process of publication itself as an experience of proof and proofing. Working on the proofs – in all senses – of Spark's autobiographical pieces, the *New Yorker* fact-checkers can seem a bit like research assistants for the pre-archival sections of *Curriculum Vitae*. For instance, having written that 'everyone who came to the house was offered a cup of tea, as in Dostoyevski', and been told that 'the checker has reported an objection from a Russian-literature professor, who says he's certain that tea was not regularly served in any book of Dostoyevski's', Spark replies: 'I am separated from my Dostoyevski books. I have it fixed in my mind that the hero/anti-hero of Crime and Punishment is always offering cups of tea to people [. . .]. Please can you check?'[24] They do; he is. And there are other times when Spark, in order to find evidence for a challenged impression or unsubstantiated memory, turns fact-checker herself and turns up more early documentation for her archive. In response to a query about the trust fund belonging to her school, she faxed the magazine a dossier of legal documents, and when told by *The New Yorker* that her former art master couldn't have exhibited a painting at a particular gallery in Glasgow, as it didn't exist, she appealed for help to Nigel Billen, Features Editor of *Scotland on Sunday*. Billen replied confirming the existence of the gallery and dates of the painting's exhibition and purchase, adding its current location in the local author-ity's collection, stock number, and prices for its photographic reproduc-tion ('£45 or so for colour, £3.20 for black and white').[25] Spark's delight (she 'love[d] to pile up details') was obvious: 'I'm really excited to see the painting which could possibly be reproduced in my memoirs which I'm writing now', she wrote back in a pile-up of subordinate clauses, so pleased with the haul of potential evidence for *Curriculum Vitae* that it had got right into her syntax.[26]

5

There was something 'fixed in [Spark's] mind' about Raskolnikov's tea-drinking which the fact-checkers had been sent to find, and her conviction that Arthur Couling had exhibited and sold a painting in Glasgow prompted her to challenge *The New Yorker*'s fact-checkers; but often the situation was reversed, and what was 'fixed' was the cor-rected checked fact, which in her correspondence with *The New Yorker* Spark either accepted without comment or herself sought to corroborate further. So, having originally written that a draper's shop had 'a system of overhead wires that carried containers of money', she accepted the checker's suggestion that they were actually 'pneumatic tubes'; this is in the next set of proofs, but an accompanying fax reports that 'the proofreader thinks she may have made a mistake suggesting "pneumatic tubes" for "overhead wires"; is "pneumatic tubes" what you meant?'[27] Spark replies that '"pneumatic tubes" is agreed by two of my con-temporaries in Edinburgh to be correct'.[28] Her desire for an adequate 'defence against inaccuracies' meant that she used the *New Yorker*'s fact-checker first to correct and then to corroborate not only her proofs but her otherwise-undefended (and to her mind, therefore, indefensible) memory.

Spark wasn't alone in this curious reading-back from magazine to world: there's a letter in one of the Spark Archive's *New Yorker* files which attests to the store its readers also set by its accuracy. It picks up on the erroneous claim, made in Spark's article on Masefield, that 'between 1885 and 1887 he worked in a bar in Greenwich Village':

> Now, even if New York in the 1880's bore some strong resemblance to Dickensian London, I would have appreciated a little clarification here, something along the lines of: 'Like many youngsters of the day, Masefield joined the Merchant Marine when he was five years old. Two years later, at the age of seven, he jumped ship in New York and went to work in a bar in Greenwich village,' Or: 'Mrs Masefield told John, then seven years old, that because he'd been late for tea, she was sending him to New York to work in a bar in Greenwich Village.'
>
> At any rate, if the dates of Masefield's Greenwich Village experience are not a misprint, how the hell did he get to New York, what did he do in the bar, was he precocious and looked much older than his age?
>
> Yours truly,
> Bill Boyd[29]

Boyd's faux-nonplussed plain-speaking is both entertaining and diagnostic: hang on a minute, this letter hollers, there's some funny business going on in these here backwoods. The presence of an error in the supposedly fact-checked world of *The New Yorker* creates a chink in its error-proofing through which anything might have slipped, and which Boyd's imagination immediately sets itself to stopping up with alternative explanations (anything but admit that this stable universe is liable to error); the elaborated stories in the first paragraph and the rapid stacked questions in the second are rhythmically and tonally different ways of sounding out an unexpected situation. But instead of querying the standards of *The New Yorker*'s fact-checking department in the early 1990s, Boyd mock-investigates New York in the 1880s; feigning to assume (and implying that he's entitled to assume) that 'the dates of Masefield's Greenwich Village experience are not a misprint', he first corrects the city with reference to the magazine (and a supporting reference to Dickens), and then complains only that the magazine doesn't give him enough detail about this textually-created place. However lightly he expresses it, he's showing the way in which *The New Yorker*'s facts demand to be taken: as a world, as everything that is this case. And in which case its silences are terrible.

6

There are occasions, in her correspondence with *The New Yorker* concerning her autobiographical writing, when Spark comes out against its world of fact and on the side of memory. In 'Bread, Butter, and Florrie Ford' her aunt takes her to the theatre, where 'Miss Ford reclined glittering in the middle of the stage beside an enormous wireless set with multicoloured illuminated "valves," which looked like light bulbs.'[30] In the proof, McGrath had queried 'light bulbs', writing 'tubes?' beside it, but Spark snapped in response: 'I have explained in the previous sentence that they looked like light-bulbs. They did not look like tubes. For a memory-piece, it is memory that counts; technical knowledge is non-essential?'[31]

This insistence on how things 'looked' to her, distinct from 'technical knowledge' – that 'for a memory-piece, it is memory that counts', which you might think was essential, and is certainly usual, in autobiography – contrasts with much of her stated intent and demonstrated method. Introducing her biography of Mary Shelley, Spark had explained that she has 'always disliked the sort of biography which states "X lay on the bed and watched the candle flickering on the roof beams" when there is no evidence X did so'; the changes made to her autobiographical writings between their first appearance in *The New Yorker* and their publication as part of *Curriculum Vitae* suggest that, rather more problematically, she sometimes disliked the kind of autobiography in which such statements were made by X herself.[32] In 'Bread, Butter, and Florrie Ford', Spark describes an American couple, the Rules, who stayed with her mother and father; Mrs Rule

> taught me to read, egged on by Andrew K. Rule, D.D., as I found out her husband was, when I was well able to read his name on an envelope. I was between the ages of three and four. It was an early start, although in Edinburgh at that time it was not unusual for children to read and write fluently before they were five. The firelight played on Mrs. Rule's hands and face, on Professor Rule's bearded smile, and on my lettered, red-backed cards on a tray before me, as I sat at the fire on a low puffy stool, while Mrs. Rule declared that a 't' and an 'h' together sounded 'th'. The Rules went home to America, from where they wrote letters to my mother, leaving with me the precious cards.[33]

In *Curriculum Vitae*, she added:

> It is only more recently that I have been able to confirm the reality of my impressions of this exciting and kind couple. [. . .] The daughter of Andrew K. Rule's second marriage, Barbara Below, has been a valuable source of corroboration of the images of my infancy. When I told her, for instance, that

her father taught us to make popcorn (and I can still see the popping corn in the pan held over the fire), Mrs Below confirmed that her father told her how, all those years ago, he showed his Scottish friends how to make popcorn.[34]

In the later paragraph, Spark's own eyewitness account '(and I can still see the popping corn in the pan held over the fire)', is suppressed into a parenthesis, while Below's hearsay evidence 'that her father told her how, all those years ago, he showed his Scottish friends how to make popcorn', echoes, matches and guarantees Spark's having 'told her, for instance, that her father taught us to make popcorn'. 'I told her' fits over 'her father told her'; 'for instance' balances 'all those years ago'; 'her father taught us how to make popcorn' agrees with 'he showed his Scottish friends how to make popcorn': the syntactic congruence slots together information and confirmation like a two-part entry code, unlocking Spark's vivid and personal memory, which is only thereby validated as 'the reality', warranted fit and released for publication.

In this light, the earlier passage reveals itself as a similar structure in which documentary evidence and its interpretation enclose and under-write a narrative memory. 'The popping corn in the pan held over the fire' was flanked by the exchange between Spark and Below; here, little Muriel's learning to read 'th' appears in a similarly privileged position, between the written traces of the Rules' presence in and absence from her home (the addressed envelope bearing the letters 'Andrew K. Rule, D.D.' which she would learn to decipher, and the letters her mother would receive and the alphabet cards left with Muriel herself). Spark's conversation with Below centred on one memory about learning '(and I can still see the popping corn in the pan held over the fire)'; here, what is happening by the fire is another kind of unfolding and another kind of learning, in which 'I sat at the fire [. . .] while Mrs. Rule declared that a "t" and an "h" together sounded "th".' And both moments reach forward into the present: as with her memory of the popping corn, Spark 'can still see' 't' and 'h' blooming into a digraph; for example, as she writes and reads 'a "t" and an "h" together' in the word 'together' in 1989.

Reading is a special sort of eyewitnessing. But learning to read is an experience involving an even more special kind of evidence, both eyewitness and documentary, because it can occur only by means of the irreversible creation of the latter out of part of the former, as visual data pass from funny squiggles to letters and words. In doing so, it emphasises certain aspects of the relation between ocular and written proof. For instance: that the kind of seeing which constitutes reading allows words written elsewhere and at another time to be eyewitnessed here and now, as Andrew K. Rule, D.D. left letters to be read on envelopes around the house, and sent back letters to be read after he left Edinburgh. And the memory of learning to read which is at the centre of this story, the memory of putting letters together to make more than the sum of their parts, is validated by these two experiences of written evidence because it's the origin of Spark's ability to see them, in reading them, *as* evidence. *Curriculum Vitae*, too, is partly founded upon the process of putting letters together: Spark's learning to read by the fire prepares a reading of her later story about popcorn which is also to do with letters and reading, because it was added to the text after 'people [. . .] wrote to me to confirm, modify and elaborate on what I had written' in *The New Yorker*.[35] Below and Spark repeat the earlier correspondence between their parents, following rules and Rules; their putting 'together' the story in letters repeats – and in Spark's case at least, can trace its first beginnings back to – Mrs Rule's orthographic manoeuvre with 'the precious cards'.

Willy Maley claims that 'Spark's version of memory lane is more like a mugger's alley, where you're as likely to get brained by a cobblestone as have an epiphany'; *Curriculum Vitae*, though, like the *New Yorker* articles which contributed to it, is at once less violent and murkier than this description suggests.[36] In particular, Spark's memories of her pre- and early literacy, in both memoirs, are mysterious in their clarity: 'It seems to me that my parents' friends and the people who called at our small flat were endless. I can remember the names and faces of people dating from my pre-school years far better than any others at any period of my life.'[37] These two sentences don't quite fit together. She can remember these names and faces 'far better than any others', but the people 'seem' – not 'seemed' – to her 'endless'; this part of her past survives into the present as her first archive, a vast reservoir of potential future recollections, unknown in extent and structure but whose content is easily identifiable when parts are fetched. This is where, 'groping for the luminous past of my first infancy I never fail to find it gleaming here and there [. . .]. My childhood in Edinburgh [. . .] occurs in bright flashes, illuminating every detail of the scene.'[38] Again, the present tense focuses on memorial reconstruction: her childhood 'occurs in bright flashes', and the 'scene' most illuminated is that of writing. Spark as autobiographer resembles the successful archival researcher described by Alice Yaeger Kaplan, 'something like a miner who has struck gold [. . .], a gem that made him glow for days', discovering that 'the gold is all in the dust'.[39] Many, although not all, of these early memories will have pre-dated her learning to read, and so her archive of 'names and faces of people' stretches back beyond and comprehends this important boundary between personal pre-history and personally literate record.

It's important not least because the identification reading makes possible between faces and written names is presented by Spark as a kind of aboriginal fact-checking: the man staying in young Muriel's house was 'Andrew K. Rule, D.D., as I found out [Charlotte Rule's] husband was, when I was well able to read his name on an envelope'. The child 'found out' rather than 'found' who he was, edging discovery into detection: so while it could be that the sense of this phrase is 'when I read our lodger's full name on an envelope I saw that it contained three other letters which nobody ever said out loud', there's also a way in which this written evidence is felt as proof of something: 'it wasn't until I could read our lodger's name on an envelope that I could properly establish his identity'.

'Names', Spark had insisted in *Curriculum Vitae*'s second paragraph, 'have a magic [. . .]. Most of the names in this, the following account of the first thirty-nine years of my life, are unknown to the public. For that reason they are all the more precious to me.'[40] Spark's is an autobiography in which the author's glinting personal memories are not so much dodgy areas as taboo objects, in that it deals with them as if they are 'magic', both 'precious' and hazardous, hidden in an endless occult realm of vulnerable but illuminating truth and polluting untruth (X might or might not have watched the candle flickering on the roof beams). And it can only be navigated by means of the proofs and procedures of fact-checking, because these constitute ritual behaviours designed to guarantee the fit between the world and the author's account of it, domesticating rogue memories into text safe to be read. The double focus of the sentence about popcorn makes this clear: while its syntax orbits around Spark's vividly present, centrally placed, and typographically highlighted memory, the dramatic situation of Below, who has heard about the incident from both Andrew K. Rule, D.D. and Muriel Spark and is therefore its designated fact-checker, is the centre of narrative importance and attention. Under these circumstances the fact-checker appears as a powerful and symbolic figure: a gatekeeper, Proof itself, against error; guarantor of all writing. 'A "t" and an "h" together sounded "th".' ✓

7

There's no need for *The New Yorker* to keep records of its fact-checking: the record of its fact-checkers is *The New Yorker*, and meanwhile, 'the proofs of published stories are locked away in some inaccessible place, so it's almost impossible to get at them, and after a short time they are destroyed'.[41] Robert Henderson's suggestive words – these are galley proofs, but his phrasing makes it sound as if they could be legal or mathematical – are prompted by a letter sent to *The New Yorker* from Dr Gordon W. Bertram, a Canadian academic, in response to a quotation printed in Spark's story 'The First Year of my Life'.[42] Bertram is asking for the source

> of the Asquith quotation 'All things have become new. In this great cleansing and purging it has been the privilege of our country to play her part.' This was apparently delivered by Asquith before the House of Commons just after World War I [. . .] but it would take me an enormous amount of time to find the precise reference in the British House of Commons records.[43]

This, then, as well as bearing further witness to the trust placed in *The New Yorker*'s factual accuracy by its readers, is another story about mysterious depositories and their gleaming contents. To Spark's vast paper archive and 'the luminous past of [her] first infancy' it adds 'the British House of Commons records', in which this 'precise reference' is buried, and the 'inaccessible place' in which the *New Yorker* proof has been – if not destroyed – 'locked away'. And there's another depository too, because the conceit behind Spark's story is that 'the young of the human species are born omniscient. Babies [. . .] know everything that is going on everywhere in the world; [. . .] it is only after the first year that it is brainwashed out of us.'[44] This infant narrator shares Spark's birth date as well as her 'luminous past' in some of its recollections; and her omniscience – to which Bertram, perhaps not entirely consciously, responds – makes her the very type of the fact-checker. Or almost; or, with a tragic flaw, for this fact-checker, although absolutely infallible, is etymologically 'infant', unable to speak, and therefore completely incapable of communicating her knowledge and opinions.[45] The story's running joke that this baby knows everything (and therefore doesn't smile) runs alongside a second, bleaker joke which makes her into a sort of miniature Cassandra: her actions are without fail misinterpreted by those around her (including her failure thus far in her life to smile).

There's a third joke, though, which saves the plot from science-fictional neatness, and it centres on the quotation that Bertram wanted to cite. At her first birthday party, the baby hears Asquith's statement quoted, and

> That did it. I broke into a decided smile [. . .]
> 'It was the candle on her cake,' they said.
> The cake be damned. [. . .] when I really mean a smile, deeply felt from the core, then to all intents and purposes it comes in response to the words

uttered in the House of Commons after the First World War by the distinguished, the immaculately dressed, and the late Mr. Asquith.[46]

With this, the story ends; nothing is added to explain why 'That did it'; why she's so fond of Asquith, or so patriotic, or so pleased that all things have become new. No clues were given earlier. The answer just can't be known, and this infant, as she said they all do 'after the first year', disappears into the silence at the end of the story and the incomprehension you alone have been spared during its course; Spark's story confirms that, like *New Yorker* proofs, babies' omniscient minds are 'locked away in some inaccessible place and it's almost impossible to get at them, and after a short time they are destroyed'. Wittgenstein didn't say 'If a baby could talk, we could not understand her', but he could have.

But then, as Miss Jean Brodie tells her girls:

> 'It is well, when in difficulties, to say never a word, neither black nor white. Speech is silver but silence is golden. Mary, are you listening? What was I saying?'
>
> Mary Macgregor [. . .] who was later famous for being stupid and always to blame and who, at the age of twenty-three, lost her life in a hotel fire, ventured, 'Golden'.[47]

When in her later difficulties, however, Mary will make never a sound: 'She heard no screams, for the roar of the fire drowned the screams; she gave no scream, for the smoke was choking her. She ran into somebody on her third turn, stumbled and died.'[48] Not only babies are infant, and the details of Mary's unknown and unknowable death – her three silent turns in the corridor, which after a short time will be destroyed – are locked away in another of the precious and inaccessible spaces from which Spark's proofed and proven narratives emerge and around which they circle, fascinated. *The Prime of Miss Jean Brodie* contains a number of reflections from and details about Spark's own schooldays, some of which will be repeated in *Curriculum Vitae*, and is constructed out of the gaps and inferences and surmisings of childhood, the mysteries in them of 'other people's Edinburghs' and 'other people's nineteen-thirties' and other people's minds and motives.[49] Mary's death, the most private and self-enclosed moment in the novel, is marked out in Spark's narrative with little flecks of recollected silent gold: Miss Brodie's advice before it, and immediately afterwards some 'pale gold cubes' of pineapple which taste to Sandy of 'a special happiness, which was nothing to do with eating, and was different from the happiness of play that one enjoyed unawares'.[50] Her negative definition edges round something which its comparisons attempt to confirm, but which unlike the fact-checked

personal memories of *Curriculum Vitae* remains ungraspable, uncorrob-
orated by outside sources. Pure gold is too malleable and ductile for most
uses, needing an alloy of less precious metal (silver, say) to strengthen it.

Miss Brodie's golden silence will ring in your ears later in the novel
('are you listening?') when she addresses the now adult Sandy:

> '[. . .] in the autumn of nineteen-thirty-one I entered an affair with Gordon
> Lowther [. . .]. That is the truth and there is no more to say. Are you listening,
> Sandy?'
> 'Yes, I'm listening.'
> 'You look as if you were thinking of something else, my dear. Well, as I
> say, that is the whole story.'
> Sandy was thinking of something else. She was thinking that it was not the
> whole story.[51]

But Miss Brodie protests too much: her conversations with her former
pupils are driven by a need to find out 'something else' about herself
accessible only through them: she wants to know which of them
'betrayed' her, causing her to be forced into early retirement, and only
then will she have the 'whole story'. Her researches are autobiographical, and they repeat in reverse her previous attempts to create and to
discover her pupils' life stories, cultivating characteristics for which they
would become locally 'famous' and persuading them to inform on each
other's private lives, their luminous infancies. They do, but they also
don't, completely; like Sandy's happiness and Mary's death, some things
here are exempt from and unsusceptible to current investigation. After
her own affair with the art master, Sandy's 'mind was as full of his religion as a night sky is full of things visible and invisible'; Spark's novel,
too, finds its poise between things evident and things hidden.[52] For
what was used to 'pin [. . .] down' Miss Brodie weren't her possible or
actual love affairs but the Fascist beliefs which were in any case clearly
documented in the 'pictures [. . .] pin[ned] on the wall' of her classroom;
and in the meantime the rest of her wondered-at life remains as it were
unbetrayed, something else, things invisible, no more to say.[53]

But the something else that Sandy is thinking just now is 'It is seven
years since I betrayed this tiresome woman', and this part of the story
at least was susceptible to proof and reproof.[54] Spark had originally
written 'twelve years', but just before *The Prime of Miss Jean Brodie*
was first published, as a nearly-whole novel which took up almost the
whole of one issue of *The New Yorker*, her editor made a calculation
and sent a hurried telegram:

> If Brodie died 1946 and Sandy betrayed her in the fall of 1938, should sen-
> tence not read 'It is eight years, thought Sandy, since I betrayed this tiresome

woman.' Please cable collect. Proofs here and everything fine except for this detail. The figure you use is twelve. Love Rachel MacKenzie.[55]

In this story two and two, like 't' and 'h', can sometimes be put together. A reply came the next day: 'Book Page 71 implies conversation early 1946 therefore Sandy says seven years and four months sorry am not famous arithmetic love Muriel Spark.'[56] *The New Yorker* is famous proof, though, and while Spark's English publisher rounded it down to 'seven years', page 92 of *The New Yorker*, on 14 October 1961 reads, 'it is seven years and four months, thought Sandy...'. It may only be a scruple but you feel it, as you feel *The New Yorker*, shift the balance of *The Prime of Miss Jean Brodie* and of Sandy and of Muriel Spark who was famous for documentary evidence.

('Thank you so much', Henderson had written to Spark, about the proofs of 'The First Year of my Life', 'for your painstaking help with sources, and so on. I wouldn't have minded if you had made it all up, the anecdotes sound so probable, but our checking department will be happier.'[57] 'I received a copy of this from another part of the wood some time ago', she wrote to him, about Dr Bertram's request, 'and replied accordingly'.[58] Her reply isn't in Acc: 10607/200, or Acc: 10607/201 either. It'll be in another part of the wood. Miss Jean Brodie told her girls: 'It is well, when in difficulties, to say never a word, neither black nor white. Speech is silver but silence is golden.')

Notes

1. J. Malcolm Maclaren, *Gold: Its Geological Occurrence and Geographical Distribution* (London: Mining Journal, 1908), p. v.
2. Muriel Spark Archive, National Library of Scotland (hereafter NLS), Acc: 10989/50; Muriel Spark, *Curriculum Vitae: A Volume of Autobiography* (Harmondsworth: Penguin, 1993), hereafter CV, p. 185.
3. Carolyn Steedman, *Dust* (Manchester: Manchester University Press, 2001), p. 17; Richard Bentley, *A Dissertation Upon the Epistles of Phalaris* (1699), cited in the *Oxford English Dictionary* online (hereafter OED), available at <http://www.oed.com/view/Entry/58683?rskey=5PSfVb&result=1&isAdvanced=true#eid5853523> (accessed 1 May 2014).
4. Muriel Spark, 'The Goose' (c. 1960), in *All the Poems* (New York: New Directions, 2004), p. 75.
5. CV, p. 164.
6. Muriel Spark, *The Golden Fleece: Essays* (Manchester: Carcanet, 2014).
7. Muriel Spark, 'The Order of the Golden Fleece', *Argentor*, 3.1 (1948), pp. 29–32, 70 (p. 30).
8. CV, p. 11. The factual details of Spark's publication in *The New Yorker* are very usefully collected and tabulated by Lisa Harrison, in '"The Magazine That is Considered the Best in the World": Muriel Spark and the

New Yorker', in David Herman, ed., *Muriel Spark: Twenty-First-Century Perspectives* (Baltimore: Johns Hopkins University Press, 2010), pp. 39–60.

9. Strabo, *Geography*, trans. by H. L. Jones, 8 vols (Cambridge, MA: Harvard University Press, 1968), XI.2.19, V.215.

10. Freya Johnston, *Samuel Johnson and the Art of Sinking: 1709–1791* (Oxford: Oxford University Press, 2005), p. 169.

11. Charles McGrath, 'Muriel Spark: Playing God', *New York Times*, 22 April 2010, available at <http://www.nytimes.com/2010/04/25/books/review/McGrath-t.html?pagewanted=all&_r=0> (accessed 1 May 2014).

12. *CV*, pp. 189–91.

13. Muriel Spark, 'Personal History: Visiting the Laureate', *The New Yorker*, 26 August 1991, pp. 63–7 (pp. 63–4).

14. Ibid., p. 64.

15. Ibid., p. 66.

16. Ibid., p. 67.

17. Muriel Spark, 'Bread, Butter, and Florrie Ford', *The New Yorker*, 11 September 1989, pp. 36–46; 'Personal History: The School on the Links', *The New Yorker*, 25 March 1991, pp. 75–85; 'Personal History: Venture into Africa', *The New Yorker*, 2 March 1992, pp. 73–80.

18. *CV*, pp. 11–12.

19. Cited in John McPhee, 'Personal History: Checkpoints', *The New Yorker*, 9 February 2009, pp. 56–63 (p. 56).

20. Cited in ibid., p. 59.

21. *CV*, p. 11.

22. McPhee, 'Personal History: Checkpoints', p. 59.

23. Muriel Spark, *The Prime of Miss Jean Brodie* (London: Macmillan, 1961); *The Driver's Seat* (London: Macmillan, 1970). These novels were first published in *The New Yorker* in slightly reduced form as 'The Prime of Miss Jean Brodie', 14 October 1961, pp. 52–161, and 'The Driver's Seat', 16 May 1970, pp. 38–102. *The Mandelbaum Gate* (London: Macmillan, 1965); the sections first published in *The New Yorker* were 'The Mandelbaum Gate: Freddy's Walk', 15 May 1965, pp. 54–9; 'The Mandelbaum Gate: Barbara Vaughan's Identity', 10 July 1965, pp. 25–52; 'The Mandelbaum Gate: A Delightful English Atmosphere', 24 July 1965, pp. 26–54; and 'The Mandelbaum Gate: Abdul's Orange Groves', 7 August 1965, pp. 28–65.

24. Julia Just, fax to Muriel Spark, 29 August 1989; Muriel Spark, fax to Julia Just, 29 August 1989, NLS Acc: 10989/226.

25. Nigel Billen, fax to Muriel Spark, 21 June 1991, NLS Acc: 10989/237.

26. *CV*, p. 11; Muriel Spark, fax to Nigel Billen, 21 June 1991, NLS Acc: 10989/237.

27. Corrected proof of 'Bread, Butter, and Florrie Ford', 9 March 1989; Julia Just, fax to Muriel Spark, 29 August 1989, NLS Acc: 10989/226.

28. Muriel Spark, fax to Julia Just, 29 August 1989, ibid.

29. Mr Bill Boyd, letter to *The New Yorker*, 19 September 1991, NLS Acc: 10989/129.

30. 'Bread, Butter, and Florrie Ford', p. 38.

31. Muriel Spark, letter to Charles McGrath, 29 March 1989, NLS Acc: 10989/226.

32. Muriel Spark, *Mary Shelley*, rev. ed. (London: Constable, 1998 [1951]), p. xii.
33. Spark, 'Bread, Butter, and Florrie Ford', p. 39.
34. *CV*, p. 26.
35. *CV*, p. 12.
36. Willy Maley, 'Prime Scene Investigation: Muriel Spark's Grave Humour' (text of a lecture delivered at the Aye Write! Bank of Scotland Book Festival, 7 March 2009), available at <http://www.willymaley.com/downloads/AyewriteSpark.pdf> (accessed 31 October 2013).
37. *CV*, p. 25.
38. *CV*, p. 17. This passage does not appear in 'Bread, Butter, and Florrie Ford'.
39. Alice Yaeger Kaplan, 'Working in the Archives', *Yale French Studies*, 77, *Reading the Archive: On Texts and Institutions* (1990), 103–16 (pp. 105, 107, 116).
40. *CV*, p. 11.
41. Robert Henderson, letter to Muriel Spark, 12 August 1975, NLS Acc: 10607/200.
42. Muriel Spark, 'The First Year of my Life', *The New Yorker*, 2 June 1975, pp. 37–9.
43. Dr Gordon W. Bertram, letter to *The New Yorker*, 26 June 1975, NLS Acc: 10989/200.
44. Spark, 'The First Year of my Life', p. 37.
45. The English 'infant' derives from the Latin *infāns*, meaning 'unable to speak' (*OED*).
46. Spark, 'The First Year of my Life', p. 39.
47. Spark, *The Prime of Miss Jean Brodie*, pp. 13–14.
48. Ibid., p. 15.
49. Ibid., p. 33.
50. Ibid., pp. 13–16.
51. Ibid., p. 60.
52. Ibid., p. 123.
53. Ibid., pp. 124, 44.
54. Ibid., pp. 125, 59–60.
55. Rachel MacKenzie, telegram to Muriel Spark, 27 September 1961, New Yorker Records, box 789, folder 9.
56. Muriel Spark, telegram to Rachel MacKenzie, 28 September 1961, ibid.
57. Robert Henderson, letter to Muriel Spark, 15 April 1975, NLS Acc: 10607/201.
58. Muriel Spark, letter to Robert Henderson, 7 September 1975, NLS Acc: 10607/200.

Chapter 6

Sylvia Plath and 'The Blessed Glossy *New Yorker*'

Linda Freedman

'I have wanted to efface myself', says the speaker of Plath's 1961 poem 'Tulips'.[1] In the context of its original publication in a spring issue of *The New Yorker* in 1962, the line is both ironic and oddly appropriate. Plath's relationship with the magazine was intimately tied to her own obsessive self-fashioning as a young and promising writer, yet the process through which she absorbed *The New Yorker* into her ongoing conceit of rebirth and resurrection was one of continual self-effacement. Despite *The New Yorker*'s reputation at midcentury for publishing mainly light verse and sentimental poetry, 'break[ing] in' to its pages promised something weighty to the young Sylvia Plath.[2] Ted Hughes could never understand it. He was particularly dismissive of the American magazine, describing it as full of 'gaucherie'. For Hughes, *The New Yorker* was 'eminently a magazine of parlour pieces, and not of serious writing, not the poems. Teaparty pieces. Birthday card rhymes. The kind of ornament on the page that the designs of advertisements also provide. A place for the eye.'[3] But for Plath, who referred to *The New Yorker* as one of her 'unclimbed Anapurnas', appearing in its pages was part of proving herself, a way of making her name, and lending it substance.[4]

This essay is concerned with the making of Sylvia Plath in the context of *The New Yorker*, and with her sense of her own materiality, or immateriality, as a writer in that context. In Jacqueline Rose's positioning of Plath in the terrain of contemporary periodicals, *The New Yorker* figures as the most desirable destination for her writing, even though her work appears more frequently in other periodicals such as the *Ladies' Home Journal*, *Mademoiselle* and *Seventeen*.[5] Rose points out that Plath published in a range of magazines with quite different markets. She went for highbrow and middlebrow, literary and popular, with exposure her overriding concern. *The New Yorker*'s initial reluctance to publish Plath made acceptance in its pages still more attractive. In March 1953 she wrote to her mother:

My personal rejection from *The New Yorker* has made me realize how hard I want to work at writing this summer. I'll never get anywhere if I just write one or two stories and never revise them or *streamline them for a particular market*. I want to hit *The New Yorker* in poetry and the *Ladies' Home Journal* in stories and so I must study the magazines the way I did *Seventeen*.[6]

It seems that Plath was somewhat encouraged by the personal letter of rejection that she received from *The New Yorker*. She had also just received a rejection from *Mademoiselle* – presumably a form letter – and felt she had little chance of making her name there. 'Twenty top girls from Smith are trying out [for a summer editorship]', she complained.[7] *The New Yorker* became still more alluring: Plath enjoyed juxtaposing her own grubbing hard work with the magazine's seemingly effortless charm: 'I will slave and slave until I break into those slicks', she wrote to her mother in 1957, and, 'I would really like to get something in *The New Yorker* before I die, I do so admire that particular, polished, rich, brilliant style.'[8]

'Tulips' provides a way into thinking about the paradoxical thread of self-making and self-erasure that runs through Plath's writing about *The New Yorker*. The passivity of the speaker's position in the hospital bed stands in stark contrast to the assertive way in which she willingly renounces all signifiers of identity: 'I have given my name and my day-clothes up to the nurses / And my history to the anesthetist and my body to surgeons.' There is a perverse and disruptive pleasure in the way this speaker maintains her watchful control through the processes of sur-render, her head 'between the pillow and the sheet-cuff / Like an eye between two white lids that will not shut.' The forcefulness of refusal in 'will not shut' makes this scene of passivity somewhat grotesque because it suggests that the speaker's prone and still form is at odds with the activity of her mind and the strength of her will. Her hospitalisation is a kind of baptism, with abasement a curiously exciting form of sanctifica-tion: 'They have swabbed me clear of my loving associations [. . .] / I am a nun now; I have never been so pure.' Like Christ, incarnate in the 'Communion tablet' of the fifth stanza, the speaker of 'Tulips' embodies self-sacrifice – and enjoys it.

The tropes that carry the paradox of self-effacement and self-fashioning in this poem localise a larger set of figurations in Plath's writings about *The New Yorker* magazine. The first of these emphasises smooth polished surface. The speaker's body in 'Tulips' is illegible, its signifiers erased: 'My body is a pebble to them; they tend it as water / Tends to the pebbles it must run over, smoothing them gently.' This illegible surface contrasts with the allusiveness of the speaker's voice, which is actively engaged in authorial self-fashioning, positioning itself in a literary, cultural, and political terrain. Plath simultaneously invokes and inverts the Emersonian cry in 'Nature' for egoless participation in a 'Universal Being': 'I am nobody' echoes Emerson's 'I am nothing. I see all.'[9] But instead of a 'transparent eyeball', she has, and is, a 'stupid pupil', the pun making a further play of imitation and allusion. 'I have nothing to do with explosions', she says, distancing herself from the 'excitable' eruption of spring flowers, and from Cold War terror, along with Emersonian disclosures of interiority. Later, when she sees herself, 'flat, ridiculous, a cut-paper shadow', the familiar American trope of double-consciousness reveals nothing but two-dimensional surface.

The insubstantial, lightweight quality of that 'shadow' surface is the second tropological thread in Plath's self-creation that runs through the context of *The New Yorker*: Plath's comments about the magazine repeatedly return to matters of weight, substance, and shape. In 'Tulips', the speaker is not only reduced to a two-dimensional cut-paper shadow; she is insignificantly small like a 'pebble', travels light, having 'lost herself sick of baggage' and wants to be 'utterly empty'. In juxtaposition with this identity-free weightlessness are the tulips, which have a grotesquely animated materiality and a heavy, monstrous, corporeal presence:

> Even through the gift paper I could hear them breathe
> Lightly, through their white swaddlings, like an awful baby
> [. . .]
> They are subtle: they seem to float, though they weigh me down
> [. . .]
> A dozen red lead sinkers round my neck.

On the one hand, the tulips intrude on the speaker's fetishised diminishing, their lightness only a deception as they impose their plump solidity on her small thinness. On the other, the tulips fulfil the process of self-effacement as Plath's speaker is remade in their image:

> And I am aware of my heart: it opens and closes
> Its bowl of red blooms out of sheer love of me.

This central paradox of self-fashioning and self-effacement with its defining tropes of smooth surface, weight, substance, and shape makes 'Tulips' a complex and conflicted poem about the self's undoing and remaking. Yet *New Yorker* readers encountering Plath's poem – and perhaps Plath – for the first time in 1962 might have expected a poem called 'Tulips' to be about spring. *The New Yorker*'s habit of publishing timely and seasonal verse and fiction was well known. Frances

Kiernan, fiction editor at the magazine between 1966 and 1987, recalled the importance of seasonal themes and references in the process of scheduling:

> Having a large reserve of fiction on hand made it relatively easy to sustain the long-standing *New Yorker* tradition of publishing stories in their proper season – not merely running a Christmas story in the latter half of December but running a story that mentioned a ginger jar of daffodils in early spring. Sometimes, when a story had to be rushed into print because it was going to come out in a book (in which case the magazine insisted on a lag time of at least three months), the daffodils had to be changed to roses or dahlias or whatever was appropriate.[10]

The 7 April issue in which 'Tulips' appeared was full of advertisements for spring clothing. Women readers could admire 'the crisp spring look', luxurious lightweight fabrics of silk and chiffon, floaty nightgowns ('Drifting on spring – a blithe shift dips its edges into demure blue or pink checks' [Fig. 6.1]), and jewelled spring blossom brooches; men could enjoy the prospect of crisp cotton suits, short-sleeved shirts, and refreshing cocktails. The first cartoon in the issue took the season as an opportunity for Cold War comedy. With the Kremlin in the background and two short, fat Russians in the foreground, it was captioned: 'Every spring I feel faint stirrings of free enterprise within me.'[11] Then, in the middle of a light-hearted story about the publishing industry, the reader encounters 'Tulips'. Poetry editor Howard Moss surely scheduled the poem for this issue for the same reason that he published Plath's 'Blackberrying' in the autumn; but it is hard to know whether Moss read them as poems that were appropriate to the season or whether he relished playing on the expectation that they might be; for 'Tulips' is no more a spring poem than 'Blackberrying' is an autumnal one. Either way, 'Tulips' clearly caught its readers' attention. Moss wrote in 1962: 'I have heard nothing but the most extravagant praise of "Tulips." Everyone I know thought it extraordinary. So do I.'[12]

If the strangeness of 'Tulips' caught the eye in *The New Yorker* of 1962, the retrospective biographical framework in which the poem is now often read is also something that *The New Yorker* helped to construct. 'Tulips' was reprinted in a double issue of 23 and 30 August 1993, out of season this time, and as part of the 'Annals of Biography' department in a long piece by Janet Malcolm that featured the first three sections of 'The Silent Woman' (later developed into a book) together with a number of Plath's poems. The piece was prefaced with the following explanation: 'Since her suicide in 1963, the poet Sylvia Plath has drawn a succession of biographers to her unquiet grave. In death, as in

Figure 6.1. Advertisement, Lord & Taylor, *The New Yorker*, 7 April 1962, p. 13. Sylvia Plath's 'Tulips' appeared in the same issue.

life, she raises uncomfortable questions about her identity – and about the nature of biography itself.'[13] Opposite was a full-page picture of Hughes and Plath, smiling out at the camera shortly after their wedding in the summer of 1956. With his arm encircling her waist and her hand affectionately clasping his, the tragic unfolding of Plath's romance and life-story was immediately manifest. 'Tulips' appears in the middle of the text of the third section, which focuses on the unreliability of witnesses in the making of biography, and on Plath's growing disillusionment with Hughes.[14] An innocent reader encountered Plath's 'Tulips' in *The New Yorker* in 1962, but a reader familiar with Plath's life-story saw the poem in *The New Yorker* in 1993. In this context there could be no mistaking it for a spring poem. Readers were encouraged by its context to construe it as a poem about identity-formation, breakdown and violence.

Malcolm began her career at *The New Yorker* as a women's writer, covering Christmas shopping specials and children's literature, and writing a regular column on interior design called 'About the House'. But under the auspices of a magazine known for its satiric stance and exacting eye she developed a strong signature style. In many respects, Malcolm's writing, with its precise deconstruction of biographical narrative, dense accumulation of information and analytic focus, learns from and feeds into *New Yorker* style. It was Malcolm who first saw that the story that surrounded Plath was the construction of the story. At their core, these articles, and the book they became, are about the effacement and re-fashioning of Plath. They are about the way she became whoever her biographers wanted her to be, silently subject to their stories and projections. Malcolm reads the history of Plath's biography as a repetitive staging of a battle between true and false selves. For Hughes, Plath's late work was about the emergence of her true self which he described along Blakean lines of imaginative release. For her mother, Plath's true self was obscured by the not-nice persona of *Ariel* and *The Bell Jar* who, she argued, was the product of sickness and falsity. Malcolm suggests that this story of a battle between a true and false Plath gained momentum at least partly because of the way it allowed Plath to epitomise a duplicitous historical moment when it felt as though honesty were just about to surface.

The reception that Malcolm deconstructs must also be a result of Plath's own thematic preoccupation with duality. Plath's personal, political, and aesthetic formulations often pivot on the possibility of smooth, blank surfaces and their temporary disclosures of violence. Writing 'for' *The New Yorker* and about *The New Yorker*, she made the magazine's flawless surface part of her own self-production. Continuing that project after her death, the magazine played a distinctive role in shaping and commenting upon Plath's posthumous reputation – and Malcolm was well aware of *The New Yorker*'s role in the tussle for ownership over the young, ill-fated poet that it had once published.

The double printing of 'Tulips' in April 1962 and August 1993, with its implications for contextual interpretation, and the poem's theme of self-effacement aligned with the process of self-fashioning, poses a question: to what extent did *The New Yorker* shape Plath into a writer, both in terms of her own ambition to see her name in its print, and in terms of the magazine's role in developing her posthumous reputation? Plath wanted to take up space in the magazine's pages, but she was also fixated on the seductive possibilities of vanishing into the smooth polished surfaces they offered. When two contrary identities clash, as they so often did for Plath, one frequently promises to efface the other. In her writing about the magazine, she repeatedly juxtaposed the weighty gain of recognition with the sometimes attractive and sometimes troubling possibility of simply melting into thin air. In a sense this reflects Plath's worry about the transitory nature of magazine publication, but it also embodies a tendency to turn the process of self-fashioning into self-effacement, with Plath looking to *The New Yorker* to provide a release from the stodgy domesticity of suburban life.

'The exquisite several-paged surface'

'The Munich Mannequins' begins with a now famous rewriting of Greek wisdom: 'Perfection is terrible, it cannot have children.'[15] This echoes Herodotus, 'Count no man happy until he is dead', and recurs in 'Edge', the last poem Plath wrote. The rhetorical suicide at the start of this last poem, heavily shadowed by Plath's actual suicide only hours later, cannot help but invite biographical reading. It is harder to read the deaths of the children in 'Edge', despite, or perhaps because of, the way they resist biographical interpretation.

> Each dead child coiled, a white serpent,
> [...]
> She has folded
>
> Them back into her body as petals
> Of a rose close when the garden
>
> Stiffens and odors bleed.[16]

The image is a tightening of form and an inversion of fertility. Like the uncomfortable alignment in the first stanza of death with perfection, it derives its power from a duplicity whereby symbols of innocence (child) and experience (serpent) resist singular interpretation, and stories of movement (generation and decay) are 'folded' into the smooth surface and effaced by stillness. The verb suggests that separation was never fully enacted: childbirth becomes a temporary disclosure, a brief revelation of depth.

The relationship between surface and voice was a fundamental part of the erotic and creative interplay between mastery and submission that was intimately connected to Plath's desire for effacement. 'The Munich Mannequins' ends with a strikingly pertinent image of silencing:

> And the black phones on hooks
> Glittering
> Glittering and digesting
> Voicelessness. The snow has no voice.

If 'Edge' and 'The Munich Mannequins' illustrate Plath's preoccupation with smooth surfaces, 'Mary's Song' shows the hold that the transparency of melted form had on her imagination. It is a disturbing poem, not least because of the way in which the Holocaust retains its etymological connection to the older Hebrew notion of a sacrificial burnt offering. The poem begins with a rendering of fat in a deliberately crass conceit that holds the image of a sizzling Sunday roast together with the suggestion of God on the cross.

> The Sunday lamb cracks in its fat.
> The fat
> Sacrifices its opacity [. . .]

The 'crack[ed]' surface bears the marks of struggle and surrender. Like Christ on the cross, the sizzling meat gives up the ghost only after a period of suffering. The poem's final lament returns to the lamb as a signifier of innocence and a victim of cyclical violence. The speaker both mourns and celebrates the sacrifice in an emotional apostrophe that sanctifies the killing as much as it is horrified by it: 'O golden child the world will kill and eat.'[17]

The poem has been read as a testament to the fear of the dispossessed mother, unable to protect her child from the historical repetition of divine cruelty.[18] Yet the image of Christ on the cross is at least partly one of willing self-sacrifice. As in 'Tulips', where the speaker is purified and translucently 'swabbed clear' by the abasement she suffers at the hands of hospital staff, 'Mary's Song' displays a fascination with the degree to which transparency, thinness and the melting of solid form involves, or necessitates, a sacrifice of self. Moreover, it suggests that such self-sacrifice is empowering. The suggestion is deliberately distasteful. The melted fat is 'holy'; the ovens in Auschwitz glow 'like heavens'; the rendered fat and melted flesh of history's sacrificial lambs retain a resistance that the perpetrators of violence cannot destroy.

> Their thick palls
> Float over the cicatrix of Poland, burnt-out
> Germany. They do not die.

Aerial and dissolute, the dead also have a 'thick' presence. They matter because the fire in 'Mary's Song' sanctifies.

Unsurprisingly, neither 'The Munich Mannequins' nor 'Mary's Song' were published in *The New Yorker*. But Plath *did* imagine *The New Yorker* performing a similar thinning and thickening of the poems it undertook to bring out. This was her reaction to first seeing her work in *New Yorker* print:

> I am awestruck, excited, smiling inside creamy as a cat: the day has evaporated, quite gone, in a rapt contemplation of my poem 'Mussel Hunter At Rock Harbor' which came out in the August 9 issue of the blessed glossy <u>New Yorker</u> – the title in that queer wobbly, half-archaic type I've dreamed poem & story titles in for about eight years. Queerest of all, I dreamed the poem would come out last night! Luckily I told Ted my dream – about Howard Moss & some poet who'd 'finally got into the <u>New Yorker</u>', even though he had a note in italics at the bottom of the page saying it had been almost completely revised & edited by a woman named, I think, Anne Morrow (a sense of Moss changing my lowercase-letters to capitals, adding commas & subtracting hyphens?) – in my dream, my poem was clipped, as on a dummy copy, on the left-hand side of a page between a left-hand column & right page of ads. I was amazed when Florence Sultan called me up & told me my poem was in. I went over, drank wine with her & admired the baby Sonia, who has suddenly got to be a dark curly haired blue eyed image of Florence, sweet & solid. There the poem was in her copy, <u>the</u> first poem in the magazine, page 22, taking up <u>almost</u> a whole page on the left, except for about an inch & a half of a 3-column story at the bottom – plenty of shiny white New Yorker space around my two column poem, about 45 lines in each column. Well, this week will soon be over: I have the naive idea people all over the world will be reading & marveling at the poem! Of course, it inhibits my poetry in one way (what other work could achieve this grandeur!) & yet, deep in me, it encourages my prose immensely – that I, too, may work my stories up to the exquisite several-paged surface of the ones next to & following my poems seems less like a mad goal.[19]

Plath is fully aware of what context does to voice. This entry is obsessed with context; the dream, the intimacy of confession, the niceties of neighbours, and most of all the slick format of *The New Yorker* are exercises in contextual self-fashioning as Plath imagines and records the way she might be perceived. It is interesting to see that she worried about *New Yorker* editing because she always agreed to suggested changes. Here the change of surface, the reproduction of her work as a *New Yorker* piece is a source both of concern and of excitement. Her dream obliterates her and reveals irritation with Howard Moss, but her irritation and effacement do not lessen her desire to appear as a *New Yorker* writer. On the contrary, she embraces her absorption into the magazine's signature style. The thrill of disappearing beneath 'the exquisite several-paged surface' is erotically charged. Here is the 'unclimbed Anapurna', the snow-capped pristine mountain that over-whelms even the successful climber who manages to make his mark upon it.

In contrast with the achievement of 'finally' getting in, there is a material lightness about everything to do with *The New Yorker* in this entry. Beginning with the way her happiness 'evaporated' the day, Plath goes on to describe her 'queer wobbly' printed words as if they were likely to collapse or disappear at any moment. Moreover, she knows that any recognition *The New Yorker* confers is fleeting: 'Well, this week will soon be over: I have the naive idea people all over the world will be reading & marveling at the poem!' The implication is that she will be easily forgotten, her work discarded in favour of newer poems in newer issues. Plath is clearly sending up her own ambition, laughing at the idea that the luxury of wasted paper around a single poem makes her special, and fully aware of the fleeting nature of magazine publication, especially publication in a weekly magazine. That worry hangs over her celebration, yet at the same time, Plath does not hide her pleasure. The 'sweet and solid' baby, plonked inelegantly in the middle of the scene, stands as a reminder of the clumsy and heavy 'fat' domesticity from which writing provides an escape. In her desire to take up space in the magazine, to cover more of its 'exquisite' surface with stories than might be possible with poems, she paradoxically suggests that she might become thinner and lighter, but stronger and further removed from the world that Florence and Sonia inhabit, as she 'work[s] up' her material presence in *The New Yorker*.

'Break[ing] in' and getting thin: a *New Yorker* arrival

The dead woman in 'Edge' has arrived. A sureness of tone and deliberateness of activity governs her persona. When news of Plath's death reached *New Yorker* poetry editor Howard Moss, he was told that her mother, Aurelia, was the 'proper recipient for flowers'.[20] He sent the appropriate tribute to Plath's mother and she replied with the following letter:

> When I received the beautiful arrangement of exquisite flowers in memory of my daughter Sylvia Plath, from you, I recalled her phoning me a few years ago – her voice vibrant with joy – 'I've arrived Mother! A New Yorker acceptance at last!' Thank you, Sincerely yours, Aurelia S. Plath.[21]

The phone call that Aurelia Plath remembers would have taken place in 1958 when her daughter was still enthused by a romantic and naïve vision of life with Hughes as one of literary ambition and shared creative focus. Arrival meant something with a future, a beginning rather than an end. This is important because the pattern of Plath's relationship with *The New Yorker* changed dramatically as her relationship with Hughes broke down. By the time she took her own life in 1963, nearly two years after she had secured a coveted first-reading agreement with *The New Yorker*, acceptance seemed to matter only in that it paid well. Functioning as a single parent with two small children in a cold London winter where both she and the children caught endless feverish colds, she was exhausted and desperate to afford the childcare that would enable her to continue writing. The cost of living allowance from her first-reading agreement had very significant practical benefits, as did the cheques she received for her poems. But she no longer cared whether the magazine would make her name. And she had stopped trying to write for its market.

During the 1950s at least, the story had been quite different. Plath talked about sending poems to *The New Yorker* as early as February 1953. 'Poems sent out make blind hope spring eternal,' she wrote, 'even if rejections are imminent.'[22] In her journals of 1956 to 1958 her desire to appear in the magazine's pages seems to have become an obsessive performance of ambition, but nowhere do we see any sign of respect for the quality of writing associated with *The New Yorker*. The tone, therefore, is a curious mix of covetousness and self-deprecation. It is performative not because Plath was insincere in her desire to become one of *The New Yorker*'s favoured few, but because writing for *The New Yorker* became intimately involved with the identity that she was part-fashioning and part-fantasising in those years. Every journal entry toys with shrinkage, assuming a self-diminishing stance and playing with notions of smallness and thinness. In 1956 she writes, 'I depend too desperately on getting my poems, my glib poems, so neat, so small, accepted by the *New Yorker*.'[23]

Her self-deprecation here entails direct criticism of *The New Yorker*'s choice in poetry; she implies that 'glib . . . neat . . . small' poems are the kind of thing that could and should get in. In the same year she talks of 'build[ing]' herself up to combat the corrosive power of jealousy: 'When I start getting jealous of the five editors of Mlle for being married [...] or Philip Booth for writing poems for the NY and having a wife and all that, it is time to build up some inner prowess.'[24] The performance intensified in 1958: 'My identity is shaping, forming itself – I feel stories sprout, reading the collection of New Yorker stories – yes, I shall, in the fullness of time, be among them – the poetesses, the authoresses.'[25] And finally, on the day she received her first notification of acceptance:

> One letter stuck up out of the mailbox, and I saw The New Yorker on the left corner in dark print. My eyes dazed over. I raced alternatives through my head: I had sent a stamped envelope with my last poems, so they must have lost it & returned the rejects in one of their own envelopes. Or it must be a letter for Ted about copyrights. I ripped the letter from the box. It felt shockingly, hopefully thin. I tore it open right there on the steps, over mammoth marshmallow Mrs Whalen sitting in the green yard with her two pale artificially cute little boys in their swimsuits [. . .] The black thick print of Howard Moss's letter banged into my brain. I saw 'MUSSEL-HUNTER AT ROCK HARBOR seems to me a marvelous poem & I'm happy to say we're taking it for the New Yorker . . .' – at this realization of ten years of hopeful wishful waits (& subsequent rejections) I ran yipping upstairs to Ted & jumping about like a Mexican bean. It was only moments later, calming a little, that I finished the sentence '. . . as well as NOCTURNE, which we also think extremely fine.' Two POEMS – not only that, two of my longest – 91 and 45 lines respectively: they'll have to use front-spots for both & are buying them in spite of having a full load of summer poems & not for filler.[26]

The New Yorker acceptance again intrudes on a mundane domestic scene. The stolid everyday surroundings, stodgily rendered by 'mammoth marshmallow Mrs Whalen' with her appropriately bulky name, stand in stark contrast to the sophisticated urbane magazine and its 'hopefully thin' letter of acceptance. Yet at the same time as she exploits the opposition between fatness and thinness, Plath complicates the trope by announcing: 'the black thick print [. . .] banged into my head'. Weighty is not the same as stodgy, just as taking up space is not the same as being used for 'filler'. While it clearly strikes her as momentous, the *New Yorker* acceptance accentuates Plath's own lightness and smallness as if the self-sacrifice involved in publication had rendered away her metaphorical 'fat'. Plath is aware, writing this entry, of the ridiculousness of the situation – the absurdity of her jumping 'like a Mexican bean' and 'yipping' like a small dog. This is slapstick comedy, pleasantly chaotic and full of knowing incongruity, and her self-portrayal is tightly controlled. Plath deliberately contrasts her own thin, innocent, youthful haphazardness with the experienced, polished performance that she associates with *New Yorker* gloss, and to the lumpy immobility that characterises suburban domesticity.

There is a striking intellectual and stylistic similarity between this journal entry and an entry she wrote while waiting to hear if some of her short stories would be published in the magazine. The stories came out of a desire to take up more *New Yorker* space, and so to gain notice and recognition, rather than from a feeling that *The New Yorker* published great fiction. Plath approached story-writing for *The New Yorker* as a self-conscious, studied and imitative exercise. 'I guess I better begin on Emmet Hummel,' she wrote in her journal entry of 31 May 1959, 'a New Yorker piece? If only I were one of their people?'[27] Plath never wrote 'Emmet Hummel', but she planned the plot, and it sounds as if she was trying to write the sort of comic piece for which James Thurber had become famous. Emmet Hummel is a 'clerk in a bank, or some such . . . immaculate, spartan, chaste', constantly dragged down by ordinary life and people.[28] *New Yorker* stories that were light-hearted in tone tended to appear near the front of the magazine, and nostalgia pieces at the back. Plath was going for a front piece with 'Emmet Hummel', and, in the absence of a contents page, for the prominence that went with that up-front position.

'Emmet Hummel' never materialised, but Plath did finish a number of other stories. Among them were two pretty uninspiring pieces: 'The Shadow' (in which we can see Plath forming ideas for *The Bell Jar* and rehearsing some of the anxieties that she would capture in 'Daddy') and 'Sweetie Pie and the Gutter-Men'.[29] Plath didn't seem to enjoy writing them. She recorded her struggle in her journals, simultaneously dismissive of the magazine and desirous of its approval: 'this week have kept all mornings free and must work on my Sweetie Pie story and figure what it's about. Sometimes, with the NYorker, I'm not so sure that matters!'[30] On 25 May 1959 she sent the two stories to fiction editor William Maxwell at the suggestion of Alfred Kazin. In the accompanying note she explained: 'Although I have had poems published in *The New Yorker*, I have not previously sent in any fiction. Other stories of mine have appeared in *Seventeen* and *Mademoiselle*.'[31] While waiting for a response from the magazine, she had the following dream:

> I picked up a New Yorker, opened to about the third story (not in the back, this was important, but with a whole front page, on the right, to itself) and read 'This Earth --- That House, That Hospital' in the deeply endearing New Yorker-heading type, rather like painstakingly inked hand-lettering [. . .] Felt radiant, a New Yorker glow lighting my face. Precisely analogous to

that young British Society girl Susan who, after being deflowered in a canoe house, asks her handsome young deflowerer: Don't I look <u>Different</u>? Oh, I looked different. A pale, affluent nimbus emanating from my generally podgy and dough-colored face.'[32]

The exaggerated tone and self-deprecating silliness of this passage, mixing images of transfiguration with virginal deflowering bears comparison with Plath's account of her first *New Yorker* acceptance: 'the realisation of ten years of hopeful wishes and waits (and subsequent rejections)'. In both cases she imagines her arrival along the lines of sexual gratification and material dissolution, becoming weightless and insubstantial, a floating 'nimbus' and a tiny 'bean'. The similarities between these two journal entries highlight the erotic aspect of Plath's attraction to the glossy magazine and the perfect surface in which she might delete and re-make herself. In both instances, she creates a narrative set-piece which depicts the surrender of self-sacrifice. In both cases she juxtaposes *The New Yorker*'s smoothness, sophistication and 'thin[ness]' with a release from the 'podgy' flab of everyday life. As with the 'Sunday lamb', her self-sacrifice leads to renewal and rebirth.

Taking up space

On 24 February 1961, Moss sent Plath a first-reading agreement with *The New Yorker* together with a very welcome hundred dollar signed bonus and a cost of living agreement.[33] Between February 1961 and February 1963, she sent him seventy-three poems (including nearly every poem that would go into *Ariel*) and he rejected sixty-four, publishing only 'Tulips' in the spring of 1962 and 'Blackberrying' in the autumn. When Plath died in February 1963, Moss still had seven of her poems in reserve. After her death, he sought permission to publish them in a single issue, which contained no other verse. They appeared on an otherwise bare double-page spread under a heading that read simply 'Seven Poems'. At the bottom right corner of the right-hand page was Sylvia Plath's name and the bracketed dates of her short life: (1932–1963).[34] It was unprecedented for a double-page spread to be devoted entirely to showcasing a single poet's work. The startling visual effect together with the dates at the bottom sent a clear message. Readers had no choice but to construe the poems within the narrative of Sylvia Plath's life and premature death.

The poems were 'Two Campers in Cloud Country', 'The Elm Speaks', 'Mystic', 'Amnesiac', 'Mirror', 'Among the Narcissi' and 'The Moon and the Yew Tree'. For Plath, who had in 1958 fixated on the 'shiny white New Yorker space around [her] two column poem', the appearance of seven works surrounded by the luxury of empty space would no doubt have seemed a triumph. The double-page spread of 'Seven Poems' was not only free of cartoons, advertisements and other *New Yorker* distractions, but was also positioned between two short stories, so acting itself as a kind of story, and not a 'place for the eye' to rest while perusing a longer work. The bracketed dates of Plath's birth and death did not give any sense of when the individual poems were written, nor of their order of composition. Readers would not have known that only 'Mystic' was written in 1963, close to the time of Plath's suicide. In this context, even a comparatively early poem such as 'The Elm Speaks' (April 1962) might be taken as a suicide note.[35] Its last few stanzas bear testimony to a mind under pressure and fear:

> I am terrified by this dark thing
> That sleeps in me;
> All day I feel its soft, feathery turnings, its malignity.
>
> Clouds pass and disperse,
> Are those the faces of love, those pale irretrievables?
> Is it for such I agitate my heart?
> [...]
> Its snaky acids kiss.
> It petrifies the will. These are the isolate, slow faults
> That kill, that kill, that kill.

The transition in this poem from movement to stillness is particularly affecting, given the context of recent suicide that would govern a reading of the poem in the 1963 magazine. The unnameable internal force of destruction is aligned with a loss of control. The 'feathery' creature is difficult to grasp and 'snaky', so epitomising deception and evil. This is compounded by the intangible 'pale irretrievables' who float like ghosts out of the speaker's reach. Not knowing, of course, that Plath lived a full year after writing this poem, readers might well have taken it to be indicative of the breakdown and suicide that shadowed her final days.

'Seven Poems' was a beginning, rather than an end, to Plath's significant presence as a *New Yorker* writer. Olwyn Hughes, who was in charge of the Plath estate, continued Plath's relationship with the magazine. On 11 December 1969 Olwyn sent Moss six newly discovered Plath poems. Moss accepted all six for publication, and in the 6 March 1971 issue repeated the format used in 1963. Once again, Plath occupied her own double-page spread, with the heading 'Six Poems' in the top centre of the left-hand page and her name in the bottom right corner of the right. This time, though, no dates followed her name; instead, each poem carried a date of composition. The poems printed were 'The Babysitters' (1961), 'Pheasant' (1962), 'The Courage of Shutting Up' (1962), 'Apprehensions' (1962), 'For a Fatherless Son' (1962) and 'By Candlelight' (1962).[36] Unlike the 1963 issue, where readers might assume all the poems had been written near the time of Sylvia Plath's death, readers of 1969 would recognise these as late, but not last works. The uninterrupted format would again have been startling, with the poems once more displayed between two short stories, without any distractions and as if they formed their own narrative. The layout encouraged people to take notice, to pause, and actually read the poems.

Moss had never accepted an entire batch of poems while Plath was alive. His immediate acceptance of these six must have been at least partly because their discovery was newsworthy. 'The Babysitters' is particularly poignant in this setting: the retrospective gap which is the focus of the opening would have seemed especially pertinent to the 1971 reader of a 1961 poem: 'It is ten years now since we rowed to Children's Island.' The ending, too, has an uncanny resonance:

> What keyhole have we slipped through, what door has shut?
> The shadows of the grasses inched round like hands on a clock,
> And from our opposite continents we wave and call.
> Everything has happened.

It would be hard for a reader of the 1971 *New Yorker* not to be affected by this voice, which speaks as if from outside time and yet takes the feeling of lost time as the subject of its lament. Readers looking for a story that would end in suicide might well have found one here.

The 1971 spread was indicative of the way in which Plath had become 'one of their people', a *New Yorker* writer whose career the magazine had helped shape. Moss was still selective, as was the fiction department, which rejected Plath's late short story, 'Mothers', when Olwyn Hughes sent it in 1970.[37] In the same year, shortly after sending Moss the six poems, Olwyn sent *The New Yorker* three other recently discovered Plath poems, 'Last Words', which she made a point of telling Moss was 'composed late 61', 'Lyonnesse', 'composed in 1962', and 'Gigolo', 'composed only a few days before Sylvia's death, late January 63'.[38] Moss accepted 'Gigolo', which, perhaps unknown to Olwyn, he had already read. Plath had sent him the poem along with 'Child', 'Totem', 'The Bald Madonna' and 'Paralytic'. They were the last poems she sent him, and he had rejected them all on the 7 February 1963.[39] Perhaps guilt made him accept the poem posthumously, perhaps he then saw the merits that he had earlier overlooked, or perhaps 'Gigolo' read differently as a posthumous poem.

Apart from the posthumous publication of Plath's poems, *The New Yorker* published extracts from Plath's journals on 27 March 2000. Titled, 'What in the author's diaries did her mother not want us to read?' the spread included prominent pictures of Hughes and Plath, and college photos of Plath among friends at Smith. An abstract for the article announced a transatlantic coup. It claimed that the diary extracts were only to be published in England so *The New Yorker* would be the only American publication to print them.[40] This turned out to be wrong but it shows that *The New Yorker* was keen to claim ownership of Plath. The spread not only presents her as 'one of their people', it also shows that she was most interesting to them when she gave them something that they could display as 'news'.

The title immediately suggests something salacious, an insight into the 'not-nice' girl that Aurelia tried to prove false. It suggests that *The New Yorker* was both aware of, and a participant in, the divisions, antagonisms and personal antipathies that have dominated Plath's biography and inflected so much of the criticism of her work, trying, like the rest of the world, to reveal the 'true' Sylvia Plath. It also suggests a sense of ownership and privileged insight into a writer the magazine had long considered its own. As Anita Helle has argued, *The New Yorker*'s selections reveal a carefully constructed romantic story.[41] Beginning with courtship, it moves to marriage with all its first hopes and later disillusionments, and ends with motherhood: the birth of Plath's second child, Nicholas. The selections from Plath's journals are long, the kind of length she had wished for, taking up fourteen pages of *The New Yorker*'s 'exquisite several-paged surface' – more than a short story might have been likely to warrant. *The New Yorker* had once provided a focus for Plath's ambitious self-fashioning and fetishised self-effacement. As she dreamed of a *New Yorker* identity and a strong material presence in the 'glossy' pages and 'white space' of the magazine, she imagined herself into an ideal of authorship removed from solid domesticity, becoming physically immaterial, thinner, lighter, and translucent. In death she finally achieved the *New Yorker* presence that had animated her earliest efforts. *The New Yorker* did finally make Sylvia Plath 'one of their people', and it did so when she could no longer control the process of her own effacement. Suicide is the final paradox of narrative assertion and loss of narrative control. The closing irony of Plath's taking her own life was that she could then only be what others made her.

Notes

1. Sylvia Plath, 'Tulips', *The New Yorker*, 7 April 1962, p. 40; *Collected Poems* (London: Faber, 1981), p. 160.
2. Sylvia Plath, letter to Aurelia Plath, 9 January 1957, *Letters Home: Correspondence 1950–1963*, selected and edited with commentary by Aurelia Schober Plath (New York: Harper Perennial, 1992), p. 290.
3. Ted Hughes, letter to Sylvia Plath, 9 or 10 October 1956, *Letters of Ted Hughes*, ed. Christopher Reid (London: Faber, 2007), pp. 65–70 (p. 68). This view of *New Yorker* poetry as lightweight was long and widely held. In Wallace Stevens's view, for example, publication in the magazine would be disastrous for the reputation of a serious poet. Ben Yagoda, *About Town: 'The New Yorker' and the World it Made* (New York: Scribner, 2000), pp. 172–3.
4. Sylvia Plath, letter to Aurelia Plath, 25 April 1953, *Letters Home*, p. 109. 'I am unrecognized', she proclaimed after an early rejection from the magazine. See *The Journals of Sylvia Plath 1950–1962: Transcribed from the Original Manuscripts at Smith College*, ed. Karen V. Kukil (London: Faber, 2000), 17 April 1958, p. 371.
5. Jacqueline Rose, *The Haunting of Sylvia Plath* (London: Virago, 1991), pp. 172–3. The *Ladies' Home Journal* has received the most attention from Plath scholars. See, in particular, Marsha Bryant, 'Ariel's Kitchen: Plath, *Ladies' Home Journal*, and the Domestic Surreal', in *The Unravelling Archive: Essays on Sylvia Plath*, ed. Anita Helle (Ann Arbor: University of Michigan Press, 2007), pp. 211–35.
6. Plath, *Letters Home*, p. 107. The italics are Plath's.
7. Ibid. Langdon Hammer focuses on Plath's position, in 1953, as student guest editor at *Mademoiselle*, and refers also to her *New Yorker* aspirations. See 'Plath's Lives: Poetry, Professionalism, and the Culture of School', *Representations*, 75 (Summer 2001), 61–88 (pp. 78–9).
8. Plath, *Letters Home*, pp. 290, 207.
9. Ralph Waldo Emerson, 'Nature', in *The Collected Works of Ralph Waldo Emerson*, ed. Joseph Slater, Robert E. Spiller, Alfred Ferguson et al., 6 vols (Cambridge, MA: Harvard University Press, 1971–2003), vol. 1 (1971), pp. 7–45 (p. 10).
10. Frances Kiernan, 'Fiction at the New Yorker', *The American Scholar*, 67.4 (Autumn 1998), 81–92 (p. 83).
11. Ibid., p. 34.
12. Howard Moss, letter to Sylvia Plath, 18 April 1962, New Yorker Records, box 795, folder 4.
13. *The New Yorker*, 23 and 30 April 1993, pp. 84–159 (p. 84).
14. Ibid., p. 136.
15. Plath, *Collected Poems*, p. 262.
16. Ibid., p. 272.
17. Ibid., p. 257.
18. Susan Bassnett, *Sylvia Plath* (London: Macmillan, 1987), pp. 142–3.
19. Plath, *Journals*, 8 August 1958, p. 413.
20. Peter Davidson, letter to Howard Moss, 20 February 1963, New Yorker Records, box 802, folder 13.

21. Aurelia Plath, letter to 'Editor of the *New Yorker*', 23 March 1963, New Yorker Records, box 802, folder 13.
22. Plath, *Journals*, p. 177.
23. Ibid., p. 199.
24. Ibid., p. 215.
25. Ibid., p. 327.
26. Ibid., 25 June 1958, p. 397.
27. Ibid., p. 489.
28. Ibid.
29. Sylvia Plath, *Johnny Panic and the Bible of Dreams and Other Prose Writings* (London: Faber, 1977), pp. 330–52.
30. Plath, *Journals*, 3 May 1959, p. 481.
31. Sylvia Plath, letter to William Maxwell, New Yorker Records, box 771, folder 17.
32. Plath, *Journals*, 6 June 1959, p. 492.
33. New Yorker Records, box 788, folder 15.
34. *The New Yorker*, 3 August 1963, pp. 28–9.
35. The amended, more explanatory title was the magazine's choice, though Plath had agreed to it before she died. The poem was later published as 'Elm' (Plath, *Collected Poems*, p. 192).
36. *The New Yorker*, 6 March 1971, pp. 36–7.
37. New Yorker Records, box 851, folder 6.
38. Olwyn Hughes, letter to Howard Moss, 8 April 1970, New Yorker Records, box 851, folder 6.
39. New Yorker Records, box 802, folder 13.
40. Anita Helle, 'Reading the Paratexts of Plath's Unabridged Journals', available at <http://www.iun.edu/~nwadmin/plath/vol3_Supp/Helle.pdf> (accessed 13 September 2013), pp. 1–13 (p. 5).
41. Ibid., p. 6.

Chapter 7

The Distractions of John Cheever

Tamara Follini

In a Rolex advertisement that appeared in four issues of the 1980 *New Yorker*, a pencil sketch of John Cheever – dapperly attired in waistcoat and bow tie, the intense gaze of his three-quarter profile diverted to his right, as if scrutinising his next subject – is balanced by a slogan and short text, at the foot of which nestles an image of the expensive timepiece (Fig. 7.1). The text declares with unimpeachable assurance a natural alignment between this 'best-selling novelist and master of the short story' and the master craftsmen who create Rolex watches, while also implying that it is the writer, not the watch, who may be more flattered by this association. 'Rolex. For those who set the measure of the times' – the lead slogan confers an award, legitimising and celebrating the efforts of the writer who 'savors the bittersweet taste of American life in timeless narration'.[1] Such promotional copy, accomplishing a commodification of the writer's work and evoking a system of exchange in which writer, horological craftsman, watch and book exist on a plane of interchangeable value, easily generates critical ironies. Yet this image and text in regard to Cheever and his work nonetheless invites numerous speculations. Why, for example, does this particular ad, one of a series, depart from the more common practice of using photographic images of its celebrated figures? Might the pencil sketch have been a condition for his appearance imposed by Cheever himself, one functioning so as to blur the line between creative author and public figure, and thus reflect, in a highly self-conscious modernist mode, the author's wily comment on his partial transformation into a commercial 'character'? If such is the case, could Cheever's appearance be taken in turn as a parodic remark on his publication history, in which the majority of his short stories as well as chapters from his novels also appeared amidst the lures and distractions of glossy consumer spaces, were jostled by the sensuous satisfactions and aura of confident allure emanating from advertisements that crowded magazines such as *The New Yorker* or *Esquire* or

Rolex. For those
who set the measure
of the times.

John Cheever

Best-selling novelist and master of the short
story. An award-winning author who savors the
bittersweet taste of American life in timeless
narration. Detail illuminates John Cheever's
writing. Just as detail inspires every Rolex
craftsman. Created like no other timepiece in
the world. With an unrelenting, meticulous
attention to excellence in a world fraught
with compromise. The Rolex Oyster Perpetual
Day-Date Superlative Chronometer. A great work
designed to stand the test of time.
Write for brochure. Rolex Watch, U.S.A., Inc., Dept. 111C, Rolex Building, 665 Fifth Avenue, New York, NY 10022. World headquarters in
Geneva. Other offices in Toronto and major cities around the world.

ROLEX

Figure 7.1. Advertisement, Rolex Watches, *The New Yorker*, 7 April
1980, p. 69.

Harper's Bazaar, in all of whose pages his work made its own bid for attention?

If the Rolex advertisement can be read as the writer's comment, poised between self-mockery and self-congratulation, on his lifelong tussle with the marketplace and the conditions of magazine publication, then it may have a special bearing on Cheever's engagement with *The New Yorker*. From 1935, at the start of his career, until 1981, the year before his death, 120 of Cheever's stories made their initial appearance in the magazine, an archive whose bulk and time-span was instrumental in establishing him as a major *New Yorker* writer and one who contributed powerfully to the perception of its literary style.[2] Yet while this was an affiliation from which Cheever frequently benefited, it was also one increasingly marked by financial frustration, creative limitation and personal discord with the editors with whom he was most closely associated. More damagingly, his reputation, both during his lifetime and in subsequent decades, was perceived as so deeply entangled with that of the magazine that, as critical comment on Cheever often notices, the association undoubtedly hindered, and may continue to unsettle, a just evaluation of his work.[3]

Can we read Cheever without reading him through or in *The New Yorker*? Are his stories best encountered on independent ground, extracted from original contexts and gathered in more dignified settings, such as the 1978 compilation, *The Stories of John Cheever*, the volume which secured him the Pulitzer Prize, and, consequently, that laudatory aura of 'timeless narration'? When an interviewer remarked that his stories 'could take place anytime and almost any place', Cheever agreed that that had been his 'intention'.[4] Certainly to experience these works undisturbed by the cluttered spaces and various ephemeral appeals of a weekly would not only help to secure the atemporal, ahistorical quality he wished to impart to them, but would allow greater measures of contemplative readerly attention and critical objectivity. Yet to read Cheever in this form may also be a kind of deprivation. It muffles a particular aspect of our being to which his imaginary enterprise repeatedly attends and which can be defined as the workings, the pleasures, dangers, and complications of readerly and experiential distraction. Distraction, of different kinds and degrees – as an experience that, in its most extreme forms, is potentially wasteful, ruinous, or tragically affiliated to self-destruction and yet also conducive to transcendent understanding or exhilaration – is a pervasive current shaping Cheever's narrative preoccupations, a force he recognises as an essential element of daily life and the peregrinations of mental thought and imagination.

Cheever looking away as we look at him, in the Rolex ad, may thus signal an artful *jeu d'esprit* on the writer's part: the pose implicitly acknowledges how rarely we focus, steadily, on even the most compelling objects or actions directly within our line of vision, of how we are moved endlessly, or removed from one actual or imaginary scene to another, by mental vicissitudes. The argument could be made that any useful re-evaluation of Cheever's work would do best to separate it decisively from the magazine's enclosure and the critical prejudices that so-called 'New Yorker fiction' easily arouses. Yet restored to that environment, an exploration of distraction as a quality of both everyday and reading experience, particularly that which belongs to the short story within the conditions of magazine publication, may be seen to emerge in several of Cheever's most provocative experiments in the form. The nature of our imaginative movements, as we follow a story intensely while yet letting eyes drift and mind dwell on enticements at the corner of our vision or side of the page, these fluctuations parallel vital features in the dramatic situations of Cheever's characters, many of whom also wander, bewildered, amidst his relentlessly thwarted narratives, in which expected sequences are subject to disruption, action seemingly ebbs and flows without direction, and characters are stranded outside the lives they had anticipated or desired.

An association between issues of distraction and matters of context looms large in movements in literary modernism, particularly those that developed in the 1920s. In an exposition of modernism's distinct periods, Michael Levenson has shown how early concerns, particularly the exaltation of an aesthetic experience of such vivid immediacy as to deliver the participant to a transcendent sphere, free of the constraints of social being, gave way to a more flexible, earth-bound but inspirationally riotous aesthetic of 'the exalted Relation'. In this bias, context was not seen as a constraint but accepted, albeit with the vital distinction that contexts themselves were applauded as changeable, creatively unsteady, never settling into a given form or frame but 'only as fabricated [. . .] in the combinatorium of part and part' and endlessly exemplifying 'the conundra of source and surrounding, parallel and precedent'.[5] Cheever's work is part of this developing twentieth-century aesthetic, especially regarding qualities of narrative montage or collage that have often been identified as inherent in his narrative experimentation.[6] But contexts, for a writer bound to the commercial conditions of *The New Yorker*, whose participation in this phase of modernism is apparent in its play with generic juxtaposition, combinations of the visual and written, the trivial and serious, offer unique provocations. While writers who exemplify experimentation with contextual expansion, Woolf or Joyce for example, exert a measure of control over their readers' cognitive travels, such influence is obviously severely limited for the writer surrendering his work to a magazine of this kind. Cheever was certainly aware that the beguiling vistas magazines offered for the wandering mind made skills of self-defence necessary, especially if art was to keep pace with the changes wrought by modernity's commercialism. In his 1976 *Paris Review* interview, responding to a query about his striking way with narrative beginnings, he wryly acknowledged the necessity of such a technique: 'Well, if you're trying as a story-teller to establish some rapport with your reader you don't open by telling him that you have a headache and indigestion and that you picked up a gravelly rash at Jones Beach.' He went on to explain: 'advertising in magazines is much more common today than it was twenty to thirty years ago. In publishing in a magazine you are competing against girdle advertisements, travel advertisements, nakedness, cartoons, even poetry. The competition almost makes it hopeless.' Yet he also ruled out a more sensationalist approach, one that was perhaps uncomfortably close to that of the rivals he wished to oppose:

> One is tempted because there has been a genuine loss of serenity, not only in the reading public, but in all our lives. Patience, perhaps, or even the ability to concentrate. At one point when television first came in no one was publishing an article that couldn't be read during a commercial. But fiction is durable enough to survive all of this.[7]

Fiction may have such resilience, but Cheever also knew that his readers might not be so robust, and that 'in a world that changes more swiftly than we can perceive' – as the narrator of a late satiric story, 'The Death of Justina', describes the nonsensical conditions of his existence – control of attention, the ability to identify significance amidst the assault of daily encounters, social exchanges, visual and aural stimuli, is inhibited by both our own responsive sensibilities and our vulnerability to modernism's forms of the artificial and absurd.[8] In one of Cheever's most well-known and chilling stories, 'The Five-Forty-Eight', which appeared in the 10 April 1954 issue of *The New Yorker*, the callous protagonist, en route to his commuting train, pauses in the vicinity of Madison Avenue before a window display that reproduces a contemporary living room; he believes he has evaded a woman whom he fears to be following him, a former secretary he has sexually used and cruelly fired. The mirroring of the man's figure superimposed by the reflecting glass on the lifeless, counterfeit scene offers a momentary tableau of his own emotional barrenness and that of the wronged woman's empty life, and as his image merges with the illusory environment, his boundaries of self-protection and self-determination also seem subject to encroachment:

> The window was arranged like a room in which people live and entertain their friends. There were cups on the coffee table, magazines to read, and flowers in the vases, but the flowers were dead and the cups were empty and the guests had not come. In the plate glass, Blake saw a clear reflection of himself and the crowds that were passing, like shadows, at his back. Then he saw her image.[9]

The narrative denies a causal relation between the forces of commercialism and ethical being; the pathos of the two characters involved has as much to do with the poverty of their inner lives as any specifically modernistic predicament. Yet the scene enacts how easily, almost surreptitiously, that which divides us from potentially harmful fantasies, delusions, distractions, can dissolve, or how susceptible the mind is, even in moments of great intensity, to the trivial, the inconsequential and incongruous. As the story proceeds, and a prolonged confrontation occurs between the man and his unbalanced former lover, all of which takes place on 'the five-forty-eight' commuting train, Cheever repeatedly depicts the mind's ceaseless receptivity even amidst moments of concentrated experiential intensity. When the woman threatens Blake with a gun, he tries to persuade himself of an eventual rescue by his fellow passengers even as his gaze follows changing atmospheric illuminations: 'out of the window he saw the river and the sky [. . .] a streak of orange light on the horizon became brilliant'. Later, as Blake realises a general obliviousness to his predicament, panic is intermingled with impressions of the mundane:

> Blake could see the southbound platform [. . .] There was a workman with a lunch pail, a dressed-up woman, and a man with a suitcase. They stood apart from one another. Some advertisements were posted on the wall behind them. There was a picture of a couple drinking a toast in wine, a picture of a Cat's Paw rubber heel, and a picture of a Hawaiian dancer. Their cheerful intent seemed to go no farther than the puddles of water on the platform and to expire there.[10]

These images of conviviality, intimacy, pleasure combined with a glimpse of human isolation could easily be aligned alongside the relation of Blake and his pursuer. Even the advertisement for rubber *heels*, as a play on slang nomenclature, may associate itself with the insensitive shallowness of the protagonist. Yet to do so may miss the point of Cheever's provocative narrative arrangements, his teasing presentation of detail that at once constitutes a realistic depiction of the physical environment while seemingly offering symbolic richness. Considering how the mind of a distracted person is not simply daydreaming, drifting idly away from a dominant claim, but rather attracted to 'a rival interest', Michael Wood makes an important distinction: 'the point in this context is not to redefine relevance – that is what recuperative readings are always doing – but to understand irrelevance, to find in it the hints and lessons it holds *as* irrelevance'.[11] Through this description of Blake's momentary fixations, Cheever may be accentuating not so much the symbolic import of that upon which Blake's nervous eye alights, these standard fixtures of railway platforms, but their very innocuousness, their short-lived but ultimately inconsequential value. That he includes such detail tethers his story to verisimilitude, while also glancing at other possible narratives, a different journey for his character lurking at the sidelines of this evening's events, and thus something of his chosen drama's own fragility. Yet the narrative also divines the arbitrary or unstable nature of these people and objects, their unreliability as pathways to intenser experience or as spiritual signs of immanent meaning in the surrounding order. Mere glimmers of import that assume momentary vividness and then fade, they are untrustworthy omens for a flight into transcendent understanding or even a more durable daily existence. As the reflections of the toasting couple, the rubber heels, the dancer 'expire' in the dirty puddles of the station platform, they confess the falsity of their seductive attractiveness, the insubstantiality and ephemerality that make any symbolic import a reader might desire to attach to them, or any escape they may offer the besieged protagonist, equally tenuous, transient, subject to dissolution.

The major portion of 'The Five-Forty-Eight' takes place on a commuting train, a conveyance expressive of rituals of professional and domestic regularity, and an often tedious journey relieved at its end by deliverance to a 'time to go home, time for a drink, time for love, time for supper'.[12] The biblical cadence offers the solace of custom, while the list tempts supplementation: is it also time to put aside the diversions of newspaper or magazine? An intimation of this tale is that it could be read on a commuting train identical to that which it depicts and that the passing images that capture Blake's attention are not unlike those that might become entangled in a reader's absorption of its drama. How aware we may be of such phenomena, how conscious of the effect of the images we receive, the physical sensations we undergo, the environments we inhabit as we read 'The Five-Forty-Eight', is one of the tale's recurrent preoccupations. As a story whose central concern is the opposing perspectives of its two warring characters regarding the import of their relation, of the relational, it teases us with the significance we might attribute to narrative details once we become aware of how interpretation may be conditioned by highly random associations or subjective forces. Any effort to pin down or to elevate its brief, flickering images thus risks a degree of unreliability or fabrication, may ignore the kinds of disordered, undisciplined indeterminacy that permeate our reading experiences. As the tale ends, and Blake warily raises himself from the ground after his tormentor, Miss Dent, has extracted her revenge, he perceives her waiting on the station platform: 'her figure in the dim light looked small, common, and harmless [. . .] she had forgotten him'.[13] Even the magnitude Miss Dent has claimed is subject to diminishment, and even her attention, once she has completed her task, cannot be sustained but disappears like wavering images in shrinking puddles. What will happen to our own hold on her story once we complete our journey and close the pages of the magazine?

Cheever had ample reason to lament the tumultuous spaces of *The New Yorker* and the multiple diversions it offered through a motley assortment of what he once called its 'bland poetry' and 'bad cartoons'.[14] He was also sharply aware of the strategies for capturing a reader's attention that formed the foundation for ever more sophisticated advertising methods in 1950s and '60s America. In a study of cognitive learning processes and ways in which attention functions, Cathy N. Davidson analyses how highly skilled advertising professionals direct the viewer to the most positive aspects of their products and condense a 'panoply of [a] culture's values [. . .] into a powerful and compelling narrative', one so expressive of instinctual desires and cultural beliefs as to allow its manipulations to remain unnoticed.[15] Mocking the exclusion of troubling content that such affirmative narratives perform, Cheever's late parody, 'The Death of Justina', follows the actions of an exasperated copywriter charged with devising the monologue for a tonic, Elixircol, that claims to reverse processes of physical deterioration and emotional malaise. The protagonist, Moses, finds himself in the ludicrous situation of being unable to dispose of the body of his visiting aunt, Justina, who has died suddenly on the family sofa, but who cannot be removed due to preventive zoning laws. As he confronts this forensic absurdity – the law decrees that '"you can't bury anything [in his neighbourhood] and you can't die there"' – Moses' advertising copy becomes ever more wildly irreverent.[16] He reverses techniques of deploying soothing reassurances to potential buyers and instead accentuates precisely the anxieties regarding physical infirmities and ageing that the tonic is meant to cure. Perhaps unsurprisingly, given the generic oddity of the story and its fantastical but unsparing critique of the advertising culture on which the magazine depended, the story was rejected by *The New Yorker*. In

Cheever's words, his editor, William Maxwell, had decided '"the satire lacks support and I suppose he means that it is over-intense"'.[17]

Yet the miraculous Elixircol reappears in Cheever's work in a way to imply that commercials, and by extension the kinds of fantasies they evoke, did not always function for him merely as parodic targets. His comments about his 1982 television play, 'The Shady Hill Kidnapping', are suggestive:

> It might seem pretentious and absurd to compare TV as a performing art to the changes that were inaugurated in Grand Opera in the 19th century but in TV we do find a new use for the music we sing, a new spectrum of love and anxiety and a completely new rapport between the audience, the performers and the playwright. In my screen-play I attempted to exploit the level of sentiment one finds in TV, and to exploit the mysterious role that is played by commercials.[18]

Although print and television media cannot be compared unqualifiedly, the statement encourages speculation as to the ways a Cheever short story might also exploit and intertwine itself with the very competing attractions and distractions – the advertisements, the cartoons, the poetry – that a reader of *The New Yorker* would inevitably encounter in pursuing the lines and columns of his narratives. It opens the possibility that being waylaid could be an appealingly indirect path to certain kinds of readerly appropriation or that similar phenomena in one's daily life, diversions interrupting habitual or expected destinations, to the extent that they break familiar frames of comprehension or habit, may offer liberating, inspiriting ways by which to appropriate experience. It cannot be said with certainty that Cheever regarded the publication conditions of *The New Yorker* as inspirational in this manner. Yet in their repeated recognition of our vulnerability to the unscripted, his stories reflect the pleasures as well as the dangers of distraction amidst conditions of contextual disorder, and play with how often we are set adrift from customary anchorage, subject to diversion and detour, caught in circulations of lives adjacent to our own, and unsettled, in ways ranging from traumatic to joyful, by unexpected encounters or what might be called improvised experience.[19]

Critical discussions of distraction frequently acknowledge the significance of Walter Benjamin's remarks on this concept in relation to modern art forms, yet often without incorporating the historical resonance of the term or the different attitudes involved in Benjamin's key phrase, '*Die Rezeption in der Zerstreuung*', or 'Reception in Distraction', which he defines as '*the sort of reception which is increasingly noticeable in all areas of art and is a symptom of profound changes in apperception*'.[20]

In an essay that takes his title from this phrase, Howard Eiland does much to clarify these complexities and, crucially, the noteworthy inconsistencies in Benjamin's attitude towards this concept.[21] Drawing on Benjamin's writings on Bertolt Brecht, Eiland distinguishes one aspect of distraction that aligns it with kinds of entertainment for the '"sated class"' and works by allowing the audience empathic identification with characters and their illusory dramatic situations.[22] This kind of distraction may be associated with a form of stupefying, self-satisfied participation in an artwork without critical distance, an activity of self-reflecting diversion into which emotional or intellectual discomfort does not intrude. Yet Benjamin also uses the term, Eiland demonstrates, to refer to kinds of '"intoxicated experience"', of being carried away, an experience which 'does not necessarily exclude a certain profane illumination'.[23] Thus, he persuasively proposes, to appropriate Benjamin's essay in a modern context, it must be understood 'beyond the simple opposition of distraction and concentration' and conceived instead in terms of '*mere* distraction and [. . .] productive distraction – between distraction as a skewing of attention, or as abandonment to diversion, and distraction as a spur to new ways of perceiving', one which revivifies our ways of being in the world.[24]

Cheever's work often makes explicit challenges to the 'sated' class, especially as they might be defined in postwar America as those unwilling to expose themselves to threatening, accidental, or unexpected occurrences and intently desirous of perpetuating social norms. Although his treatment of such characters is often accompanied by compassion, it is propelled by an ironic, unsparing clarity. In 'The Season of Divorce', for example, the unnamed narrator who maintains a barrier around his sensibility, as if to guard himself against a certain kind of distraction in a world he describes as 'full of accidental revelations, half-heard cries for help, and strangers who will tell you everything at the first suspicion of sympathy', meets his comeuppance in the form of an acquaintance whom he fallaciously believes has 'no more bearing on the businesses of [his family's] lives' than the interruptions suffered from a 'blind man' or the 'elevator man', but whose passionate desire for his wife unsettles the fragile construction of their marriage.[25] The story ends with the importunate lover expelled, domestic harmony reestablished, and a luminous tableau of near-perfect familial contentment. The narrator, going to his children's room with his wife, is greeted by a fantastical edifice his children have made, 'something out of an orange crate, something preposterous and ascendant'. A resolution of dramatic turbulence is offered alongside a whispered challenge to credulity: 'preposterous' exhales an insinuation of continued unrest while the evening light illuminating this scene recalls a moment, earlier in the narrative, when 'the markings of light' on a bitter winter afternoon 'convinced [the narrator] that it was the season of divorce'.[26]

This story adopts a traditional narrative form adhering to temporal sequence, perhaps reflecting the narrator's unwillingness to depart from familiar emotional trajectories. Cheever's more experimental stories, however, repeatedly abandon such comforting forms and are imbued with qualities of waywardness, shaped by disorientating fluctuations of events and loosely bound, scattered pieces of distinct human experiences. Elizabeth Hardwick's alert, albeit intentionally disparaging, comment on Cheever's novels could also be applied to these most casual seeming of stories: they 'fly apart, shred, and shed as if some wind of inattention had overtaken them'.[27] Such a creative practice has made a number of wind-blown critics, perhaps too inclined to stability, perceive these stories as reliant on inner structures of symbolism, imagery and lyrical repetition to bind flightiness into coherent wholes.[28] Yet while such structures are unarguably present, rescue work need not be overdone. '[S]traighforward narrative is inadequate', Cheever declared to himself, and to one interviewer: 'linear plot is unreal, debased, useless, false'.[29] Narrative looseness is equally suggestive in terms of the stories' permeability, their willingness to entertain openness, their desire to startle us by their disjunctions, or what might be called, returning to Benjamin's terms, their embodiment of, and attempt to inspire, 'productive distraction'. If, as Hardwick observed, these stories come to the reader as if dismembered, the result of 'inattention', that is because they represent experience, at its inward, emotional, psychological level, as fragmentary, disjointed, and subject to varieties of randomness, eccentricity, and sometimes unsettling synchrony. As Samuel Chase Coale has argued, for Cheever 'the essence of contemporary life was its jagged metamorphoses, its sudden leaps and diversions', while his plots, such as they are, 'reveal modern psychological existence as essentially chaotic and disconnected'.[30] Yet although they reflect such disorder, these seemingly ungainly plots do not understand its essence as solely negative, as debilitating or destructive, and suggest that Cheever may deploy such a narrative technique purposefully to startle his reader. In this way his stories operate in a manner not dissimilar to that which Benjamin described as allowing for 'the discovery of situations [. . .] accomplished by means of the interruptions of sequences', gaps that provide imaginative space for unforeseen reflections and sensations, and which characterise art forms which inspire the kind of 'intoxicated experience' that is consequent on an art of 'productive distraction'.[31] For repeatedly, in Cheever's stories, narrative disarray, and the circumstantial and experiential disorder it reflects, are intimate with psychological release and emotional elation. While characters and readers who abandon conventional social and emotional pathways risk harmful, even violent fates, they may perchance also discover forms of momentary elation or transcendence by which needs for spiritual sustenance or psychological release from the mundane are assuaged.

Distraction in contemporary usage is most often used in accordance with its second definition, 'the drawing away (of the mind or thoughts) from one point or course to another' and a 'diversion of the mind or attention' (*OED*). This usage could be said to reflect something of the flirtatious invitations to waywardness that many of Cheever's stories make to the reader in their encouragement to liberate the self from fixed historical and temporal co-ordinates. Yet the more ominous primary definition of the term also has a bearing on his creative preoccupations: '[a] drawing or being drawn asunder; pulling asunder; forcible disruption, diversion, or severance' (*OED*). Two of the most impressive stories Cheever published in *The New Yorker* bring these meanings into disturbing conjunction, flitting restlessly between notions of a potentially amusing, satisfying or enlightening diversion and a deleterious or sinister departure from a prearranged course; these tales may be said to exemplify qualities of Cheever's narrative methods at their most disconcerting while also hinting at his often agonised relation to the magazine and its readers.

'The Events of That Easter' was published in the 16 May 1959 issue of *The New Yorker*. The story's title and its appearance approximately six weeks after the Easter holiday of that year (29 March) suppose a documentary dimension to the actions recounted, and accordingly an explanatory background to these 'events' is given by retrospective description: Mr Freeley, the manager of a splendid, newly opened grocery store, whose business is suffering because the town's capricious ladies are 'incapable of fidelity' to the store's attractions, is ordered to organise an Easter egg hunt. The eggs contain a variety of vouchers, but the most desirable, five golden eggs, promise prizes of luxurious vacations abroad. Elaborate arrangements are made, meant to preserve the utmost secrecy under cover of darkness, but Mr Freeley never gets to hide his treasures on Easter eve. A humiliating event, in which he is mugged by three violent youths while taking a walk, interferes and the job falls to his youthful assistant, Charlie, who remains in ignorance of what has happened to his boss. Does this violent attack have anything to do with the scene with which the story begins, in which Freeley, while attending his daughter's school concert, reprimands several obstreperous students whose antics 'made it difficult for him to give all his attention' to the performance? The story refuses to confirm a certain linkage and alights instead, abruptly, on Charlie's conscientious efforts to carry out his task – although he in turn is interrupted when he is discovered engaged in his work. As word of Charlie's activities rapidly spreads abroad, on the telephone wires of the night, he is pursued by an ever-growing posse of white robed, slipper shod matrons, all mad to discover one of the golden eggs, in a scene of absurdist melodrama that releases the story from the boundaries of realism and projects the reader into an almost hallucinatory, dream-like realm. These frenzied matrons recall the fourth meaning of distraction, '[v]iolent perturbation or disturbance of mind or feelings, approaching to temporary madness' (*OED*). And yet to Charlie the mildly crazed, middle-aged women appear 'so like angels in their night clothes' as to induce a kind of revelation: the story ends with the youth, exhausted but serene as the sun rises and having managed to hide the eggs despite his pursuers, listening joyfully to 'all the birds singing in the trees like a band of angels whistling to their dogs'.[32]

'The Events of That Easter' in generic, tonal and affective terms is a highly unstable compound. Its title claims consanguinity with realistic documentary while evoking quasi-mythic chronicle, it swings between comedic scenes, depictions of repellent violence, moments of surrealism, and rhapsodic naturalism; it disturbs any possible readerly equanimity when it lingers on Freeley, humiliated by his tormentors, experiencing 'an eruption that twisted all his purpose and left his loves and his works senseless and his memory a spot of filth on the floor', and yet invites participation in the ecstatic happiness of the innocent Charlie. Moreover, it splices these stories together, subjecting the reader to Freeley's trauma just as Charlie, his task completed, apprehends the women's frantic search as a scene of 'pure revelation and glory'.[33] Cheever seems intent on emphatically reminding his reader of the most devastating forms of distraction, especially how certain detours may result in varieties of disruption or severance so savage or ungovernable as to sully memory, destroy continuity, expel hope. No explanation is provided for Freeley's puzzling diversion during his evening walk into a derelict district of town, but the obverse of Cheever's repeated validation of 'the sinuous and fragile constructions of love and self-esteem that human beings are continually building' to sustain their lives is here given fearsome expression.[34] Freeley is led to his doom as if distraction carries within it the impulses of self-destruction or is the domain of a fugitive self who resists both such 'fragile constructions' and the comedic settings of our social and domestic occupations, and whose violence, threatening the story's progression, seems almost to put the author himself at its mercy.[35] Yet Charlie's contrasting story seems equally to insist on kinds of experience, and perhaps of knowledge, only to be discovered *by* distraction, by yielding to feelings or responding to unexpected events in which we are 'drawn away from one course or direction to another'. Although Charlie's plans go awry, his willingness to persist in his task in an improvisatory way, outwitting his pursuers to accomplish his mission, delivers him from past apprehension, fears of an imminent catastrophe or an unexpected, senseless death. Again, no logical reason is given for this mysterious, visionary influx of contentment, his joyful sensation 'that the illustrious and peaceful works of man would go on forever', but he is released into a world remade as if by the conjunction of serendipitous and spiritual powers.

To read this story within the covers of *The New Yorker* heightens both its farcical nature and its strangeness, imparting to readers a more vivid sense of the vertiginous world they and the characters are inhabiting. At times, the narrative mimics the mild, benevolent humour that also characterises seven cartoons that interrupt its progress over nine pages in addition to an embarrassingly silly Updike poem and a whimsical column filler at the story's end; at others, it starkly opposes such amusement as if fiercely impatient of casual interruption. In direct and indirect ways, the reader is made conscious of surroundings even while the story solicits their attention, an effect that is amplified by what may be instances of editorial humour as well as authorial design. One suspects an ironic hand at work in the placement of a cartoon, on the page on which Charlie sets out to fulfil his mission, whose captain extols the benefits 'of getting the right man for the right job' in a store's complaints department. Likewise, one can suppose that Cheever was familiar enough with the frequency of glamorous travel advertisements in *The New Yorker* to anticipate his story being read alongside the contending enticements of these glossy fantasies, a probability influencing interpretation of the story's presentation of its Dionysian housewives. Was Cheever offering his readers a way to critique, while enjoying, the upper-class consumer appeals that flooded the magazine's pages, enabling a self-conscious resistance, by such readers, to their social positions? Was he anticipating the need for a more nuanced understanding of our psychological relation to advertised pleasures beyond those often constructed for critical purposes in oppositional terms?[36] Although, despite Charlie's elevating vision, Cheever's matrons are objects of mild mockery, succumbing to commercially driven temptation, and perhaps of more pointed critique in their debasement of the Easter vigil, they simultaneously function as a sly interrogation of the reader's own vulnerability to the affective nature of 'the mysterious role' of advertisements and the justifiable, fundamental yearnings they stimulate to take flight from everyday lives.[37]

The cover image of this issue also serves as a reminder of the human inclination to indulge in dreams, like the matrons, that may miraculously come to be satisfied against inauspicious odds: a drawing of a night-time race-track lit by spotlights, the picture recalls fantasies of luck and chance and perhaps by extension the diverse emotional and psychological currents that move in tandem with everyday actions and make us creatures of our own interruptions. Uncannily, the image also echoes a dimension of Cheever's personal relation to *The New Yorker* and the wagers risked in writing, especially the precarious task of keeping a story on track and keeping one's reader engaged. Fifteen years earlier, in 1944, when initiating a formal arrangement with the magazine, he had confided to his journal: 'In signing a contract with the New Yorker there are certain apprehensions as if writing were a mystery, something as chancey [*sic*] as a long shot on a wet track with mud all over the silks and the bums crowded in under the grandstand out of the rain.'[38] Anxiety about his own literary ability may factor in this remark, but it also reflects Cheever's concern as to whether he could adjust his creative vision to the magazine's requirements and its editors' tastes. Numerous letters from the period of Cheever's early association with *The New Yorker* are notable for editorial scepticism regarding the same qualities that his critical champions cite as essential characteristics of his narrative style. On 6 December 1944, for example, Gus Lubrano, Cheever's first editor, explained his rejection of a story thus: 'The general feeling is that the combination of realism and something that comes close to fantasy doesn't work out very well.' Three years later, Lubrano returned another two stories, explaining that William Maxwell had concurred with him in believing 'the reader is left with the obligation to provide a disproportionate share of interpretive imagination'.[39] Unsurprisingly, in 1950, Cheever summarised a potential danger of continuing his association with *The New Yorker* as it had become apparent after attending a literary gala: 'A lot of people complimented me on my stories, and I hope that I can at least take from this some confident feeling that people are interested in seriousness and that I have been able to preserve in spite of the pages of The New Yorker, many of my own characteristics.'[40]

Documentation of the relation between Cheever and *The New Yorker* reveals a complex web of association veering between mutual appreciation and aesthetic antipathy, emotional support and rejection, with factors of financial generosity and need, candour and insincerity, complicating the relation further. Certainly, as well, Cheever's sense of the 'contemptible smallness' that he felt the magazine sometimes imposed on him was undoubtedly accentuated through his long-time struggle to launch himself as a novelist. Efforts to transcend his private sense of limitation by finishing his first novel, *The Wapshot Chronicle* (1957), went hand in hand with a desire to overcome the demeaning opinion of being regarded merely as a '"*New Yorker* writer"'.[41] Yet an exchange of letters, at the time of the novel's completion, between Cheever and those editors with whom he was most intimate, William Maxwell and Katharine S. White, illustrates an attachment that was often as supportively vital to Cheever as it was creatively frustrating. When White wrote to him on 20 August 1956, praising *The Wapshot Chronicle* and expressing her delight that *The New Yorker* would be publishing several chapters from it, Cheever replied without delay:

> My life seems to be a series of perils from which I am rescued again and again by the kindness and bravery of the magazine. This was never so true [. . .] as in the case of the novel. Harpers *seemed* to like it but it was very hard to tell [. . .] and had not you and Bill Maxwell told me you liked it I would have had a miserable time.[42]

And yet, despite similar expressions of gratitude to his editors and, in public statements, the magazine itself, the history of Cheever's subsequent relation to *The New Yorker*, fraught with pay disputes, feelings of being undervalued, and his own increasing psychological instability, suggests undercurrents of bitterness may frequently have infected even relatively tranquil periods, especially in regard to the magazine's readership. In 1959, he counselled himself, 'nearly every time I think of a story I see it set up in the magazine opposite a cartoon; and I must realize that the people who read my fiction have stopped reading *The New Yorker*', and in 1971, perhaps as a consequence of *The New Yorker*'s rejection of 'The Jewels of the Cabots', when Cheever believed his relation to the magazine was at an end, a bitter fantasy is recorded in his journal, 'I will write a story beginning: Noone reads the fiction in the New Yorker anymore.'[43]

Cheever liked to imagine that his most sympathetic readers inhabited the woods outside his study window, but what did he make of those on commuting trains or in their homes or a doctor's waiting room needing diversion? At the time of writing 'The Events of That Easter' benign tolerance may have been dominant, but a few years later his attitude seems to have become more severe. 'Christmas Eve in St. Botolph's' eventually formed the opening chapter of Cheever's second novel, *The Wapshot Scandal* (1964), but was published three years earlier in *The New Yorker* and hazards a direct affront to the magazine's readership. In a manner similar to 'The Events of That Easter' it places passages of lyrical exuberance in disturbing proximity to repellent violence, but unlike the earlier work deprives the reader of a concluding consolatory epiphany.

For the majority of its length, five and a half of its six pages, running in the magazine, it is disarmingly celebratory, describing the seasonal activities of the denizens of St. Botolph's on a snowy Christmas Eve with cinematic objectivity but casting a degree of communal compassion and absolution over foibles and weaknesses. Composed of a series of sketches of the townspeople in their holiday activities and preparations, the story offers a brief glimpse of each as if reminiscent of the harmless curiosity and innocuous surprises of an advent calendar. These sketches are not uniformly happy ones – broken marriages, drunkenness, vagrancy, lurk here – but the narrative moves briskly, seemingly unfettered of more sustained attention to any individual, until the carollers arrive at a house 'some greeting-card artist [. . .] might have drawn, brick by brick, room by room, on Christmas Eve', and where an old woman recites a poem for the assembled company.[44] Although unidentified, this is Emerson's 'The Snow-Storm', the first five lines of which are given in the text.[45] As if emulating the poem's triumphal opening and its closing evocation of 'the frolic architecture of the snow', Cheever's story itself appears as a frolic, a harmless seasonal greeting that spirals to a transcendent expression of joy as the carollers, re-entering the snowy landscape, are imbued with the sensation 'that there was happiness everywhere, happiness all around them'. Then, unexpectedly, the story turns. The final five paragraphs linger on 'one lonely figure on the scene, lonely and furtive', who sees in the storm only 'the mortality of the planet' and whose Christmas Eve mission is to drown a sack of kittens in an icy river, a task that results in his own accidental death as well.

Emerson's poem, in lines absent from Cheever's text, evokes a force that is not only extravagantly inventive but also possessed of such riotous, undisciplined energy as to be almost brutal in its effects:

Speeding, the myriad-handed, his wild work
So fanciful, so savage, nought cares he
For number or proportion.

The hidden allusion invites the conjecture that Cheever's story emulates a similar untamed, unpredictable ferocity. Is this Cheever's savage mockery of an unsuspecting reader, a fierce challenge to anyone expecting easy amusement or the promotion of untroubled self-contentment? The tale's disturbing climax is like the Christmas token left for sinners and which its closing sentence judges appropriate for at least some inhabitants of St. Botolph's: 'where in an hour or two the souls of men would be sifted out, the good getting toboggans and sleds, skates and snowshoes, ponies and gold pieces, and the wicked receiving nothing but a lump of coal'. The story's violent conclusion, with its departure from the steady movement and formal proportion evoked by the 'greeting-card' dwelling, forces the reader into a harsh landscape and bitterly rebukes an incapacity for literary seriousness or unwillingness to attend to 'accidental revelations, half-heard cries for help', like those of the old man's anguished screams: '"Help! Help!" he cried [. . .] "I'm drowning!" But no one heard him, and it would be weeks before he was missed.' Cruelly, unforgivingly, the story unsettles the complacent reader wishing only for the most puerile pleasures of distraction while providing its own kind of 'profane illumination' by this ruthless juxtaposition of scenes and cunning change of atmosphere. 'Christmas Eve in St. Botolph's' appeared in the 23 December 1961 issue of *The New Yorker*. It may not have been the variety of seasonal entertainment readers were expecting and it may be another sign of Cheever's bid to emerge from the confinement in which the magazine had too long immured him. Yet it was brave of *The New Yorker* to print this tale, so like 'the mad wind's night-work' of Emerson's storm, and to collaborate in its ingenious disruptions.

Notes

1. The four issues were: 7 April, p. 69; 19 May, p. 27; 9 June, p. 125; 23 June, p. 11. I have been unable to find other Rolex ads that similarly do not use photographs of celebrity subjects, with the exception of one that depicts Christopher Columbus.
2. Cheever's two biographers, Blake Bailey and Scott Donaldson, give the number of his contributions to the magazine as 121: Bailey, *Cheever: A Life* (New York: Alfred A. Knopf, 2009), p. 80; Donaldson, *John Cheever: A Biography* (New York: Random House, 1988), p. 205. His son makes the total 120, which accords with my own count. See *The Letters of John Cheever*, ed. Jonathan Cheever (London: Jonathan Cape, 1989), p. 61.
3. Cheever's growing stature and wider public recognition as a writer, in the 1960s and '70s, coincides with the period in which *The New Yorker* was repeatedly attacked as a trivializing, pretentious publication supposedly catering to a self-congratulatory readership and their concerns for literary propriety and social respectability. Contemporary critics often find it necessary to defend his work against adverse association with the magazine. For a summary of these views see Francis J. Bosha, 'John Cheever: Critical Reception', in *John Cheever: Critical Insights*, ed. Robert A. Morace (Pasadena, CA: Salem Press, 2012), pp. 89–119 (pp. 89–91).
4. 'John Cheever: The Art of Fiction LXII', interview with Annette Grant, *The Paris Review* (Fall 1976), repr. *Conversations with John Cheever*, ed. Scott Donaldson (Jackson and London: University Press of Mississippi, 1987), pp. 95–112 (p. 106).
5. Michael Levenson, 'Novelty, Modernity, Adjacency', *New Literary History*, 42.4 (Autumn 2011), 663–80 (pp. 669, 670, 671).

6. See, for example, Wayne Stengel, 'John Cheever's Surreal Vision and the Bridge of Language', *John Cheever: Critical Insights*, pp. 136–48 (p. 136), while Bailey describes the ending of 'The Country Husband' as a 'virtuosic montage' (*Cheever: A Life*, p. 210).

7. 'John Cheever: The Art of Fiction LXII', *Conversations with John Cheever*, pp. 107–8.

8. John Cheever, *The Stories of John Cheever* (1978, repr. London: Vintage Edition, Random House, 1990), pp. 549–60 (p. 549); hereafter *SJC*. This story was rejected by *The New Yorker* and thereafter sold to *Esquire*; see note 17.

9. John Cheever, 'The Five-Forty-Eight', *The New Yorker*, 10 April 1954, pp. 28–34 (p. 28); *SJC*, pp. 308–22 (p. 309).

10. *The New Yorker*, 10 April 1954, pp. 31, 32; *SJC*, pp. 316, 318. In *SJC*, 'a man with a suitcase' is given as 'a woman with a suitcase'.

11. Michael Wood, 'Distraction Theory: How to Read While Thinking of Something Else', *Michigan Quarterly Review*, 48.4 (Fall 2009), 577–88 (p. 582).

12. *The New Yorker*, 10 April 1954, p. 34; *SJC*, p. 320. Cheever's title may be ironically alluding to a poem by the popular American Roman Catholic poet Joyce Kilmer, 'The Twelve-Forty-Five', which sentimentally eulogises a late night train: 'The midnight train is slow and old, / But of it let this thing be told, / To its high honor be it said, / It carries people home to bed. / My cottage lamp shines white and clear. / God bless the train that brought me here.' *Trees and Other Poems* (1914), in *Joyce Kilmer: Poems, Essays and Letters*, ed. with a memoir by Robert Cortes Holliday, 2 vols, vol. 1: Memoir and Poems (London: Hodder & Stoughton, 1917), pp. 174–7.

13. *The New Yorker*, 10 April 1954, p. 34; *SJC*, p. 320.

14. *The Journals of John Cheever* (New York: Alfred A. Knopf, 1991), p. 121; quoted by Bailey, *Cheever: A Life*, p. 276.

15. Cathy N. Davidson, *Now You See It: How the Brain Science of Attention Will Transform the Way We Live, Work, and Learn* (New York: Viking, 2011), pp. 28–9. That Cheever's stories so often reflect the culture of advertising during this period seems to have been noticed by the writers of the television serial based on 1950s and '60s New York advertising culture, *Mad Men*, which makes abundant references to his work and personal life, and whose narrative techniques of montage may also owe something to Cheever's literary methods. See, for example, Peter Applebome, 'Decoding the "Mad Men," Ossining and Cheever Nexus', *New York Times*, 22 July 2010, A20(L).

16. *SJC*, p. 555.

17. Quoted in Bailey, *Cheever: A Life*, p. 279. Bailey's remark that 'Cheever loved the story, and for the rest of his life he generally chose to read it at any public gathering' is confirmed by Benjamin Cheever, who also notes that his father 'liked to tell his audience that the story had been turned down by *The New Yorker*', and quotes him as explaining that '"They thought of it as an art story"' (*The Letters of John Cheever*, pp. 159–60).

18. John Cheever Collection of Papers, 1969–1982, Untitled [notes, vignettes, personal reflections. . .]. 54 TS leaves. Backlog Cheever, Box 5, folder 5 (uncatalogued). The Henry W. and Albert A. Berg Collection of English

and American Literature, The New York Public Library, Astor, Lenox and Tilden Foundations; hereafter: John Cheever Untitled, Berg Collection.

19. Cheever declared to himself: 'the only sense of the future I can hold out to my children is the sense of the future as an improvisation with the understanding that improvisation can be as rich or richer than dogma' (John Cheever Untitled, Berg Collection).

20. Benjamin discusses this concept in his well-known essay 'The Work of Art in the Age of its Technological Reproducibility', in *Selected Writings*, ed. Howard Eiland and Michael W. Jennings, trans. Edmund Jephcott and others, 4 vols, vol. 4. (Cambridge, MA: The Belknap Press of Harvard University Press, 2003), pp. 251–83 (p. 269), italics in original. For an historical analysis of this term, I am grateful to Paul North, *The Problem of Distraction* (Stanford: Stanford University Press, 2012).

21. Howard Eiland, 'Reception in Distraction', *boundary 2*, 30.1 (Spring 2003), 51–66.

22. Ibid., p. 52.

23. Ibid., pp. 55–6. Eiland sees this attitude as explicit in Benjamin's comments on kinds of intoxication and enchantment linked to the flâneur, the gambler and the collector in *The Arcades Project*.

24. Ibid., pp. 57, 60.

25. John Cheever, 'The Season of Divorce', *The New Yorker*, 4 March 1950, pp. 22–7 (p. 24); *SJC*, pp. 181–92 (p. 185); in this edition, 'accidental revelations', in the quoted phrase, is singular: a probable erratum.

26. Ibid., pp. 27, 26; *SJC*, pp. 192, 190.

27. Elizabeth Hardwick, 'Cheever, or the Ambiguities', *New York Review of Books*, 20 December 1984, pp. 3–4, 6, 8 (p. 6).

28. See, for example, Robert A. Morace, 'From Parallels to Paradise: The Lyrical Structure of Cheever's Fiction', and Samuel Chase Coale, 'Cheever Through the Lens of Language: Bridges of Entanglement and Bewilderment', both in *John Cheever: Critical Insights*, pp. 183–216, pp. 41–56.

29. John Cheever Untitled, Berg Collection; Interview with Samuel Chase Coale, 3 June 1975, cited by Samuel Chase Coale, 'John Cheever: Suburban Romancer', in *John Cheever: Critical Insights*, pp. 149–67 (p. 153).

30. Ibid., pp. 153, 165.

31. Walter Benjamin, 'What is Epic Theatre?' (1931), first version, cited by Eiland, 'Reception in Distraction', p. 53. Eiland importantly traces Benjamin's positive understanding of distraction to his interest in Brecht's theatre. Cheever's frequent testimony to his delight when, in life or in narrative, 'totally disparate facts come together' has relevance here. See 'John Cheever: The Art of Fiction LXII', *Conversations with John Cheever*, p. 98.

32. John Cheever, 'The Events of That Easter', *The New Yorker*, 16 May 1959, pp. 40–8 (pp. 40, 48); the story was not reprinted in *SJC*.

33. Ibid., pp. 47–8, p. 47.

34. John Cheever, 'Keep the Ball Rolling', *The New Yorker*, 29 May 1948, pp. 21–6 (p. 22).

35. North's proposal that distraction may be considered as 'a capacity to receive specters' or 'non-beings' may be appropriate to describe the experience related here (*The Problem of Distraction*, p. 13). Anne Stillman also writes suggestively of T. S. Eliot's apprehension of the destructive aspects of

distraction, with its 'frayed edges of perception, severance; division . . . time wasted; violent scatterings of cognition'. See 'Distraction Fits', *Thinking Verse* II (2012), 27–67 (p. 54), available at <http://www.thinkingverse. com/issue02/Anne%20Stillman,%20Distraction%20fits.pdf> (accessed 1 May 2014).

36. These are questions asked by Trysh Travis in relation to the culture of advertising in *The New Yorker*. See 'What We Talk About When We Talk About *The New Yorker*', *Book History*, 3 (2000), 253–85.

37. This issue of *The New Yorker* contains a double-page spread on the attractions of Canada, four full-page ads for Bermuda, France, Massachusetts and Nassau, as well as BOAC, Pan Am, SAS Airlines and Sheraton Hotels, in addition to numerous smaller ads for other destinations, cruises and tours.

38. Bailey, *Cheever: A Life*, p. 111.

39. New Yorker Records, box 403; 24 February 1947, New Yorker Records, box 445.

40. Bailey, *Cheever: A Life*, p. 166.

41. Ibid., p. 222.

42. 24 August 1956, New Yorker Records, box 742.

43. John Cheever, *The Journals* (London: Jonathan Cape, 1991), p. 121; Bailey, *Cheever: A Life*, pp. 448–9. An otherwise blank sheet in New Yorker Records, box 853, records, 'William Maxwell, May 24, 1971. Rej: The Jewels of the Cabots'.

44. John Cheever, 'Christmas Eve in St. Botolph's', *The New Yorker*, 23 December 1961; this and all subsequent quotations, p. 30.

45. 'Announced by all the trumpets of the sky, / Arrives the snow, and, driving o'er the fields, / Seems nowhere to alight: the whited air / Hides hills and woods, the river, and the heaven, / And veils the farm-house at the garden's end', *The Collected Works of Ralph Waldo Emerson*, 10 vols, vol. IX, *Poems: A Variorum Edition*, Historical Introduction, Textual Introduction, and Poem Headnotes by Albert J. von Frank, Text Established by Albert J. von Frank and Thomas Wortham (Cambridge, MA: The Belknap Press of Harvard University Press, 2011), p. 90; 'farm-house' is not hyphenated when these lines are reprinted in Cheever's story in *The New Yorker*.

III Lightness and Gravity

Chapter 8

Portrait of the Rabbit as a Young Beau: John Updike, *New Yorker* Humorist

Thomas Karshan

1

In 1945, John Updike, then only twelve years old, wrote to two of his heroes, James Thurber and Saul Steinberg, requesting examples of their work that he had seen in *The New Yorker*. With the gratifying responsiveness that would come to characterise *The New Yorker*'s dealings with Updike, Thurber sent him one of his dogs, and Steinberg a drawing which Updike had specifically asked for, a scene of two men greeting one another (Fig. 8.1).[1] The man on the right tips not only his hat but with it his head, with a courtesy that seems as aggressive as it is impassively self-destructive. The man on the left, his more ordinary manners thoroughly trumped, returns a look of fear, tempered or perhaps intensified by confusion. It's not quite clear how we are to take this scene. Are we seeing here how civilisation, by severing our egos, decapitates us? Or is this a horrid hallucination of the aggressive competitiveness always implicit in civility? Either way, the cartoon will have offered Updike an early initiation into what he would later recognise as 'the overall topic' of William Shawn's *New Yorker*: 'civilisation and its discontents', the governing topic of all Updike's writing.[2]

Updike's Aunt Mary had given the family a subscription in the Christmas of 1944, and Updike 'fell in love with the magazine as a child, from what seemed an immense distance'. 'I wanted to appear in *The New Yorker* – indeed, as would-be writer, I wanted little else.'[3] Updike went on to publish over 850 items in *The New Yorker*, from 1954 to his death in 2009, becoming the most distinguished product and most complete embodiment of what he was to call 'not only the best general magazine in America, but perhaps the best that America ever produced'.[4] Granted one of the magazine's famously generous first-reading agreements in September 1954, when he was only twenty-two,[5] he contributed to nearly every department of the magazine, writing

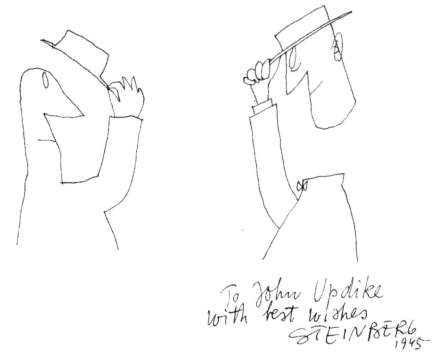

Figure 8.1. Saul Steinberg, untitled drawing, inscribed 'To John Updike with best wishes STEINBERG 1945', originally published in John Updike, *Due Considerations* (New York: Alfred A. Knopf, 2007), p. 608. © The Saul Steinberg Foundation/Artists Rights Society (ARS), New York/DACS, London.

whimsical 'Talk of the Town' and major political 'Commentary' pieces, parodies and humorous casuals, reviews of fiction, theology and biography, light and serious verse, and dozens of short stories. He even supplied *The New Yorker* with a number of 'Newsbreaks', those humorous examples of the stylistic solecisms of other newspapers and journals that *The New Yorker* uses to fill gaps left in the bottom of columns.[6] Updike was what he said he had set out to be, a consummate 'magazine writer', enamoured of 'the book-making process', turning his hand to whatever task *The New Yorker* required of him, plugging odd gaps in columns with verse of the requisite length, and making brilliant play out of the restrictions of his medium.[7] Ever poised, amused, and curious, like the top-hatted and monocled beau who in Rea Irvin's famous *New Yorker* cover image inspects every butterfly of passing fashion, Updike brought to its apogee the house style of *The New Yorker*: the long unfaltering sentences and masterful mixture of tones; the omnivorousness with which it digests even the most difficult ideas into mass readability; the cosmopolitan sophistication softened by a distinctly American humour – what might be called its democratic *sprezzatura*, a capacity to present even the most threatening material with the unfailing good manners of Steinberg's man doffing his hat.

Updike was before all else a *New Yorker* humorist, just as *The New Yorker* was first of all a humour magazine, founded by Harold Ross on the model of *Punch* and *Judge*. Updike's early passion for the magazine was 'mainly for its humor and cartoons',[8] and he 'grew up, in a sense, within *New Yorker* cartoons – bending my mind around their outlines, blissfully losing myself in their clouds of half-tone wash'.[9] Each Christmas he would ask for a *New Yorker* cartoon anthology, and his childhood reading was in large part the *New Yorker* humorists – Thurber, Robert Benchley, Stephen Leacock, S. J. Perelman.[10] 'As a boy', he said, 'I wanted to be a cartoonist', not a writer.[11] He drew cartoons for his high-school newspaper, the *Chatterbox*, and more sophisticated ones for the *Harvard Lampoon*, the humour magazine which, as he later wrote, 'had begun life in the 1890s as an imitation of *Punch* and had imitated *Judge* and *Life* in the Twenties, [but] by the Fifties was an imitation of *The New Yorker*'.[12] While a high-school and college student, Updike submitted many cartoons to *The New Yorker*, but without success.[13] It was instead in the related mode of light verse, 'a kind of cartooning with words', that he gained entry into the magazine, when his 'Duet, with Muffled Brake Drums' appeared on 14 August 1954.[14] Katharine White then wrote to him:

> Light verse is one of our most precious ingredients and light verse writers are rare nowadays, so I hope you will keep up the good work and will bombard us with verse. I had read yours in the <u>Lampoon</u> and had hoped you might become a contributor. Of course we are equally anxious to get humorous prose, so if you ever write what we call 'casuals', in office jargon, please send them along too.[15]

In 1957, White would write again to say 'we need your help to maintain our status as a magazine that publishes humor, and you're one of the few funny writers left'.[16]

Updike had been hired to join the staff of *The New Yorker* on 15 August 1955, and though he left the staff in March 1957, the magazine continued to exhort him for more of his brilliant 'Talk of the Town' pieces and commentaries. *The New Yorker* archives are full of letters from Katharine White, William Maxwell and William Shawn begging him for more; Brendan Gill would later say that 'it was perfectly obvious that he was writing better Talk pieces than anyone who had ever written them'.[17] From as early as 1955, Updike was, in William Maxwell's words, 'a member of the family', privy to William Shawn's private notes on his work, and able to call on Shawn's secretary to help him find an apartment for his family when, as it happened, they wanted to stay in New York for a month one summer.[18]

Updike was, then, *The New Yorker*'s favourite child. Yet the relationship was a complicated one. Against the sunny secular liberalism the magazine embodied, Updike, a neo-Christian and critic of Enlightenment since his Harvard days, would over the late 1950s develop a sophisticated theological critique, informed by deep reading in Chesterton, Lewis, Tillich, Unamuno, and, above all, Kierkegaard and Barth. As he tells us in his autobiography *Self-Consciousness*, against the dovishness of *The New Yorker* he was a hawk, on Vietnam, on sex, on God:

> I was, by upbringing, a Lutheran [. . .] faith alone, faith without the false support of works [. . .] a certain contempt for the world and for attempts to locate salvation and perfection here. The world is fallen, and in a fallen world animals, men, and nations make space for themselves through a willingness to fight. [. . .] Peace depends upon the threat of violence [. . .] down-dirty sex and the bloody mess of war and the desperate effort of faith all belonged to a dark necessary underside of reality that I felt should not be ignored, or risen above, or disdained.[19]

The argument of this chapter is that Updike was able to develop a fifth-column position by drawing upon discontents already implicit in *New Yorker* humour. In its cartoons and light verse Updike found a humorous cloud of secular anxiety which he could distil, with deceptive courtesy, into an internal critique of *The New Yorker*'s culture. Cartoons showing savages acting like Manhattanites, or vice versa, betrayed a sense of the hidden affinity between civilisation and the discontented primitive instincts; cartoons about cannibals, the fearful possibility that life was a violent matter of eat-or-be-eaten;[20] cartoons about urban anxiety, the false support of work, and works; while light verse playing on speed and slowness hinted at an underlying desire to see in a human life an un-modern norm of shape and pace. And *The New Yorker*'s very many cartoons and jokes about advertising could be radicalised by Updike into a subversive investigation of the network of signs and signals, words and letters, of his culture. As he wrote in his 1963 *New Yorker* essay on light verse, in words which have applicability to the lightness of his writing more broadly:

> modern light verse, as it was created by Calverley, calls into question the standards of triviality that would judge it. [. . .] a universe of importance is pulled down [. . .] the figures by which men have agreed to swear and live are tripped up by metrics, flattened by the simple inopportuneness of rhyme.[21]

In radicalising *The New Yorker*'s light culture, Updike helped take the magazine in a new direction. As early as May 1959, William Maxwell told Updike, then still only twenty-seven, that 'it is a slightly different magazine because you are now published in it'.[22] Updike was one of the principal figures in reinventing *New Yorker* humour for the new, more sophisticated era that began in 1951 when Ross died and was replaced by Shawn. Like his heroes Saul Steinberg and Vladimir Nabokov, who had started before him in the late 1940s, Updike took many of the stock themes of *New Yorker* humour in the Ross era, giving them a metaphysical twist which carried them forward into the raw material for his serious fiction.

Updike did make a sharp distinction between his writings for *The New Yorker* and his novels, which he viewed as 'a thing apart', carefully excluding them from his first-reading agreement.[23] It may appear, then, that there are two Updikes: the cosmopolitan beau who helped sustain the butterfly lightness of *The New Yorker*, and another, earthier writer, rooted in the poor Lutheran world of rural Pennsylvania he had grown up in, whose *Rabbit* books express the mortal gravity and encumbrance of existence. As Updike wrote in his poem 'Earthworm', published in *The New Yorker* in May 1962:

> We pattern our Heaven
> on bright butterflies,
> but it must be that even
> in earth Heaven lies.[24]

In the final stanza the earthworm turns and repudiates the butterfly's claim to unrestricted lightness:

> Immersed in the facts,
> one must worship there;
> claustrophobia attacks
> us even in air.[25]

Revealingly, the editors of *The New Yorker* claimed not to understand and refused to print this final stanza, which to Updike 'held the kernel of [his] philosophy',[26] though he tried to explain himself in a series of letters: 'What I meant was that, just as the earthworm is immersed in the earth, so we are immersed in facts that make us claustrophobic. So we should take this lesson from the earthworm, of living and worshipping in the medium in which we find ourselves.'[27]

Ten years earlier, while a freshman at Harvard, Updike had presented a similar idea to his parents, in a letter that attests to the influence of such prominent anti-modernist Harvard professors as Douglas Bush:[28]

> We do not need men like Proust and Joyce; men like this are a luxury, an added fillip that an abundant culture can produce only after the more basic literary need has been filled. This age needs rather men like Shakespeare, or Milton, or Pope; men who are filled with the strength of their cultures and do not transcend the limits of their age, but, working within the times, bring what is peculiar to the moment to glory. We need great artists who are willing to accept restrictions, and who love their environments with such vitality that they can produce an epic out of the Protestant ethic.[29]

Updike sketches here a blueprint for what would later become the *Rabbit* novels, which attest to a love for the restrictive Pennsylvania Dutch Protestant environment he was born into, making an epic out of its ethic. There is, however, a surprising detail here, in the odd conjunction of Milton and Pope, grave Puritan epic and the light mock-epic writing which at that very time Updike was doing in the pages of the *Lampoon*, as in his 1953 'Reverie, Induced by Simultaneous Exposure to *Paradise Lost*, Book IX, and a Host of TV Commercials'.[30]

As it turned out, the epic novelist of *Rabbit* wrote with the pen of a wit; the witty beau pulled a rabbit out of his top hat; the butterfly embraced gravity and restriction; and the earthworm came to see its writing as a form of metaphysical lightness, saying, in *Self-Consciousness*, that 'writing [. . .] is a presumptuous taming of reality, a way of expressing lightly the unbearable', and that 'writing, in making the world light – in codifying, distorting, prettifying, verbalizing it – approaches blasphemy'.[31] The ironies of Updike's situation were that in submitting to the restrictions of *The New Yorker*'s lightness – the 'restriction', 'environment', or 'medium' in which he happened to find himself – he was not betraying but fulfilling his own commitment to his earthworm project; conversely, in abiding by these restrictions, he could achieve freedom within and then beyond them, as the rabbit leaps from the earth to which he returns and in which he lives. As Updike's mentor Kierkegaard wrote: 'we speak colloquially of making ourselves light by casting off burdens, and this view is the basis of all banal life-views. In a higher, in a poetical and philosophical sense, the opposite holds true: one becomes light by means of weight; one soars high and free by means of – a pressure.'[32]

Saul Steinberg expressed a similar idea in an insightful drawing he sent Updike on his sixtieth birthday in 1992, forty-seven years after his first gift (Fig. 8.2). In it a Rabbit draws the work-bench which contains and upholds him, but then extends the line until it becomes something

Figure 8.2. Saul Steinberg, untitled drawing, inscribed 'John Up. 60!
Love from Saul ST March 1992', originally published in John Updike,
Due Considerations (New York: Alfred A. Knopf, 2007), p. 609. ©
The Saul Steinberg Foundation/Artists Rights Society (ARS), New
York/DACS, London.

like a treble clef, turning work into music, structure into play, constraint
into freedom.[33]

2

Updike's first productions at the *Chatterbox*, the newspaper at
Shillington High School, were cartoons, mainly recording the wins and
losses of the school's baseball, football and basketball teams, such as the
one reproduced in Figure 8.3, from December 1945. Fifteen years later,
Updike would set these scenes of competition in basketball in motion in
the opening scene of *Rabbit, Run*, in which Harry 'Rabbit' Angstrom – a
one-time high-school basketball star – gets into a game with some teen-
agers. There, as already in the sports cartoons Updike was drawing at
the age of thirteen, the good humour and grace of sporting competition
thinly veil the violence of the desire to beat one's opponent. Towards the
end of his time at high school Updike had already begun to articulate
the violence of his humour, in a poem, 'Laugh, world, laugh', of January
1949, written when he was 17, and, he says, 'prompted by the rash of

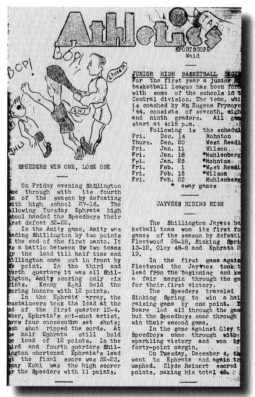

Figure 8.3. John Updike, cartoon, Chatterbox, 7 December 1945, p. 3. © Estate of John Updike.

magazine articles, and newspaper columns on the great curative power of laughter':

> Let's hear you roar when you read the news,
> (Hitler grinned as he butchered Jews)
> [. . .]
> Satan is laughing, but (God only knows why)
> I can't see the twinkle in St. Peter's eye.[34]

That violent humour began to proliferate outwards into the cartoons Updike drew for the *Harvard Lampoon*, many of which recapitulate the theme of the cartoon the young Updike had requested from Steinberg. In May 1953, for instance, he once again made a joke about the courtesy that decapitates, in a cartoon of a man approaching the hangman's steps: mind your step, reads the legend, with grave Shakespearean wit. A cartoon of the previous month has two besuited men jovially clinking glasses: the danger of the alcohol, supposedly sublimated into social

Figure 8.4. John Updike, cartoon, *Harvard Lampoon*, February 1953, p. 15. © Estate of John Updike.

ritual, is unleashed in the last panel, which shows them transformed into demonic haters. In a third cartoon from February of the same year, Updike portrays himself as *Lampoon* jester salting himself in the pot, in a witty variation on *The New Yorker*'s staple cartoons about savages and cannibalism (Fig. 8.4). Civilisation requires that artists, and maybe all men, destroy themselves for our nourishment, though here the jester hardly looks like a victim: somehow, he thinks he's won, as he adds his own salt to the pot, like the man in the Steinberg cartoon grinning triumphantly as he removes his own head.[35]

In a cartoon published in the *Lampoon* in September 1954, after his graduation and his first publications in *The New Yorker*, Updike took a well-known cartoon by Garrett Price showing a series of ever bigger fish eating one another, and merely altered the direction of the last fish's eye, so that it glances back to see who in turn is going to eat it (Fig. 8.5).[36] Life is not just a matter of trying to be the biggest fish: there will always be another, bigger fish behind you, so that life is essentially fish-eat-fish, or, as Updike says in explaining his hawkish position on Vietnam, 'dog eat dog', and you had better find in that what gaiety you can – the gaiety we see in Updike's last fish's eye, which recalls that of the jester salting himself for the pot, and, indeed, of Steinberg's self-decapitating man.[37] The cartoon expresses an idea that goes back at least as far as Jonathan Swift's 1733 poem 'On Poetry', that:

September, 1954

Figure 8.5. John Updike, cartoon, *Harvard Lampoon*, September 1954, p. 21 © Estate of John Updike.

Hobbes clearly proves that ev'ry Creature
Lives in a State of War by Nature
[. . .]
So, Nat'ralists observe, a Flea
Has smaller Fleas that on him prey;
And these have smaller Fleas to bite 'em,
And so proceed *ad infinitum*.
Thus ev'ry Poet, in his Kind,
Is bit by him that comes behind[38]

This maxim of lightness passes from Swift through Hilaire Belloc and on to Updike and *The New Yorker*. It only took the Freudianism of the twentieth century to see in its dark pessimism a hidden erotic longing, as in Updike's 1968 short story 'Under the Microscope', where one sexy young water mite suggests that being eaten is 'what we all want . . . subconsciously, of course'; her interlocutor, a version of Updike, turns round and eats her.[39] A matching thought had been expressed in Nabokov's first contribution to the magazine, a poem entitled 'A Literary Dinner', of April 1942:

Come here, said my hostess, her face making room
for one of those pink introductory smiles
that link, like a valley of fruit trees in bloom,
the slopes of two names.
I want you, she murmured, to eat Dr. James.[40]

As Updike later would, Nabokov here plays on and deepens into seriousness the modes and conventions of *New Yorker* light verse: civilisation – the difference between wanting to meet people and wanting to eat them – hangs, with delicious precariousness, on a single letter. There is an aggression in light verse that is always threatening to eat life back to its original alphabet; it is specific to Nabokov, and after him Updike, only to lend this aggression a sly, dashing eroticism.

Updike wrote a diptych of stories in the late 1960s, 'Under the Microscope' (1968) and 'During the Jurassic' (1967), in which he developed this vision of literary cocktail-party cannibalism via a mock-epic play on extremes of scale by drawing on two staples of *New Yorker* cartoons, dinosaurs and microbes. They were two of the only four Updike stories ever printed with accompanying cartoons (not by him), all of which appear in his 1972 collection *Men and Women*. In 'The Baluchitherium', the only one of these four stories to have been published in *The New Yorker* (though without its cartoons), Updike interviews the largest mammal to have lived on land, extinct but now resurrected from its fossils.[41] Like a number of Updike's light stories, 'The Baluchitherium' is wittily disguised as a 'Talk of the Town' piece. Many of Updike's 'Talk' pieces, like his light verse, were about extinctions and survivals, such as one from July 1956 on the fossil relics of the dinosaur 'Tritylodonts', or another from April 1958 on 'the oldest egg in New York – a dinosaur egg a hundred and twenty million years old'.[42] Extinction was a persistent concern of *The New Yorker*: life, as seen through the melancholy monocle of the humorist, is a sequence of butterflies, of ephemeral lives and fashions all fated to swift extinction. Between October and November 1956, Updike published a poem, 'Old Faces of '56', about all the creatures thought to have been extinct that had been discovered still alive; a 'Talk' piece marvelling, among other things, that 'paper collars' were 'not extinct'; and another piece 'in defense of the dip pens Postmaster General Summerfield is ousting from post offices across the nation' that builds to the following sombre reflection: 'it seems that Progress, in order to maintain the appearance of itself, must sacrifice to the dumb god Era its own best fruits'.[43]

Updike valiantly returned to his defence of old post offices in March 1958, having in May 1957 published a piece of light verse, 'Planting a Mailbox', fancifully imagining the 'miracle' by which 'a post office blooms'.[44] For Updike, the post office was civilisation in quintessence; more specifically, it was an indispensible staging-post between Progress and the Primitive. One of Updike's *Lampoon* cartoons from April 1951 shows a post office in some far-off imperial locale, with two 'savages' straight from the stock of old racist *New Yorker* caricatures looking over at a dishevelled colonial dandy and saying, 'Special Delivery? You'd better take it.'[45] Thirty-some years later Updike would go on to give a speech at the International PEN Congress of 1986, asking 'How Does the State Imagine?' His answer was that it is through 'the post office', for which a writer, no matter how dissident, must remain grateful, for the post office embodies the structures that make communication possible; and, adds Updike, 'the tribe seeks interconnection and consolidation'.[46]

Updike would grant the same sentiment to Rabbit Angstrom in *Rabbit Redux* (1971): 'Wonderful service, the postal. Put yourself in one of those boxes, sorted from sack to sack, finally there you go, plop, through the right slot out of millions. A miracle that it works. Young punk revolutionaries, let them try to get the mail through, through rain and sleet and dark of night.'[47] There is an instructive parallel here with Steinberg, who made many drawings of US postal offices, and who, as Adam Gopnik acutely noted in a *New Yorker* piece, 'saw that the Post Office was to America what the village church is to England, what the Mairie is to France: the small institution that sums up the local faith'.[48] And there is an equally instructive parallel, or partial contrast, with Thomas Pynchon – in this as in many other respects Updike's avant-garde anti-type – who in *The Crying of Lot 49* (1963) evoked the Trystero postal service as the necessary subversion to the violent empire of the US post.

Not that Updike ignored the primal forces subterranean to civilisation. In a 'Talk' piece of February 1956 about a conference of the weed society of America, we hear of 'the Mastery of Man over Nature'; but 'in regard to ragweed control, it is not clear who is master [. . .] ragweed is a concomitant of human civilisation'.[49] Updike's first-ever 'Talk' piece puzzled over why it was that so many half-dollar coins go out of circulation in New York City. His answer is that their heaviness, which might please 'an economically primitive people' that 'wants its currency to be a material echo of the barter system', dispirits the 'urban creature' who, 'caught with a couple of half dollars in his pocket feels burdened, jingly, archaic – as if he had reverted to wampum'.[50] Just a year later, another of Updike's 'Talk' pieces again detected the primitive irrational, this time in the subway tokens whose odour in December, 'minty, damp, cool, and secretive', was, 'after a moment, we remembered', 'the smell of subway tunnels in cold weather. We might have been a bear walking into his cave for the long season of dreams.' And the sight of a girl buying her tokens, not one at a time, but in a block of twenty, startles; but then, 'the subway doesn't seem to us such an unlikely place for an act of faith, after all. Down there, we always misread the Vermouth advertisement "N.Y. Loves G&D" as "N.Y. Loves God."'[51] In such small civic and apparently secular scenes Updike unearths not only tacit acts of faith, but also an instinct for the void below.

Updike found an exquisite opportunity to insert a sliver of metaphysics into *The New Yorker*'s secular worldview when the Russians first sent a shuttle to the moon late in 1957, inspiring in Americans the so-called 'Red Moon scare'. In 'The Lovelorn Astronomer', the very first poem he sent *The New Yorker* in July 1953, Updike had faced the terrifying interstellar vacancies seen by science, and their power to make human emotion seem trivial: 'Who bleeds to stain the moon?'[52] Now, on 16 November 1957, Updike – then still only twenty-five years old – wrote the lead 'Notes and Comments' piece for the magazine, ironically adopting the voice of the secular *New Yorker* editorial 'we' to ask why it was that 'last week, we passed several anxious days tending the moon for which previously we had never much cared', and had always been told was merely 'a mammoth stone [. . .] Yet when we read the Russians might celebrate their birthday party by splashing a red stain across a breadth of craters, it might have been our own face they were planning to spatter with ink.' Why does the moon matter so much, if it is only an old mammoth stone? For some reason, if the moon is tainted by another cause, America's sleep will be ruined:

> Troubled, we woke when it was still dark, and went to the window, to see, through a screen of leafless elm branches, the moon half submerged on the horizon – bloated, cockeyed, and, in the orange dawn, transparent. Lord, we thought, the moon has foundered! [. . .] heaven knew what strange assault awaited it. How reluctantly it abandoned the obsolescent safety of the American sky![53]

Updike's poem, 'Quilt', published in the same issue, takes up the theme, but inverts it: here it is not the moon that assures our sleep, but the nation, a quilt made of the 48 states:

> Don't kick your covers, son. The bed is built
> So you can never shake the clinging quilt
> That blanketed your birth and tries to keep
>   Your waking warm, impalpable
>   As atmosphere. As earth it shall
> Be tucked about you through your longest sleep.[54]

Updike would return to the same knot of themes in *Rabbit, Redux*, which begins with an epigraph from the moon-landings, auguring the otherworldly trip of the late '60s, and ends with Rabbit and his wife Janice, reunited in a motel room, able to sleep beside one another again: 'he lets her breasts go, lets them float away, radiant debris. The space they are in, the motel room long and secret as a burrow, becomes all interior space. [. . .] He. She. Sleeps. O.K.?'[55]

When the Russians actually 'hit the moon' two years later, in September 1959, Updike was again tasked with writing *The New Yorker*'s response, but this time an uncharacteristic acceptance of American secularism expressed itself in the withdrawal of his covert metaphysical endeavour. Folding the political story around another, homelier narrative, he told of watching an old lady in a cemetery, tending the grave of her dead husband – or so he assumed, until she moved on to another grave, leaving his sentimental, 'conventional thanatopsis' to collapse: 'it seemed not to matter whose name was on the tombstone'. Cheerfully, newsboys deliver the papers with their headlines about the moon-landing: 'There it was – democracy, indifference, persistence' – the American creed – and 'the moon fled to its proper distance', once more a mere rock, and death nameless or uncurated.[56]

More typical of Updike's 'Talk' pieces is one on a session with a life insurance salesman, published in November 1960: 'Much of our time with him was devoted to the making of vortical calculations, the empty center of the vortex being our absence.'[57] Vortex was, like void, one of the words down which Updike could slide through the surface of the newsy world into a metaphysical other space. He had slipped it into his previous contribution to the magazine, published two weeks earlier: his account of the final game of the great Boston Red Sox baseball player Ted Williams. It is a famous piece of sportswriting – and not such a famous piece of covert theology, though it is that, too. For when, improbably, Williams at his last at-bat hits a home run, Updike finds the sudden intercession of the miraculous that has made professional sport such an effective disguise for faith in the twentieth century (in a short story, 'Incest', of June 1957, *The New Yorker*'s readers had been told of a protagonist who 'like many Americans, [. . .] was spiritually dependent on Ted Williams'[58]):

> Like a feather caught in a vortex, Williams ran around the square of bases at the center of our beseeching screaming [. . .] Our noise for some seconds passed beyond excitement into a kind of immense open anguish, a wailing, a cry to be saved. But immortality is nontransferable. The papers said that the other players, and even the umpires on the field, begged him to come out and acknowledge us in some way, but he never had and did not now. Gods do not answer letters.[59]

Williams is as alien and inaccessible to human reason as God is in Karl Barth's theology. Answering no letters, he disdains the networks of worldly communication and communion. But he does play: for Updike, as also for Nabokov and Steinberg, play is one fleeting glimpse of the divine afforded to earthly existence, and as such the very type of art and its faint hesitant gestures towards immortality.

3

A feather fluttering in a vortex, Williams is an image of that saving lightness which for Updike rises above death. As Updike said in the essay on
Max Beerbohm and light verse that he published in *The New Yorker* in
March 1963, 'light verse precisely lightens; it lessens the gravity of its
subject'. For 'language is finite and formal; reality is infinite and form-
less. Order is comic; chaos is tragic. By rhyming, language calls attention to its own mechanical nature and relieves the represented reality of
seriousness.'[60] To the reprint of the article in *Assorted Prose*, he added
a footnote:

> Perhaps this sibylline sentence should be expanded. I think that order is comic
> in the sense that it is deathless. The essence of the machine is its *idea*; though
> every part is replaced, the machine persists, as the (successful) embodiment
> of certain abstract notions. There is something Platonic about machines; we
> speak, for example, of *the* 1937 Chevrolet as of a reality distinct from all
> the Chevrolets built in 1937. Likewise, a poem is a verbal machine infinitely
> reproducible [. . .] whereas that which is organic is specific and mortal.

Pitched against a world of realism, which mimics 'the massive onflowing
impersonality that has supplanted the chiming heaven of the saints [. . .]
light verse, an isolated acolyte, tends the thin flame of formal magic and
tempers the inhuman darkness of reality with the comedy of human
artifice'.[61] It is worth pausing here to expose Updike's hidden paradoxes,
so strange and unearthly they are worthy of Beerbohm himself. Reality
is inhuman and mortal; the human, conversely, expresses itself in the
magic and immortality of art; reproducibility, and therefore immortality, is characteristic of machines; ergo, machines must have a greater
share in humanity than organic reality has.

Reporting on machinery, automation and commerce was Updike's
main beat as a staff 'Talk of the Town' writer. We find him, in 1955–57,
writing about the 'Third National Electrical Industries Show'; the
motor-boat show; the annual mobile homes show; a gas-powered cork-
screw; a speech prompting device; an exhibition of old industrial products; a talking elevator; a mechanical secretary. No wonder he started
one of his pieces by remarking that 'mapping the inroads of automation
is a chore'.[62] He even wrote a piece in September 1956 on an ideally safe
car (though not on that Platonic ideal, the 1937 Chevrolet).[63] In fact
Updike's first ever contribution to *The New Yorker* was a piece of light
verse on the ideal luxury machine, the Rolls Royce, and the advertisements for it that had appeared in *The New Yorker*:

Duet, with Muffled Brake Drums

50 Years Ago Rolls Met Royce – a Meeting that made Engineering History
– Adv. in The New Yorker.

Where grey walks slope through shadows shaped like lace
Down to dimpleproof ponds, a precious place
Where birds of porcelain sing as with one voice
Two gold and velvet notes – there Rolls met Royce.

'Hallo', said Rolls. His umber silhouette
Seemed mounted on a blotter brushed when wet
To indicate a park. Beyond, a brown
Line hinted at the profile of The Town.

And Royce, his teeth and creases straight, his eye
A perfect match for that well-lacquered sky
(Has zenith since, or iris, been so pure?),
Said, 'Pleased to meet you, I am sure.'

A graceful pause, then Rolls, the taller, spake:
'Ah – is there anything you'd care to make?
A day of it? A fourth at bridge? Some tea?'
Royce murmured, 'If your afternoon is free,
I'd rather, much, make engineering history.'[64]

'The conceits and figures by which men have agreed to swear and live are tripped up by metrics, flattened by the simple inopportuneness of rhyme.'[65] What is it to meet another person? That is the question posed in the cartoon the twelve-year-old Updike had asked for from Steinberg; in Nabokov's 'Literary Dinner', with its play on 'meet' and 'eat'; and in this poem, too, as it catches at the false tone in the advertisement to tease open what we mean by 'meet'. Updike's light verse often stages its own fanciful meetings: 'An Imaginable Conference', published a year later in August 1955, imagines Henry Green and Wallace Stevens meeting in the course of business.[66] Such incongruous meetings naturally take place in light verse, turning as it so often does on zeugma: for zeugma is the rhetorical device which shows us that unlike ideas have often already met in a single word, though we had never noticed it, and by the piquancy of that discovery brings to our awareness the mismatch between the finite formality of language and the infinite informality of reality. Language is something made, an irrational or even magical machine, and Updike's 'Duet' asks what it is to 'make' (this in a poem about machines and manufacture): to make a day of it, to make a fourth at bridge, to make tea, or to make history. Pope had done the same thing with the key word 'take' in his *Rape of the Lock*, a poem that is the source of much of the modern light verse tradition. In lines about Queen Anne – 'thou [. . .] whom three realms obey, / Does sometimes counsel take – and sometimes Tea' – Pope implicitly asks what it is to 'take', in a poem about rape, possession, and consumption.[67] Updike's poem nods towards the origins of its wit in the self-consciously Popean line '(Has zenith since, or iris, been so pure?)', before capping its homage to the mock-epic satirists in the final lines of the poem: as Updike says in his notes to his *Collected Poems*, 'the concluding triple rhyme and final hexameter are devices I had noticed in Dryden'.[68]

'Duet' breaks words down into their constituent parts, exposing ordinary language as an irrational machine; but it then re-assembles them into a deathless gaiety which, as Updike says, 'tempers the inhuman darkness of reality with the comedy of human artifice'. Still more so does Updike's next *New Yorker* poem, the exceptionally brilliant 'Player Piano', published in December 1954:

Player Piano

My stick fingers click with a snicker
And, chuckling, they knuckle the keys;
Light-footed, my steel feelers flicker
And pluck from these keys melodies.

My paper can caper; abandon
Is broadcast by dint of my din,
And no man or band has a hand in
The tones I turn on from within

At times I'm a jumble of rumbles,
At others I'm light like the moon,
But never my numb plunker fumbles
Misstrums me, or tries a new tune.[69]

The perfect emblem for the reproducibility of art in an age of mechanical reproduction, the player piano would have offered an easy target for the satiric arrows of such saturnine cultural critics of the 1940s and '50s as Theodor Adorno or Dwight Macdonald, and indeed Updike's 'Player Piano' advertises its own inhumanity, the absence of man or hand or craft in 'the tones I turn on from within'. It never tries a new tune. As the opening stanza clicks and clacks around the letter *k* with a manic caged compulsiveness, we seem to hear not just a chuckle but a violent mechanical snicker. Yet with the final word of the stanza, 'melodies', the stop is let out, snickering becomes music, and the raw din of language is tamed by the formal magic of art. The abandon of words, their capacity to interlock in new patterns with new meanings, is broadcast, the poem opening out into the surrounding air as its intricate pattern of half and internal rhymes allows the irrational ear to rearrange it in a multiplicity of ways different to those forced by the line breaks upon the rational eye. The full freedom of language is allowed to sound as if within the frame of the piano, and yet, by the miracle of a hidden engineering, it remains felicitous, no matter how the ear arranges it. The din makes its own 'I', working the machinery of language to such a point that in its play it comes alive and starts speaking directly to us, with a personality, charm and vitality unimpaired by the perfect smoothness that was also the trademark of *The New Yorker* – another medium for the mass reproduction of luxury art, another organ for taking the rumbles of gossip and tuning them to perfection, without ever fumbling or losing its poise; and though the *New Yorker* beau may never try a new tune, wouldn't it be a trifle gauche to do so?

Elsewhere in Updike's light verse, the snicker retains its violence, biting into the solecisms men have learned to swear and live by, reducing their clichés back to emptily clattering syllables: as in 'The Newlyweds', a poem about the celebrity couple Eddie and Debbie Fisher, published in November 1955.

> The Newlyweds
>
> After a one-day honeymoon, the Fishers rushed off to a soft drink bottlers' convention, then on to a ball game, a TV rehearsal and a movie preview.
>
> – *Life*
>
> 'We're married,' said Eddie.
> Said Debbie, 'Incredi-
>
> ble! When is our honey-
> moon?' 'Over and done,' he
>
> replied. 'Feeling logy?'
> Drink Coke.' 'Look at Yogi
>
> go!' Debbie cried. 'Groovy!'
> 'Rehearsal?' 'The movie.'
>
> 'Some weddie,' said Debbie.
> Said Eddie, 'Yeah, mebbe.'[70]

Having rhythm and line structure create hectic speed or languorous slowness is one of Updike's favourite light verse effects, and it feels killjoy to force any lesson from this fun. Still, there is a point here, in what Katharine White praised as Updike's 'telling but unscolding humor', which proceeds from the bogus tone of the *Life* epigraph: it's only for the cameras and magazine columns that the Fishers' marriage vows have been sworn, and their life lived.[71] Their marriage is no more convincing a meeting of spirits than Rolls and Royce's had been. The effect, though, is the opposite of the earlier poems, which by entirely fulfilling the restrictions of the medium won freedom, broadcast language, and brought the mechanical to life. Here, the words are broken and diminished by the magazine's line breaks. Life is reduced to language, language to signs, and signs to advertising slogans and television messages. And with it, life is being distorted out of its proper rhythm and shape – the sort of shape one has as a half-conscious archetype at the back of one's mind, and that might be represented in the cartoon of the hill of life that Updike drew when he was seven years old, and later mentioned in his 1968 poem 'Midpoint'.[72]

4

A number of Updike's short stories published in *The New Yorker* around the same time as these poems dwell specifically on the world made out of advertising signs – in particular, three from the winter of 1955–56. 'The Kid's Whistling', from December 1955, shows Roy making signs for a department store, and struggling to make the individual letters clear.[73] In 'Snowing in Greenwich Village', from January 1956, an advertising executive hears one of his wife's ambiguous remarks as being 'like those advertisements that from varying angles read differently'.[74] Another advertising executive, Rafe, catches sight of another of these same duplicitous signs on the bus home from work in 'Toward Evening', published the next month. Back at home at the end of the story, he steps out on his balcony to see blinking on and off over the night-time cityscape a sign for Spry cooking oil: 'Rafe sometimes wondered how it had come to be there. Some executive, no doubt, had noticed the bare roof of the newly acquired waterfront plant.' His casual suggestion for a sign had been passed along, over weeks, through the chain of command – and eventually, the sign went up:

> Thus the Spry sign (thus the river, thus trees, thus babies and sleep) came to be.
> Above its winking, the small cities had disappeared. [. . .] The Spry sign occupied the night with no company beyond the also uncreated but illegible stars.[75]

This is not a happy vision: the world is all man-made signs, and then there is the illegible void. Yet set against this in early Updike is a different vision – the other side of his double-signed world – born of a wilful faith that the signs of the substantial world must always have been there, and that the means through which we communicate are not to be reduced back to the rational efforts of automation. The first poem in Updike's *Collected Poems* is written out of such an act of faith. 'Why the Telephone Wires Dip and the Poles are Cracked and Crooked' was published in the *Harvard Lampoon* in 1953, when Updike was only 21.

> The old men say
> Young men in gray
> Draped the thread across our plains
> Acres and acres ago.
>
> But we, the enlightened, know,
> In point of fact, it's what remains
> Of the flight of a marvelous crow
> No one saw:
> Each pole, a caw.

The poem ironises Enlightenment, with its analysis of the world back to signs and its militant exposure of the artificial systems that constitute civilisation. Gently but surely, the poem insists instead that the writer's job is to bury those signs back into reaffirmed myth. In his introduction to his *Collected Poems* Updike writes of how he sought to convey 'the mythogenetic truth of telephone wires [. . .] I still remember the shudder, the triumphant sense of capture, with which I got these lines down, not long after my twenty-first birthday.'[76] There is a clear contrast here between Updike's counter-enlightenment position and the secular enlightened view of Thomas Pynchon, who sought to expose as a conspiracy the communicative systems of America: the US mail, and the telephone wires, amid which Pynchon positions himself in *The Crying of Lot 49*, with the squatters 'swung among a web of telephone wires, living in the very copper rigging and secular miracle of communication, untroubled by the dumb voltages flickering their miles, the night long, in the thousands of unheard messages'.[77]

Updike was involved in a similar mythogenetic labour when, in the introduction to his *Collected Poems*, he tried to enforce the principle of 'segregation', already quoted, between his serious poetry as deriving from the 'real (the given, the substantial) world and light verse from the man-made world of information – books, newspapers, words, signs'.[78] He placed 'Why the Telephone Wires Dip' in his serious poetry, as if to complete its transformation of the lines of communication back into the given, and therefore the substantial – even though the true interest of the poem is how it occupies that uncertain space between signs and reality which it pretends to close. Another 'serious' poem comes still more dangerously close to that line of segregation. Sent to *The New Yorker* in July 1954, though only published in July 1957, 'Ex-Basketball Player' is spoken in a slow elderly voice that guides us into a little town to the gas station where there now works Flick, the town's ex-basketball star – a relic, a survivor, but not extinct. Once he played for the Wizards, was a local myth, and performed small miracles with the ball – 'In '46 / He bucketed three hundred ninety points, / A country record still. The ball loved Flick.' Now, however,

Flick stands tall among the idiot pumps –
Five on a side, the old bubble-head style,
Their rubber elbows hanging loose and low.
One's nostrils are two S's, and his eyes
An E and O. And one is squat, without
A head at all – more of a football type.[79]

This is a world fuelled by signs. Here bodies are slack and rubbery, heads are empty, and the pumps are idiots; some have no heads at all. Is this the light? Or the real, the given, the substantial?

Updike had more fully explored this subject in 'Ace in the Hole', his second story published in *The New Yorker*, in April 1955, but of all Updike's *Collected Stories* the first composed. It was only accepted by *The New Yorker* when Updike re-submitted it after the successes of his early light poems, but was written late in 1953 for a creative writing seminar at Harvard, run by the French critic Albert Guerard, in Updike's words 'the very model of a cigarette-addicted Gallic intellectual', who 'liked the story' because 'he said it frightened him, an existential compliment'.[80] A European intellectual contempt informs the portrayal of Ace, a creature of advertising stimuli, pop songs and clichés, and part of the machinery of his car. The opening paragraph could be an illustrative passage from Adorno's *Minima Moralia* (1951) or Nabokov's *Bend Sinister* (1947):

The moment Ace's car touched the boulevard heading home, he snapped on the radio. He needed the radio, especially today. In the seconds before the tubes warmed up, Ace said aloud (doing it just to hear a human voice; there was no one else in the car), 'Jesus, she'll pop her lid.' His voice, though familiar, irked him; it sounded thin and scratchy, as if the bones in his head were picking up static. In a deeper register Ace added, 'She'll murder me.' Then the radio came on, warm and strong, so he stopped worrying about his wife, and the job he had just lost. The Five Kings were doing 'Blueberry Hill'. They made a real thing of it. To hear them made Ace feel so sure inside that he plucked a cigarette from the pack on the sun shield . . .[81]

Perhaps Ace has just seen the advertisement for Kent's Micronite Filter cigarettes which was carried in the same issue of *The New Yorker*, advising consumers of 'the real assurance you can get only with KENT'S Micronite Filter'.[82] Ace's voice is an alien implant, his head merely

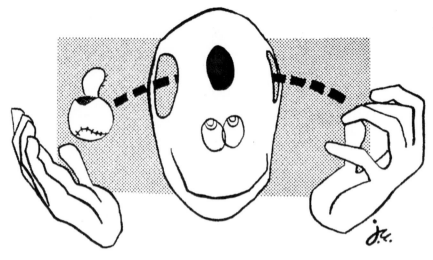

Figure 8.6. John Updike, cartoon, *Harvard Lampoon*, October 1951, p. 12. © Estate of John Updike.

Figure 8.7. Saul Steinberg, untitled drawing, originally published in *The New Yorker*, 1 November 1958, p. 41. © The Saul Steinberg Foundation/Artists Rights Society (ARS), New York/DACS, London.

a cranium radio picking up the static din of the air around him. He could, at least in this opening paragraph, be the bone-headed athlete with nothing but air between his ears that Updike had cartooned for the *Lampoon* in October 1951 (Fig. 8.6).

5

Saul Steinberg would publish in *The New Yorker* in 1958 a drawing also playing on the notion that there is nothing within the skull, or rather, that there might be anything (Fig. 8.7). At first sight Steinberg's drawing seems only an amusing image of the truism that inside every well-armoured man is a nervous rabbit. But the joke it makes turns outwards a puzzle or problem that would be central to Updike's *Rabbit* books. Twentieth-century culture has chosen to equate the self with consciousness, and consciousness with that inner chatter, the interior monologue, out of which Joyce's *Ulysses* fashioned the modern novel of subjectivity. But there is no good reason to accept any of these equations; all we know is that there is a space within the head, which in a poem of 1956 Updike called 'the great meringue we call the Void', a space ready to be filled by any of the metaphors culture finds lying to hand – the breath of the spirit, silent talk, even a rabbit.[83]

So arbitrary is it to conceptualise the inner life on the model of any external material existence: this was the lesson Updike had taken from Kierkegaard's *Fear and Trembling*, the book which he would later say most changed his life, and which he read, 'fearful and desolate', in the winter of 1955–56. The key sentence for him, as he later remembered it, was this: '"The paradox of faith is this, that there is an inwardness which is incommensurable to the outward, an inwardness, be it observed, which is not identical to the first but is a new inwardness."'[84] This is precisely the paradox that Kierkegaard's famous 'leap of faith' alone can cross; and it was this leap that Updike sought to make in the period of the mid- to late 1950s, when, as he describes it in *Self-Consciousness*, he was a young father heavy with mortality, constricted by responsibilities, and consumed by 'angst', in a time of 'remembered gray moments, in which my spirit could scarcely breathe': such as one, shortly after meeting a life insurance salesman (perhaps the meeting he recounted in his November 1960 'Talk' piece on the subject), when he was 'playing basketball [. . .] and I looked up at the naked, netless hoop: gray sky outside it, gray sky inside it'.[85]

Two years after Steinberg's drawing was published, *Rabbit, Run* came out. Its opening reworks, but entirely transforms, 'Ace in the Hole'. Once again, an ex-basketball star, Rabbit Angstrom, has just been fired from his job – advertising the MagiPeel, a cheap industrial gadget. But unlike Ace and Flick, this ex-basketball star is still something special; as people keep saying, he has a gift for life. In the opening line, 'boys are playing basketball around a telephone pole with a backboard bolted to it', their play located in the secular miracle of communication; and as

Rabbit stands ready to shoot the basketball, 'the old stretched-leather feeling makes his whole body go taut, gives his arms wings' – as if he were an angel.[86] He has the ability to combine quickness and slowness that is needed in basketball, as in lightness. As if without gravity, the ball rides towards the net on an arc of its own making; and Rabbit is capable of the lightness of the leap.

Notes

1. John Updike, *Due Considerations* (New York: Alfred A. Knopf, 2007), p. 608.
2. John Updike, *Odd Jobs* (New York: Alfred A. Knopf, 1991), p. 766.
3. John Updike, *More Matter* (New York: Alfred A. Knopf, 1999), pp. xxi, 763.
4. Updike, *Due Considerations*, pp. 100–1.
5. Katharine White, letter to John Updike, 15 September 1954, New Yorker Records, box 732, file 20.
6. See Mary Ann Leiner, letter to Updike, 11 August 1954, box 732 file 20, and Updike, letter to William Shawn, 23 May 1959, New Yorker Records, box 561, file 7.
7. Updike, *More Matter*, pp. xxi, 758.
8. Updike, *Due Considerations*, p. 102; John Updike, *Collected Poems: 1953–1993* (New York: Alfred A. Knopf, 1993), p. xxiii.
9. Updike, *More Matter*, p. 787.
10. Updike, *Due Considerations*, pp. 181, 607, 612.
11. Updike, *Collected Poems*, p. xxiii.
12. Updike, *More Matter*, p. 789.
13. According to Ben Yagoda, in *About Town: The 'New Yorker' and the World it Made* (New York: Scribner, 2000), p. 303.
14. Updike, *Collected Poems*, p. xxiii. For a discussion of light verse at *The New Yorker*, see Judith Yaross Lee's thematic account in *Defining 'New Yorker' Humor* (Jackson: University Press of Mississippi, 2000).
15. Katharine White, letter to John Updike, 17 July 1954, New Yorker Records, box 732, file 20.
16. Katharine White, letter to John Updike, 2 July 1957, New Yorker Records, box 757, file 5.
17. For the date of Updike joining *The New Yorker*, see a letter from Updike to William Maxwell of 20 July 1955, New Yorker Records, box 740, file 6. For the *New Yorker*'s enthusiasm for Updike's 'Talk of the Town' pieces, see, among many others, a letter of Katharine White to Updike, 2 May 1960, New Yorker Records, box 782, file 13. Gill's comment is quoted by Yagoda in *About Town*, p. 306.
18. Katharine White, letter to John Updike, 15 September 1954, box 732 file 20; William Maxwell, letter to John Updike, 2 August 1959, New Yorker Records, box 773, file 14; John Updike, letter to William Shawn, 14 July 1958, New Yorker Records, box 555, file 16.
19. John Updike, *Self-Consciousness* (London: Penguin, 1990), pp. 124, 129.

20. See Mary Corey, *The World Through a Monocle: 'The New Yorker' at Midcentury'* (Cambridge, MA: Harvard University Press, 1999), pp. 64–6.
21. John Updike, 'Rhyming Max', *The New Yorker*, 7 March 1964, pp. 178–9.
22. William Maxwell, letter to John Updike, 7 May 1959, New Yorker Records, box 765, file 2.
23. Updike, *More Matter*, p. 765; John Updike, letter to William Shawn, 17 August 1956, New Yorker Records, box 544, file 13.
24. John Updike, 'Earthworm', *The New Yorker*, 12 May 1962, p. 145.
25. Updike, *Collected Poems*, p. 29.
26. Ibid., p. 361.
27. John Updike, letter to Howard Moss, 12 May 1961, New Yorker Records, box 789, file 28.
28. Around the time Updike wrote this letter he was reading that other great Protestant epic, *The Faerie Queen*, with Douglas Bush, whom he much admired (Updike, *More Matter*, pp. 843–4).
29. Quoted by Sam Tanenhaus in 'John Updike's Archive: A Great Writer at Work', *New York Times*, 20 June 2010, available at <http://www.nytimes.com/2010/06/21/books/21updike.html?emc=eta1> (accessed 21 December 2013).
30. John Updike, 'Reverie, Induced by Simultaneous Exposure to *Paradise Lost*, Book IX, and a Host of TV Commercials', *Harvard Lampoon*, December 1953, pp. 2–3.
31. Updike, *Self-Consciousness*, p. 215.
32. Søren Kierkegaard, *The Crisis and a Crisis in the Life of an Actress* (1848), in *Christian Discourses*, trans. Howard and Edna Hong (Princeton, NJ: Princeton University Press, 1997), p. 312.
33. Updike, *Due Considerations*, p. 609.
34. John Updike, 'Laugh, World, Laugh', *Chatterbox*, 28 January 1945, p. 5.
35. Cartoon of man approaching hangman's steps, *Harvard Lampoon*, May 1953, p. 5; cartoon of two men drinking, *Harvard Lampoon*, April 1953, p. 13; cartoon of jester being boiled, *Harvard Lampoon*, February 1953, p. 15.
36. See Robert McCoy, 'John Updike's Literary Apprenticeship on "The Harvard Lampoon"', *Modern Fiction Studies*, 20:1 (Spring 1974), 3–12 (p. 5).
37. Updike, *Self-Consciousness*, p. 123.
38. Swift, 'On Poetry' (1733), ll. 319–20, 338–42, in *The Writings of Jonathan Swift* (New York: Norton, 1973).
39. John Updike, *The Early Stories 1953–1975* (London: Hamish Hamilton, 2004), p. 714.
40. Vladimir Nabokov, 'A Literary Dinner', *The New Yorker*, 11 April 1942, p. 18.
41. John Updike. 'The Baluchitherium', *The New Yorker*, 14 August 1971, p. 39.
42. John Updike, 'Tritylodonts', *The New Yorker*, 21 July 1956, pp. 12–13; 'Dinosaur Egg', *The New Yorker*, 19 April 1958, p. 31.
43. John Updike, 'Old Faces of '56', *The New Yorker*, 27 October 1956, p. 36;

'Convincing', *The New Yorker*, 10 November 1956, p. 44; 'Notes and Comment', *The New Yorker*, 6 October 1956, p. 33.

44. John Updike, 'Notes and Comment', *The New Yorker*, 15 March 1958, p. 31; 'Planting a Mailbox', *The New Yorker*, 11 May 1957, p. 103.
45. *Harvard Lampoon*, 15 April 1951, p. 16.
46. Updike, *Odd Jobs*, p. 120.
47. In John Updike, *A Rabbit Omnibus* (London: André Deutsch, 1990), p. 411.
48. Adam Gopnik, 'What Steinberg Saw', *The New Yorker*, 13 November 2000, pp. 141–7.
49. John Updike, 'Weed Work', *The New Yorker*, 4 February 1956, p. 20.
50. John Updike, 'The Half-Dollar Problem', *The New Yorker*, 3 September 1955, pp. 20–1.
51. John Updike, 'Notes and Comment', *The New Yorker*, 1 December 1956, p. 41.
52. *American Weave*, 19.1 (1954), p. 22.
53. John Updike, 'Notes and Comment', *The New Yorker*, 16 November 1957, p. 41.
54. John Updike, 'Quilt', *The New Yorker*, 16 November 1957, p. 54.
55. Updike, *A Rabbit Omnibus*, p. 414.
56. John Updike, 'Notes and Comment', *The New Yorker*, 26 September 1959, p. 33.
57. John Updike, 'Notes and Comment', *The New Yorker*, 5 November 1960, p. 43.
58. John Updike, 'Incest', *The New Yorker*, 29 June 1957, pp. 22–7 (p. 25).
59. John Updike, 'Hub Fans Bid Kid Adieu', *The New Yorker*, 22 October 1960, pp. 109–31 (pp. 128–31).
60. Updike, 'Rhyming Max', pp. 178–9.
61. John Updike, *Assorted Prose* (London: Deutsch, 1965), p. 200.
62. John Updike, 'Speech on the Spool', *The New Yorker*, 22 October 1955, p. 37.
63. John Updike, 'Packaged', *The New Yorker*, 29 September 1956, pp. 26–8.
64. John Updike, 'Duet, with Muffled Brake Drums', *The New Yorker*, 14 August 1954, p. 74.
65. Updike, 'Rhyming Max', p. 178.
66. John Updike, 'An Imaginable Conference', *The New Yorker*, 6 August 1955, p. 24.
67. *The Rape of the Lock* (1714), III. 7–8, in Alexander Pope, *Poetical Works* (London: Oxford University Press, 1966).
68. Updike, *Collected Poems*, p. 369.
69. John Updike, 'Player Piano', *The New Yorker*, 4 December 1954, p. 169.
70. John Updike, 'The Newlyweds', *The New Yorker*, 19 November 1955, p. 157.
71. Katharine White, letter to John Updike, 24 June 1960, New Yorker Records, box 782, file 13.
72. Updike, *Collected Poems*, p. 363. See also Steinberg's image of the hill of life in *The New Yorker*, 11 November 1967, cover.
73. John Updike, 'The Kid's Whistling', *The New Yorker*, 3 December 1955, p. 127.

74. John Updike, 'Snowing in Greenwich Village', *The New Yorker*, 21 January 1956, pp. 30–3 (p. 30).
75. John Updike, 'Toward Evening', *The New Yorker*, 11 February 1956, pp. 28–30 (p. 30).
76. Updike, *Collected Poems*, p. 3; p. xxiv.
77. Thomas Pynchon, *The Crying of Lot 49* (London: Vintage, 2000 [1966]), p. 124.
78. Updike, *Collected Poems*, p. 3; p. xxiii.
79. John Updike, 'Ex-Basketball Player', *The New Yorker*, 6 July 1957, p. 62.
80. Updike, *Early Stories*, p. ix.
81. John Updike, 'Ace in the Hole', *The New Yorker*, 9 April 1955, pp. 92–9 (p. 92).
82. Ibid., p. 43.
83. John Updike, 'Mr High-Mind', *The New Yorker*, 28 April 1956, p. 44.
84. Updike, *Odd Jobs*, p. 844.
85. Updike, *Self-Consciousness*, pp. 92–3.
86. Updike, *A Rabbit Omnibus*, p. 3.

Chapter 9

Sports at *The New Yorker*

Kasia Boddy

On 18 April 1925, two months after its launch, *The New Yorker* opened a new department with a page of short pieces on sport and its personalities. The miscellany included golf ('Jess Sweetser evidently doesn't know what do with business when it interferes with pleasure'); tennis (Vincent Richards 'is getting fat'); a Midwestern walking race (after which the victorious Italian Ugu Frigerio sent Mussolini a cable); the New York Giants (motion picture evidence of 'kidding' in the training camp); and, as the lead item, news of the up-coming fight between Gene Tunney and Tom Gibbons which was thought to be of interest to 'folks outside of Dubuque and away from the East Side' because the heavyweight title is the 'real thing'.[1] The only straightforward news item, with no jokes at all, was an update on Ivy League rowing coaches. The Sports Department fills two columns; the third contains advertisements, including one for English Sport Suits made by Banks, Inc. of Fifth Avenue. Turn the page and you're in the Books Department, where another Fifth Avenue firm, Charles Scribner's Sons, 'announces' the publication (eight days earlier) of F. Scott Fitzgerald's *The Great Gatsby*. The two advertisements, and the two pages, are not in the least at odds; as any regular reader of Fitzgerald would have recognised, sport and sportswear play an important part in his construction of an aesthetic and moral framework. Fashionably dressed athletes exemplify a particularly modern grace and style, and yet they cannot be trusted. Neither those involved in organising sport (like the gambler Meyer Wolfsheim, 'the man who fixed the World Series in 1919') nor those who participate in its games (such as former Yale football star, and still 'cruel'-bodied, Tom Buchanan, and the 'hard, jaunty' yet 'incurably dishonest' golfer, Jordan Baker) have much to recommend them. Sport may offer 'acute limited excellence', but it can also, as Fitzgerald's narrator concludes, 'play with the faith of fifty million people'.[2]

A weekly magazine like *The New Yorker* could not afford such scruples about limited excellence; moreover, as Lionel Trilling noted, *New*

Yorker readers prided themselves on being eclectic, on enjoying 'all the arts but also all the sports'.[3] Well, not all. For many years, coverage was restricted to a small number of fashionable activities, associated, for the most part, with Ivy League college competitions – rowing, hockey and football – or country club leisure pursuits – golf, polo, horse-racing, yachting and tennis (about which James Thurber wrote under the name 'Foot Fault').[4] Occasional high-profile boxing matches, as we've seen, were thought 'sufficiently elegant' to appeal to folks outside of Dubuque and away from the East Side.[5] *The New Yorker*'s problem with sports was their ubiquity; boxing and baseball titbits may not have appealed to the 'little old lady in Dubuque' but they were the staple fodder, the 'custom', of the 'clan' of patriotic Babbitts against whose tastes Harold Ross defined his magazine.[6] Ross may 'have had more interests than most people' but they were usually located in central Manhattan.[7] Sports were all very well as long they didn't take place too far from the 'elusive', much satirised and yet vitally important, 'Social Center' of the city.[8] When 'the practically extinct game of hockey' was revived at Madison Square Garden in 1925, Ross's ideal readers attended in 'formal dress' and fur coats and were soon persuaded to 'order their boxes yearly, as they do for the Metropolitan'.[9]

In the forty years leading up to the launch of *The New Yorker*, sport had assumed an increasingly important place in American mass leisure. Joseph Pulitzer became the first publisher of a New York daily paper to establish a distinct sports department – one of a series of measures that saw the circulation of the *World* rise from 11,000 in 1883 to 1.3 million in 1898.[10] Although Pulitzer recruited regular contributors on forty different sports, it was the popularity of baseball and boxing (decried as barbaric on the editorial page but heavily represented in the sports pages) that 'transformed casual readers into fervent fans'.[11] William Randolph Hearst followed Pulitzer's example when he took over the *New York Journal* in 1895, expanding the sports section and even placing sports stories on the front page.[12] 'Our growing interest in sport', announced Will Irwin in 1911, was 'the mark of an Anglo-Saxon-Celtic people passing from an era of hand labor to that of machinery'; all that Hearst and Pulitzer had done, he maintained, was observe 'our growing interest in sport' and proceed 'to cultivate the taste'.[13] Perhaps. In any case, the mutually supportive relationship between mass spectator sports and the mass media flourished and grew. In 1890, 0.4 per cent of newspaper space was devoted to sport; by 1900, that had risen to 4 per cent and by the 1920s, the popular press set aside 12–20 per cent for sports coverage.[14] In 1929, the American Society of Newspaper Editors reported that one in four readers bought a paper primarily because of its sports page; the editors voted the boxer Jack Dempsey the 'greatest stimulation to circulation in 20 years'.[15] Sports news was no longer seen as a matter of local interest; 'for the first time', Paul Gallico later recalled, athletes 'were given publicity, newspaper reportage, and space usually reserved for the doings of crowned heads, major natural disasters, and wars'.[16] Sportsmen and women also featured heavily in the advertisements that accompanied stories of their exploits, and by 1925, 70 per cent of newspaper revenue came from advertising (Fig. 9.1).[17] *The New Yorker*, for all its carefully maintained distinction between editorial and advertising, was able – through its departments – to target readers and advertisers quite precisely.[18] It didn't take long for the 'Sports of the Week' column to develop into more specific occasional departments devoted to individual sports, such as 'The Tennis Courts' or 'Hockey'. If, as the current editor David Remnick points out, *The New Yorker* has never been 'known foremost for its sports writing', that writing contributed to the magazine's identity and appeal almost from the start.[19]

Personal journalism: familiar and florid

If, as many now claim, the 1920s represented a golden age of sport, it was an age of mass consumption rather than mass participation.[20] In their 1929 study of Middletown, the Lynds noted that modern leisure was now 'mainly spent sitting down'.[21] 'A few play,' elaborated Stuart Chase, also in 1929, 'while the rest of us shout, clap hands, [. . .] crush in our neighbours' hats, and get what thrill we may from passive rather than active participation.' For Chase, this was sport 'at one remove'.[22] Worse still was listening to the radio ('sport at two removes'). Television was yet to come. Where passive participation often found its thrills, Will Irwin noted in 1911, was through a 'flippant, humorous, slangy view of sport'.[23] This is the Algonquin wit, and syndicated columnist for the *New York World*, Heywood Broun on the 1921 Jack Dempsey / Georges Carpentier contest:

> [Carpentier's] head was back and his eyes and his smile flamed as he crawled through the ropes. And he gave some curious flick to his bathrobe as he turned to meet the applause. Until that very moment we had been for Dempsey, but suddenly we found ourselves up on our feet making silly noises. We shouted 'Carpentier! Carpentier! Carpentier!' and forgot even to be ashamed of our pronunciation.[24]

Broun's report exemplifies what Leo Lowenthal, a Frankfurt School sociologist, writing twenty years later, identified as a distinctive 1920s

Southern Fashions by Saks-Fifth Avenue

The new colours are as feminine as the new lines...with baby pinks
...and blues...and other pastel shades. We are now ready
with our collection at Saks-Fifth Avenue in New York
...in Chicago...at Palm Beach...and at our
new Saks-Fifth Avenue shop at Miami.

New York   SAKS-FIFTH AVENUE   *Chicago*

Figure 9.1. Advertisement, Saks Fifth Avenue, *The New Yorker*, 21
December 1929, p. 16.

'language of directness'. At the very moment when 'modern institutions of mass communication' were promising 'total coverage', Lowenthal argued, journalists increased their use of 'you' and 'we' to create a compensatory sense of intimacy between writer and reader.[25] In a 1927 *New Yorker* Profile (written in the third-person and published anonymously), Broun described himself as 'the most thorough-going practitioner of personal journalism in New York'.[26]

But what was the nature of this 'personal journalism'? Could a 'compensatory sense of intimacy' be achieved simply with a few pronouns? Side-stepping 'total coverage' also meant speaking to readers in a language that they (and, it was suggested, only they) could understand. Broun goes on to describe the Dempsey / Carpentier fight as 'the finest tragic performance in the lives of ninety thousand persons'. It was, he joshed, 'sport for art's sake', comparable even to the work of Eugene O'Neill, 'the white hope of the American drama': 'None of the crowds in Greece who went to somewhat more beautiful stadia in search of Euripides ever saw the spirit of tragedy more truly presented.'[27] Lowenthal claimed that such allusions were designed 'to confer pseudo-sanctity and pseudo-safety on the futile affairs of mass culture', and complained that they were oddly mixed up with 'slang and colloquial speech'.[28] But this seems to miss the tone and the point. There is no 'linguistic confusion'. Like Byron and Hazlitt a hundred years earlier, writers like Broun (and Gallico, Ring Lardner, and Damon Runyon) were keen to display their mastery of both high and low argot, and while largely cultivating a 'familiar style' ('as any one would speak in common conversation') they also liked to dabble in its 'gaudy' antithesis.[29]

As did A. J. Liebling. Although, as Lee has pointed out, 'Ross explicitly defined *The New Yorker* against the current field', the contributors that he hired inevitably imported into the magazine elements associated with other publications.[30] Liebling had been a newspaper man, employed by the *New York World*, the 'writer's paper', before he joined *The New Yorker* in 1935.[31] Although it took him a while to adjust to the magazine's more leisurely style, Liebling thought he injected a newspaperman's vitality into the magazine, and often distinguished his work from his 'pretty shoddy' predecessors.[32] Although best-known for the boxing essays he wrote after the Second World War, Liebling's style owes much to the 1920s and to Heywood Broun. His most famous essay 'Ahab and Nemesis' even begins by quoting from Broun's account of the 1922 Benny Leonard / Rocky Kansas lightweight championship fight – in which Kansas, knocked to the floor, finally comes to appreciate that 'the old masters did know something [. . .] tradition carries a nasty wallop'.[33] When Liebling says that he has 'often thought of Broun's words', he is suggesting the applicability of the sentiment to the fighters he discusses in his own essay; but of course the allusion itself enacts (as allusion always does) Liebling's own desire to signal a relation both to the old master Broun and to the *kind* of words Broun used; words that are very different from what, in the same sentence, he quotes and dismisses as '*Journal-Americanese*' (the example is 'scaled the fistic summits').[34]

Withering references to the journal-americanese of ordinary sportswriting have regularly appeared in *The New Yorker*'s *belles lettres* of sport. John Updike's only baseball piece, a *tour de force* from 1960 about batter Ted Williams's valedictory home game at Fenway Park, 'Hub Fans Bid Kid Adieu', quotes a 'sample' of 'appreciative sports-page prose' before appreciating Williams himself with an allusion to Donatello's *David*; Roger Angell's 1980 profile of pitcher Bob Gibson is presented in direct counterpoint to the image constructed by the 'press'.[35] But Liebling, writing in 1955, was particularly concerned with a new threat – what he termed 'this ridiculous gadget called television': both the higher sportswriting and the higher sport had become (for Liebling and for fellow *New Yorker* contributor, John Lardner) endangered species in need of careful preservation. Between 1947 and 1951, John Lardner published a series of essays in the magazine entitled 'That was Pugilism', vividly evoking the era of his father, Ring Lardner, as a time of wild adventures and idiosyncratic figures. 'Things are not the same in the wake of the Second World War', he complained, 'The fighters are more businesslike; their training camps are respectable and dull [. . .]; the managers and "characters" on the fringe of the show are organized and syndicated.'[36]

Liebling meanwhile presented his essays as a direct response to 'the anticipated lean aesthetic period induced by television', a medium devoted (he said) to 'the sale of beer and razor blades' and whose devotees were easily duped.[37] 'The masses are asses', an old fighter called Al Thoma tells Liebling, 'There are no connoisseurs. The way most of these guys fight, you'd think they were two fellows having a fight in a barroom.'[38] In contrast to the 'big and silly television audience' was the aficionado and his far from silly readers. Neatly sidestepping the devotion of *The New Yorker* to selling things – the fact that his essays were simply nestled among ads for 'the wines you loved in Paris', instead of Pabst Blue Ribbon, and that rather than Gillette disposable razors, they shared a space with Excalibur 'legendary blades' – Liebling presents himself as the last of the purists.[39]

In order to mount his rearguard defence of 'sport for art's sake', Liebling needed to look further back than 1921 for a model; a hundred years further back to the 1820s where he found a moral and stylistic touchstone in the nineteenth-century Anglo-Irish journalist, Pierce Egan. Liebling declared Egan 'the greatest writer about the ring who ever lived' and saw his *New Yorker* pieces, collected as *The Sweet Science*, as an 'Extension of the GREAT HISTORIAN'S Magnum Opus'; the title itself is a phrase of Egan's.[40] Indeed the Regency commentator is evoked and praised as (among others) the Herodotus, Holinshed, Edward Gibbon, Philippe de Commines, Thomas Malory, Thucydides, Colly Knickerbocker and Sainte-Beauve of the English prize ring, while *Boxiana* is dubbed its 1001 nights.[41] Liebling's fascination, like Egan's, was as much with the exotic subculture of boxing as with the sport. 'Low-life was [Harold] Ross's word for what I did best', he later recalled; and Ross especially liked it when Liebling adopted the 'high-low style' that had been a feature of the magazine since Corey Ford provided an Impressionist urban sketch of an East Side boxing club in the magazine's first issue.[42] High and low got along just fine; as ever, the shared enemy is the middle.

Liebling's essays present themselves as elegies to the last of boxing's picturesque oddballs and to 'the verbal dandyism of Egan'.[43] Fred Warner argues that few readers who encountered them in *The New Yorker* cared much about boxing. They accepted 'exposure to a brutal and alien sport', he says, simply 'because they loved good prose'.[44] I think Warner is exaggerating the distaste for boxing felt by at least some *New Yorker* readers, but it's certainly true that the point of reading Liebling is a style that you either love or hate – witty, digressive, flattering his readers with frequent allusions to literature and art. Floyd Patterson, after his defeat of Archie Moore, is described as being in the position 'of a Delacroix who has run out of canvas'.[45] In 'Ahab and Nemesis', the obvious allusion is to *Moby-Dick*, but (like Broun on steroids) Liebling also brings in *bel canto*, Faust, Camus and the Myth of Sisyphus, Margot Fonteyn and Artur Rubenstein, and numerous words and phrases that Egan 'would have' used. Remnick describes Liebling's 'snaky and digressive' style as 'incapable of cliché', but it might be more accurate to say that it was a way of avoiding cliché – a perennial danger for a sportswriter.[46] Determined never to revisit a simile, Liebling developed a voice that was 'erudite in . . . [a] wised-up sort of way', or as he put it himself, 'laboriously offhand'.[47] *The New Yorker*, Robert Warshaw argued in 1947 (echoing similar remarks by Dwight Macdonald and others), 'has always dealt with experience [. . .] by prescribing the attitude to be adopted toward it'.[48] The attitude here, I think, is more than simply one of knowingness. Liebling, who – more in the style of Hazlitt than Egan – includes himself as character in his essays, sometimes expresses a certain ruefulness about taking sport so seriously.[49] But it's a cheerful ruefulness that he knows he shares with his readers, so he tells them: let's make the following of sport into a sport and a pastime in its own right; let's be playful about play, stylish about style.

An intelligent interest in the game

On 6 February 1930, Hugh Bradley, a sportswriter at the *New York Evening Post*, wrote to Harold Ross proposing a weekly baseball article 'to entertain people who are not ardent fans but who have an intelligent interest in the game'.[50] Bradley's rather defensive tone seems to anticipate Ross's reply, the following day:

> Dear Mr Bradley,
>
> The question of a baseball column has come up many times, and we don't want one. Our mind is pretty definitely settled as to this. The newspapers cover the subject so completely and thoroughly that we don't see anything in it for us.
>
> Thank you for your suggestion, however. We are always ready to listen to suggestions.
>
> Yours sincerely,
>
> H.W. Ross[51]

Baseball may have been the national sport but, under Ross, it never made more than an occasional appearance at the magazine's peripheries – in a cover image, such as Vladimir Bobritsky's strikingly modernist batter of 8 May 1926 (Fig. 9.2), or an amused and amusing 'Talk of the Town' piece. 'All we know about big-league baseball', declared a 1936 sketch on Joe Di Maggio, 'is what our office boy finds time to tell us.'[52] The second-hand report of Winchell, the office boy, allows *New Yorker* readers to indulge in a little tabloid gossip while retaining a mild superiority about both the subject and the genre: 'Winchell says he's stuck on a bubble dancer down in the Village, that his friends call him Dead Pan Joe, and that he likes to sit through movies twice – likes to get a thorough understanding of them.'[53] And even after the magazine embraced baseball wholeheartedly in the 1960s, its having-it-both ways attitude didn't entirely disappear. As late as 1973 Lillian Ross introduced a talk piece on Willie Mays as a report by 'a young friend of ours in the fifth grade', written 'after he came home from the dentist'.[54]

Roger Angell has never been coy about his interest in baseball, although the question of how intimate one should be with its stars

Figure 9.2. Vladimir Bobritsky, cover illustration, *The New Yorker*, 8 May 1926 © The New Yorker Collection.

has often been his subject. The son of Katharine Sergeant White, the magazine's first fiction editor, and the stepson of E. B. White, one of its most famous humorists, Roger Angell has been a *New Yorker* contributor since 1944 and a fiction editor since 1956.[55] He first wrote about baseball in 1962 when William Shawn told him to 'go down to spring training and see what you find'.[56] In 1930, baseball fans listened to games on the radio and then relived every run and strike-out by reading newspaper reports, but thirty years on, they could see the games live on television. What more did they need? But rather than abandon sports to the screen, Shawn decided, as did the editors of several competing publications, to commission a different kind of sports piece, one that made no pretence at offering 'news'.[57] 'People used to laugh at me because my World Series pieces came so late, sometimes after Thanksgiving', Angell recently recalled. 'Shawn didn't have a sense of deadline. [. . .] Shawn thought, *Everybody knows what the news is; now tell us something else about it.*'[58] Published in April 1962, Angell's 'The Old Folks Behind Home' initiated a new 'something else' and also a new name for the Sports Department: The Sporting Scene.[59]

Like Liebling, Angell made the difference between daily newspaper or TV coverage and writing 'at length for a leisurely and most generous weekly magazine' a subject in itself.[60] But while Liebling described the detrimental effects TV had on sports, Angell concentrated on the implications for the spectator. 'Too much with us', he maintained, televised sport was laying 'waste our powers of identification and enthusiasm' and even 'attention'. 'As more and more closing rallies and crucial putts and late field goals and final playoffs and sudden deaths and world records and world championships unreel themselves ceaselessly before our half-lidded eyes', Angell argued, 'we seem to have forgotten what we came for':[61]

> More and more, each sport resembles all sports; the flavor, the special joys of place and season, the unique displays of courage and strength and style that once isolated each game and fixed it in our affections have disappeared somewhere in the noise and crush.[62]

Television and the sports pages – 'now almost the largest single part of the newspaper', and brimful with 'salary disputes, medical bulletins, franchise maneuverings, l-star ballots, drug scandals, close-up biogs, after-dinner tributes, union tactics, weekend wrapups, wire-service polls, draft-choice trades, clubhouse gossip, and the latest odds' – produce the noise and crush that Angell's sentence mimics.[63] Each item in the list – from drug scandals to clubhouse gossip – is given equal syntactical weight, because, Angell suggests, the mass media fails to offer any sense of perspective. This is also true of television in a literal sense: TV after all is two-dimensional. 'Foreshortened on our screen, the players on the field appear to be squashed together, almost touching each other,' Angell complains, 'and, watching them, we lose the sense of their separateness and lonesome waiting.'[64] And without an understanding of the 'essential distances of the game', how can we experience 'emotion'?

What Angell promised was the kind of distance that only a 'nonprofessional baseball watcher' could have.[65] 'Free to write about whatever I found in the game that excited or absorbed or dismayed me', as he later recalled, Angell epitomised *The New Yorker*'s long-standing sense of itself as 'interpretative rather than stenographic', as a place where 'serious amateurs' could feel at home, 'with no credentials other than their own ability to observe, think, and write'.[66]

Faced with an 'unselective proliferation' of sports, Angell proposed an introspective edit. Through recourse to 'the interior stadium' or 'baseball in the mind', the fan, and writer, could play a 'game of recollections, recapturing, and visions'.[67] This is no 'mere returning' but a form of selection, a means to 'make discoveries' and 'penetrate some of [baseball's] mysteries', the 'disclosure of its truths'. Angell's primary unit is what he calls 'isolated fragments of time', leading one critic to compare him to Wordsworth.[68] But, although his mood is fundamentally Romantic and 'introspective', Angell's style is more eclectic. In some ways, he follows firmly in the footsteps of Liebling and Broun, whom he read 'just about every day' growing up.[69] One pitcher is a 'shining paladin', another faces the fate of a 'cavalryman at Balaclava'.[70] He also once wrote a Joycean eulogy to the sounds he had 'missed all winter'.[71] But most of the time, Angell's baseball pieces share their shape and feeling with the *New Yorker* short stories which he edited and with which his own pieces rubbed shoulders.[72] The issue in which 'The Interior Stadium' appeared – 20 February 1971 – featured three stories: by Jorge Luis Borges, Donald Barthelme and John Updike. He admired them all, but it is Updike, a writer whose attachment to the traditions of *The New Yorker* was almost as deep as his own, whose work most resembles his.[73] Angell recognised the connection, when, many years later, he recalled reading Updike's 'Hub Fans Bid Kid Adieu', about the Red Sox batter Ted Williams's valedictory home game in 1960. 'My own baseball writing was still two years away [. . .] and though it took me a while to become aware of it, John had already supplied my tone, while also seeming to invite me to try for a good sentence now and then, down the line [. . .].'[74] As well as Updike's tone and time-suspending sentences, Angell shared the novelist's attachment to the transcendent possibilities of the 'daily ordinary' and a 'Protestant assertion that brings the sublime down to earth'.[75] The Updike story that shares an issue with 'The Interior Stadium' is called 'Plumbing' and it centres on an old man who comes to fix the pipes in the narrator's new home. The plumber is a 'poet' and his 'musing upon eternals of corrosion and flow' offers a lesson to the narrator, a man who occupies houses 'thinly'. He, and we, 'trust' the plumber's 'spiritual aspirations' because, as Updike said of Thoreau, he gives us 'repeated examples of his practical know-how'.[76] But this proposition can be turned around so that being able 'to *do* things' is valued simply because it makes one *think* things; and bringing the sublime down to earth involves elevating a 'sudden fragment of locality', if not always to the sublime, at least to what Angell calls 'inner vision'.[77] For both writers, 'private reality' is presented as an alternative to the flood of 'news' insisted upon by the 'media'.[78]

Forty-two years later, Angell is still participating fully in a media ecology that is noisier and faster than ever. Unlike Shawn, *The New Yorker*'s current editor, David Remnick, believes in deadlines, and Angell says he tries 'to oblige'.[79] He regularly blogs on the magazine's website, including on the 2013 World Series in which the Boston Red Sox defeated the St. Louis Cardinals. During the Series, Remnick featured online one of Angell's most celebrated pieces, 'Distance', first published in 1980, and a startling example of how different a meditative essay is from an of-the-moment blog.

'Distance' is a profile of Bob Gibson, a pitcher for the St. Louis Cardinals whose glory days came during the 1968 World Series against the Detroit Tigers. Having already posted an Earned Run Average of 1.12 for the season – the lowest recorded since 1914 – Gibson went on to score an unheard-of 17 strikeouts in the first game of the Series. Sport in 1968 was racially and politically charged, but Angell makes no mention of the postponement of the baseball season's opening day, on 9 April, for the funeral of Martin Luther King; or of the impact of Jack Olsen's articles for *Sports Illustrated* on how 'dissatisfied, disgruntled, and disillusioned' the 'black athlete' really was; or of Tommie Smith's and John Carlos's Black Power salutes at the Mexico Olympics.[80] Angell's interests are elsewhere. 'Distance' is an extended meditation on the resonances of a particular concept within the sphere of baseball. Its starting point may have been 'Tao in the Yankee Stadium Bleachers (What comes from reading Chuang-Tzu between innings)', a poem by John Updike that appeared in *The New Yorker* in 1956 and which begins 'Distance brings proportion.'[81]

The most straightforward distance that Angell explores is physical – the gap between the pitcher and the plate that Gibson miraculously seems to close even as he remains socially and psychologically aloof from 'the opposition', but also the view from the stands, revealing the geometry of the game to an extent that neither two-dimensional television nor the players themselves can appreciate.[82] 'You really see how it *works* from here', the pitcher Steve Blass once told Angell, when they went together to the manager's box; 'Down there, you've got to look at it all in pieces.'[83] Temporal distance is also at stake, as Angell presents his essay as an attempt 'to try to get to know [Gibson] a little better' before the pitcher undergoes 'embronzement' in the Baseball Hall of Fame, and before the memory of watching him play is buried beneath a 'thin cement of statistics'.[84] If the sacred space of the ballpark suspends chronology – 'keep hitting, keep the rally alive, and you have defeated time. You remain forever young' – the 'end of the game' is also inevitable.[85] Angell does not see his own writing as a form of embronzement but rather as the literary equivalent of keeping the rally alive. After watching some Indian jugglers, William Hazlitt once asked 'What is there that I can do as well as this?'; to which he responded 'Nothing'. 'I have always had this feeling of the inefficacy and slow progress of intellectual compared to mechanical excellence, and it has always made me somewhat dissatisfied.'[86] When Angell evokes the 'ideal of pitching', he seems to be expressing a similar feeling – and yet, most of the time, both he and Hazlitt seem to accept that the brief form – the profile or fact piece as much as the lyric or the short story – can achieve its own kind of ephemeral excellence, its own 'perfectly arrested moment of joy'.[87] Magazine writing too can make its pitch in style, and 'play a little' in front of an adoring home crowd.[88]

More than anything, 'Distance' is about the relationship between the spectator in the stands and the athletes in the park. Watching 'at a little distance' enables the players to retain a 'heroic tinge', to exist as beings 'beyond us'.[89] Angell once more distinguishes his own approach from that of the mass media. The more the tabloids and TV insist that 'we know everything about the [players'] skills and financial worth and private lives', the more Angell emphasises their mystery. The temptation in writing about athletes – and one that he knows he shares – is 'undercomplexity' and an 'insatiable vicariousness' that threatens to undermine that mystery.[90] For Angell, it is not the athlete's fame, fortune or physical prowess that inspires identification but rather his 'pertinent hesitations' and 'personal mutability'.[91] In a piece about the pitcher David Cone, Angell admits to liking Cone most 'in confusion and pain', and asks, 'was it because he'd become more like me, to myself?'[92] Angell is both motivated by, and wary of, a desire to 'close this space a little'.[93] Bob Gibson has a 'space within him that is not quite filled' that reminds 'us' of the 'humdrum, twilight quality of all our doings of middle life'.[94] Steve Blass, a pitcher who lost his form, provokes thoughts of 'something deeper within us'; for 'the man out there is no longer just another great athlete, an idealised hero, but only a man – only ourself'.[95]

The dialectic of identification and aura can never really be resolved.

Angell recalls a conversation with Joe Wood who 'had played ball for fourteen years, all told, and people had been asking him to talk about it for nearly sixty years'. 'Old men are patronized in much the same fashion as athletes', he concludes, 'because we take pride in them, we expect their intimacy in return. I had intruded after all.'[96] If intimacy with athletes is a pernicious fantasy, intimacy with other fans is both inevitable and desirable. The 'we' who know we are 'not good enough to play'[97] can nevertheless experience the 'joy' of baseball at 'a little distance' – from the stands, from the promptings of our 'interior stadium' or from the 'game of recollections [. . .] best played in the winter' by Angell's essays.[98] Unlike those who mindlessly consume quantities of sport on TV and in the tabloids, 'we' are in the 'business of caring'. It does not matter that the object of that care is something 'frail or foolish'; 'caring deeply and passionately, really *caring*' is itself a moral good.[99] Carlton Fisk's home run in the 1975 World Series is wonderful in itself, but it is even more wonderful because of the ripples it produced beyond Fenway Park:

> [Fisk] circled the bases in triumph, in sudden company with several hundred fans, and jumped on home plate with both feet, and John Kiley, the Fenway Park organist, played Handel's 'Hallelujah Chorus', *fortissimo*, and then followed with other appropriate exuberant classical selections, and for the second time that evening I suddenly remembered all my old absent and distant Sox-afflicted friends (and all the other Red Sox fans, all over New England), and I thought of them – in Brookline, Mass., and Brooklin, Maine; in Beverly Farms and Mashpee and Presque Isle and North Conway and Damariscotta; in Pomfret, Connecticut, and Pomfret, Vermont; in Wayland and Providence and Revere and Nashua, and in both the Concords and all four Manchesters; and in Raymond, New Hampshire (where Carlton Fisk lives) and Bellows Falls, Vermont (where Carlton Fisk was *born*), and I saw all of them dancing and shouting and kissing and leaping about like the fans at Fenway – jumping up and down in their bedrooms and kitchens and living rooms, and in bars and trailers, and even in some boats here and there, I suppose, and on the back-country roads (a lone driver getting the news over the radio and blowing his horn over and over, and finally pulling up and getting out and leaping up and down on the cold macadam, yelling into the night) and all of them, for once at least, utterly joyful and believing in that joy – alight with it.[100]

The Red Sox won the game but, the following night, conceded the World Series to the Cincinnati Reds.

Baseball, Angell insists, is a 'matter of belonging', 'a family for those who care about it'.[101] Of course families can follow magazines as well as teams, and more than most, *The New Yorker* has encouraged a sense of belonging to a 'unified and continuing entity'.[102] *New Yorker* readers famously rush home 'to read the latest issues, to be part of the community that read that latest issue'.[103] That experience is too familiar to provoke the kind of intense emotion felt by Red Sox fans that October night. Until, that is, the season ends and 'Roger Angell comes along and makes it go alive again.'[104]

Notes

1. 'Sports', *The New Yorker*, 18 April 1925, p. 25. Judith Yaross Lee identifies the author as Peter Vischer, 'probably'. See her *Defining 'New Yorker' Humor* (Jackson: University Press of Mississippi, 2000), p. 70.
2. F. Scott Fitzgerald, *The Great Gatsby* (New York: Scribner, 2004 [1925]), pp. 72, 7, 58, 6.
3. Lionel Trilling, '"New Yorker" Fiction', *Nation*, April 1942, pp. 425–6 (p. 425). For example, a 1934 hockey column can be found sandwiched between an ad for early American furniture and one for Steinway grand pianos (*The New Yorker*, 3 March 1934, p. 42).
4. On Niven Busch, Jr.'s coverage of professional hockey after 1927, see Craig Monk, 'When Eustace Tilley Came to Madison Square Garden: Professional Hockey and the Editorial Policy of the *New Yorker* in the 1920s and 1930s', *American Periodicals*, 15.2 (2005), 178–95. Not all of Monk's references are correct.
5. Dwight Macdonald, 'Laugh and Lie Down', *Partisan Review*, 4.1 (1937), 44–53 (p. 52).
6. Harold Ross, 'Announcing a New Weekly Magazine' (1924), repr. in Thomas Kunkel, *Genius in Disguise: Harold Ross of 'The New Yorker'* (New York: Random House, 1995), Appendix I, p. 439; Sinclair Lewis, *Babbitt* (New York: Modern Library, 2002 [1922]), p. 154.
7. A. J. Liebling, 'Harold Ross – Impresario' (1959), in *Just Enough Liebling* (New York: North Point Press, 2004), pp. 460–8 (p. 462).
8. Frank Sullivan, 'Down the Ages with the Social Center', *The New Yorker*, 6 March 1926, pp. 13–14 (p. 13). On 'Ross's carefully contrived cosmopolitan myth', see Thomas Grant, 'Mythologizing Manhattan: The *New Yorker*'s New York', *American Studies*, 28.1 (1987), 31–46 (p. 32).
9. 'Heroes of the Week', *The New Yorker*, 9 January 1926, p. 8; Niven Busch, Jr., 'Hockey', *The New Yorker*, 22 November 1930, pp. 63–5 (p. 63).
10. Denis Brian, *Pulitzer: A Life* (New York: Wiley and Sons, 2010), pp. 72, 66, 223.
11. Ibid., pp. 251, 73.
12. Ben Proctor, *William Randolph Hearst: The Early Years, 1863–1910* (Oxford: Oxford University Press, 1998), p. 48.
13. Will Irwin, 'The American Newspaper: A Study of Journalism in its Relation to the Public', Part IV: 'The Spread and Decline of Yellow Journalism', *Collier's*, 4 March 1911, pp. 18–19, 35–6 (p. 36).
14. Stanley Woodward, *Sports Page* (New York: Simon & Schuster, 1949), p. 38. On the importance of 'the growing interest in sports' for the

development of Sunday papers, see Alfred McClung Lee, *The Daily Newspaper in America* (New York: Octagon Books, 1973 [1937]), p. 396.

15. Bruce J. Evensen, 'Jazz Age Journalism's Battle Over Professionalism, Circulation, and the Sports Page', *Journal of Sport History*, 20.3 (1993), 229–46 (p. 230).

16. Paul Gallico, 'The Mirror', in *The Golden People* (New York: Doubleday, 1965), p. 25. From 1923 to 1936, Gallico, as sports editor of the New York *Daily News*, 'wrote a seven-day-a-week thousand-word sports column' ('Foreword', ibid., p. 13).

17. Lee, *The Daily Newspaper in America*, p. 749.

18. For Harold Ross's letter to Raoul Fleischmann, 17 April 1926, outlining the importance of this distinction, see *Letters From the Editor: The New Yorker's Harold Ross*, ed. Thomas Kunkel (New York: Modern Library, 2000), pp. 24–5. Judith Yaross Lee argues that a Sports Department was only introduced 'to compensate for the end of the theater and music seasons, to maintain audiences and hence advertisers during the summer' (*Defining 'New Yorker' Humor*, p. 70).

19. David Remnick, 'Introduction', *The Only Game in Town: Sportswriting from 'The New Yorker'*, ed. David Remnick (New York: Random House, 2010). The very heft and range of this 500-page collection implies that perhaps sports have not been insignificant to the magazine after all.

20. Jesse Frederick Steiner, 'Spectatorism versus Participation', in *Americans at Play: Recent Trends in Recreation and Leisure Time Activities* (New York: McGraw Hill, 1933), pp. 100–2.

21. The Lynds, *Middletown: A Study in Contemporary American Culture* (New York: Harcourt, Brace and Company, 1929), p. 226.

22. Stuart Chase, *Men and Machines* (New York: Macmillan, 1929), p. 259.

23. Irwin, 'The American Newspaper', p. 36. His examples are the cartoonists and sportswriters T. A. 'Tad' Dorgan and [Bud] Fisher.

24. Heywood Broun, 'Sport for Art's Sake', *New York World*, July 1921, repr. in *Pieces of Hate and Other Enthusiasms* (New York: George H. Doran, 1922), pp. 64–9 (p. 67).

25. Leo Lowenthal, 'The Triumph of Mass Idols', *Literature, Popular Culture, and Society* (Englewood Cliffs, NJ: Prentice-Hall, 1961 [1944]), pp. 109–41 (p. 133).

26. R. A. [Heywood Broun], 'The Rabbit that Bit the Bulldog', *The New Yorker*, 1 October 1927, pp. 18–22 (p. 18). Broun and Ross were friends and poker buddies. See Lee, *Defining 'New Yorker' Humor*, p. 23; Richard O'Connor, *Heywood Broun: A Biography* (New York: G.P. Putnam's Sons, 1975), p. 143 and *passim*. Broun also described himself as the 'highest paid reporter in the country'. Heywood Broun, 'Personal Journalism is Coming Back – Broun', *Editor and Publisher*, 15 March 1924, p. 7.

27. Broun, 'Sport for Art's Sake', p. 64.

28. Lowenthal, 'The Triumph of Mass Idols', pp. 131–2.

29. William Hazlitt, 'On Familiar Style' (1822), in *The Selected Writings of William Hazlitt*, vol. 6, *Table Talk*, ed. Duncan Wu (London: Pickering and Chatto, 1998), pp. 217–22.

30. Lee, *Defining 'New Yorker' Humor*, p. 40.

31. David Remnick, 'Introduction: Reporting It All', in Liebling, *Just Enough Liebling*, pp. ix–xxvi (p. xvi). After Joseph Pulitzer's death in 1911, his son Ralph took over the sensationalist *New York World* and subjected it to a 'remarkable transformation', which intensified after Herbert Bayard Swope became editor in 1921. Under Swope, the *World* quickly became famous for its 'gifted and exciting assemblage of writers' but began to 'slide' after 1925 when the *Herald Tribune* took on the mantle of the 'writer's paper'. Swope resigned in 1928 and in 1931 the *World* merged with the *New York Telegram*. See George H. Douglas, *The Golden Age of the Newspaper* (Westport, CT: Greenwood Press, 1999), pp. 238–43.

32. Raymond Sokolov, *Wayward Reporter: The Life of A. J. Liebling* (New York: Harper and Row, 1980), pp. 104–5.

33. Liebling is quoting Heywood Broun's 'The Orthodox Champion', reprinted in *Pieces of Hate and Other Enthusiasms*, pp. 149–52 (p. 152).

34. A. J. Liebling, 'Ahab and Nemesis', *The New Yorker*, 8 October 1955, pp. 104–20 (p. 104). Liebling is equally concerned to distance himself from 'the boys on the quarterlies' as from 'the boys on the dailies' (p. 110): the weekly *New Yorker* seems to get it just right. '*Journal-Americanese*' is a reference to the *New York Journal-American*, an afternoon paper, born of a merger between two Hearst publications, that ran from 1937 to 1966. See Ben Proctor, *William Randolph Hearst: The Later Years, 1911–1951* (New York: Oxford University Press, 2007), p. 211. More evidence that 'fistic' was both anachronistic and a cliché of early twentieth-century sportswriting can be found in James Joyce's parody of a boxing report in the 'Cyclops' section of *Ulysses* in which the Irish fighter, Bennett, is described as a 'fistic Eblanite'. See *Ulysses*, ed. H. W. Gabler (London: Penguin, 1986 [1922]), p. 261.

35. John Updike, 'Hub Fans Bid Kid Adieu', *The New Yorker*, 22 October 1960, pp. 109–31 (pp. 110, 126); Roger Angell, 'Distance', *The New Yorker*, 22 September 1980, pp. 83–127 (p. 121).

36. John Lardner, 'That Was Pugilism: Toledo, 1919', *The New Yorker*, 6 December 1947, pp. 71–86 (p. 71). Mary F. Corey makes a different point about these pieces, arguing that their primary purpose was to remind readers 'of the bad old times' of race relations and 'how far America had come'. See *The World Through a Monocle: 'The New Yorker' at Midcentury* (Cambridge, MA: Harvard University Press, 1999), pp. 87, 89.

37. A. J. Liebling, 'Introduction' to *The Sweet Science* (Harmondsworth: Penguin, 1982 [1956]), pp. 1–12 (pp. 5, 3).

38. A. J. Liebling, 'The Neutral Corner Art Group, *The New Yorker*, 18 December 1954, pp. 71–86 (p. 75).

39. Incidentally, no advertisements interrupted Henry Louis Gates's 'Net Worth', a detailed dissection of Michael Jordan and his endorsements; it was published in the 'Annals of Marketing', *The New Yorker*, 1 June 1998, pp. 48–61.

40. Liebling, 'Introduction' to *The Sweet Science*, p. 12.

41. A. J. Liebling, 'Long Toddle, Short Fight', *The New Yorker*, 30 May 1953, pp. 33–47 (p. 33); 'Nino and a Nanimal', *The New Yorker*, 7

August 1954, pp. 52–63 (p. 52); 'Debut of a Seasoned Artist', *The New Yorker*, 4 September 1954, pp. 44–56 (p. 44); 'The Neutral Corner Art Group', p. 71.

42. Liebling, 'Introduction' to *The Sweet Science*, p. 6. See Corey Ford, 'Highlights', *The New Yorker*, 21 Februrary 1925, p. 15.

43. David Remnick, 'Reporting It All: A. J. Liebling at One Hundred', *The New Yorker*, 29 March 2004, pp. 52-61 (p. 52).

44. Fred Warner, 'Afterword' to A. J. Liebling, *A Neutral Corner: Boxing Essays* (New York: North Point Press, 1990), pp. 239–45 (p. 239).

45. A. J. Liebling, 'An Artist Seeks Himself', *The New Yorker*, 23 May 1959, pp. 96–117 (p. 98).

46. Remnick, 'Introduction: Reporting It All', p. xi.

47. Ibid., p. xi; A. J. Liebling, *The Press* (New York: Pantheon, 1975 [1961]), p. 25.

48. Robert Warshaw, *The Immediate Experience* (Cambridge, MA: Harvard University Press, 2001), p. 75. Ten years earlier Dwight Macdonald argued that the magazine 'has its tone, to which its contributors keep with faithful ear' ('Laugh and Lie Down', p. 44).

49. With its detailed account of his journey to see a (cock)fight, 'Dead Game' (*The New Yorker*, 1 April 1950, pp. 34–45) is the Liebling piece most closely modelled on William Hazlitt's 'The Fight' (1822), the essay that Tom Wolfe names as 'Exhibit A' in the essayistic tradition of 'literary gentleman with a seat in the grandstand'. See 'The New Journalism', in *The New Journalism* (London: Picador, 1975 [1973]), pp. 15–68 (p. 58).

50. Hugh Bradley to H. W. Ross, 2 June 1930, New Yorker Records, B. 1928–1930.

51. H. W. Ross to Hugh Bradley, 2 July 1930, New Yorker Records, B. 1928–1930.

52. [Fred Wittner], 'Dead Pan Joe', *The New Yorker*, 3 October 1936, pp. 12–13 (p. 12). The piece is reprinted, and attributed to Wittner, in *The Fun of It: Stories from The Talk of the Town*, ed. Lillian Ross (New York: Modern Library, 2001), pp. 103–4.

53. [Wittner], 'Dead Pan Joe', p. 13.

54. Lillian Ross, 'Mays at St. Bernards', *The New Yorker*, 9 June 1973, pp. 25–6 (p. 25); also included in *The Fun of It*, ed. Ross, pp. 254–6.

55. 'Within the office precincts' Angell reputedly referred to his mother as Mrs White. See Brendan Gill, *Here at 'The 'New Yorker'* (London: William Heinemann, 1990 [1975]), p. 294.

56. Steve Kettmann, 'Roger Angell', *Salon*, 29 August 2000, available at <http://www.salon.com/2000/08/29/angell> (accessed 10 June 2014). Elsewhere, Angell said that it was he who had approached Shawn and 'asked to see what I could do if I went to a baseball game'. See George Plimpton, 'Talk with Roger Angell', *New York Times*, 15 May 1977, pp. 1–32 (p. 32).

57. Tom Wolfe cites Gay Talese's 1962 *Esquire* piece, 'Joe Louis: The King as a Middle-Aged Man', as a groundbreaking work of New Journalism, an example of the kind of 'stylish' work that could be produced if writers were 'allowed' greater freedom and a long lead time ('The New Journalism', p. 24). Talese, in turn, credits Carson McCullers's *New*

Yorker short story 'The Jockey' (23 August 1941) as his inspiration. See *The Silent Season of a Hero: The Sports of Gay Talese*, ed. Michael Rosenwald (New York: Walker and Co, 2010), pp. 1–16 (pp. 1–4).

58. Chris Smith, 'Influences: Roger Angell', *New York Magazine*, 20 May 2006, available at <http://nymag.com/arts/books/profiles/17043> (accessed 1 May 2014).

59. Roger Angell, 'The Old Folks Behind Home', *The New Yorker*, 7 April 1962, pp. 160–71.

60. Roger Angell, 'Foreword', *The Summer Game* (London: Sportspages, 1987 [1972]), pp. vii–viii (p. viii).

61. Roger Angell, 'The Interior Stadium', *The New Yorker*, 20 February 1971, pp. 92–9 (p. 92).

62. Ibid., p. 92.

63. Ibid.

64. Ibid., pp. 94–5.

65. Roger Angell, 'Foreword', p. vii.

66. Ibid., p. vii; Ross, 'Announcing a New Weekly Magazine', p. 439; Christopher B. Daly, *Covering America: A Narrative History of a Nation's Journalism* (Amherst: University of Massachusetts Press, 2012), p. 202. Accepting an award for his critical writing in 1984, John Updike spoke 'in defense of the amateur reader' whose perspective was distinct from both journalists and academics. See *Higher Gossip: Essays and Criticism*, ed. Christopher Carduff (London: Hamish Hamilton, 2011), pp. 422–3.

67. Angell, 'The Interior Stadium', p. 92.

68. A. James Memmott, 'Wordsworth in the Bleachers', *Journal of American Culture*, 9.4 (1982), 52–6.

69. Roger Angell, 'Early Innings', *The New Yorker*, 24 February 1992, pp. 84–92 (p. 84).

70. Roger Angell, 'In the Counting House', *The New Yorker*, 10 May 1976, pp. 106–27 (p. 108); Roger Angell, 'Season Lightly', *The New Yorker*, 16 July 1973, pp. 50–65 (p. 52).

71. Angell, 'In the Counting House', p. 122.

72. 'One of the great pleasures of writing about baseball', Angell told George Plimpton, 'is that it provides me with such a radical change' (Plimpton, 'Talk with Roger Angell', p. 1).

73. From the age of eleven, Updike said, his 'sole ambition was to make the *New Yorker* myself'. See Jane Howard, 'Can a Nice Novelist Finish First?' (1966), repr. in *Conversations with John Updike*, ed. James Plath (Jackson: University Press of Mississippi, 1994), pp. 9–17 (p. 12). The closest Angell came to Barthelmian *jeu d'esprit* was in a series of pieces collected in 1970 as *A Day in the Life of Roger Angell*.

74. He also described it as 'the most celebrated baseball piece ever'. Roger Angell, 'The Fadeaway', *The New Yorker*, 9 February 2009, pp. 38–9.

75. John Updike, 'More Light on Delft', *New York Review of Books*, 18 February 1999, reprinted in *Higher Gossip*, pp. 224–31 (p. 230).

76. John Updike, 'Introduction', Henry David Thoreau, *Walden* (Princeton, NJ: Princeton University Press, 2004), pp. ix–xxiv (p. xix).

77. Ibid., p. xxiii; Roger Angell, 'Romance', *The New Yorker*, 26 May 2003, pp. 74–9 (p. 75); Angell, 'The Interior Stadium', p. 92

78. Updike, 'Introduction', p. xxiii.

79. Smith, 'Influences: Roger Angell'.

80. Jack Olsen, 'The Black Athlete – A Shameful Story; Part I: The Cruel Deception', *Sports Illustrated*, 1 July 1968, pp. 12–27 (p.15), available at <http://sportsillustrated.cnn.com/vault/article/magazine/MAG1081325> (accessed 1 May 2014).

81. John Updike, 'Tao in the Yankee Stadium Bleachers (What comes from reading Chuang-Tzu between innings)', *The New Yorker*, 18 August 1956, p. 28.

82. Angell, 'Distance', p. 92.

83. Roger Angell, 'Down the Drain', *The New Yorker*, 23 June 1975, pp. 42–59 (p. 48).

84. Angell, 'Distance', pp. 96, 98.

85. Angell, 'The Interior Stadium', p. 97.

86. William Hazlitt, 'The Indian Jugglers', in *The Selected Writings of William Hazlitt*, vol. 6, *Table Talk*, pp. 67–77 (pp. 68–9).

87. Angell, 'Down the Drain', p. 42.

88. Angell, 'Distance', p. 116

89. Angell, 'Early Innings', p. 88; Angell, 'Distance', p. 184.

90. Angell, 'Early Innings', p. 87; Roger Angell, 'The Web of the Game', *The New Yorker*, 20 July 1981, pp. 96–109 (p. 106). Updike explores Ted Williams's desire 'to sever the game from the ground of paid spectatorship'. 'Hub Fans Bid Kid Adieu', p. 109.

91. Updike, 'Tao in the Yankee Stadium', p. 28.

92. Roger Angell, 'Before the Fall', *The New Yorker*, 26 March 2001, pp. 72–82 (p. 74).

93. Angell, 'Distance', p. 122.

94. Ibid., p. 127.

95. Angell, 'Down the Drain', p. 57.

96. Angell, 'The Web of the Game', p. 106.

97. Angell, 'Early Innings', p. 92. Angell's anxiety about intrusion distinguishes him from another of the most celebrated of *New Yorker* feature writers on sport, John McPhee. McPhee's 'Levels of the Game' presented a 'double profile' of Arthur Ashe and Clark Graebner through an almost stroke by stroke, present-tense account of their 1968 US Open semi-final and he has the players 'think' and 'remember' all sorts of things about their lives, and America, while tossing the ball or adjusting their rackets. See *The New Yorker*, 7 June 1969, pp. 45–111, and 14 June 1969, pp. 44–81. When it was published as a book, Robert Lipsyte said that it 'may be the high point of American sports journalism' (*New York Times*, 4 December 1969).

98. Angell, 'The Interior Stadium', p. 92.

99. Roger Angell, 'Agincourt and After', *The New Yorker*, 17 November 1975, pp. 146–68 (p. 167). Hans Ulrich Gumbrecht contrasts the 'beholder' of sport with the 'television viewer', who is synonymous with the 'potential customer'. See *In Praise of Athletic Beauty* (Cambridge, MA: The Belknap Press, 2006), pp. 8, 144.

100. Angell, 'Agincourt and After', p. 164.
101. Roger Angell, 'Tiger Tiger', *The New Yorker*, 3 December 1984, pp. 54–99 (pp. 82–3); Roger Angell, 'In the Country', *The New Yorker*, 17 August 1981, pp. 41–78 (p. 41).
102. Ben Yagoda, *About Town: The 'New Yorker' and the World it Made* (New York: Scribner, 2000), pp. 43, 105. Alexis de Tocqueville, observing American journalism in the 1830s, argued that a newspaper or magazine 'always represents an association of which its regular readers make up the membership'. See *Democracy in America*, vol. 2, trans. Gerald Beven (London: Penguin, 2003 [1840]), p. 603.
103. Renata Adler, *Gone: The Last Days of 'The New Yorker'* (New York: Simon & Schuster, 1999), p. 48.
104. Richard Ford, quoting his wife, in 'Introduction' to Roger Angell, *Game Time: A Baseball Companion* (Orlando: Harvest Books, 2003), pp. vii–xiv (p. xiv).

Chapter 10

The *New Yorker* Life of Hannah Arendt's Mind

Duncan Kelly

In the annals of *The New Yorker*, the 'Reporter at Large' feature has been central, often dealing with major subjects of truly global significance, and occasionally taking up the entire magazine itself. Exceptionally famous instances include John Hersey's 1946 discussion of 'Hiroshima', and his nearly equally influential (in hindsight) and only slightly earlier account of JFK's wartime exploits, 'Survival' from 1944. Nearly twenty years later, Rachel Carson's 'Silent Spring' of 1962 transformed public awareness in another way, as did James Baldwin's 'Letter from a Region of my Mind' in November of the same year. Related magazine sections like the 'Annals of Crime' also come close to the genre, in the form, for example, of Truman Capote's dramatic piece of 1965 non-fiction journalism, 'In Cold Blood'. Indeed all of these deeply researched and imaginatively engaged works present, in readable and compelling prose, the sort of deeply hued argument that only a really generous publisher can provide with space, research assistance and superlative copy-editing as well as famously fastidious fact-checking. Yet although each of these essays transformed entire fields of inquiry (nuclear devastation, environmentalism, race relations, literary non-fiction), few have matched the provocative impact of Hannah Arendt's series of five features concerning 'Eichmann in Jerusalem', published between February and March in 1963. In her case, moreover, the fact that the Eichmann trial was covered under the 'Reporter at Large' feature is particularly appropriate.

Along with the fact-checkers and the typeface, the 'Reporter at Large' feature is probably the magazine's most recognizable global stamp. Part of the reason it was transformative of public journalism almost from the beginning was that the reporter herself was so much a part of the feature. Its polemical and political thrust developed in tandem with the editorial direction provided by William Shawn, and exploded in the 1960s.[1] The reportage features are highbrow and panoramic, typically concern matters of real public significance, but are equally partisan, written from a particular point of view, and designed for impact. They are judgements, forms of criticism often as recognisable for the style of engagement as for the engagement itself. Through the monocle, that is to say, you are invited to engage in a form of spectatorship whose particular form of envisioning is designed to make you imagine a world from the point of view of other people. That imaginative leap is required in order to enter into this other world, and to engage sympathetically as well as critically with it. And in this, of course, *The New Yorker* is heir both in substance and form to a great heritage of English-speaking periodicals, designed to update the classically eighteenth-century vision of the spectator as witty, ironic, sceptical and conversationally engaging. Indeed, one might say that the direct lineage of the *New Yorker* monocle can be traced right back to *The Spectator* of Addison and Steele, and particularly their most famous series of essays on 'The Pleasures of the Imagination'. Bearing that sort of intellectual inheritance in mind helps to frame the question of why, despite the fact that Hannah Arendt rarely modulated her tone of engagement whatever audience she was writing for, it was particularly appropriate that her analysis of Eichmann eventually appeared in *The New Yorker*. The features helped to crystallise aspects of her ideas about the relationship between thought, imagination and judgement, and in particular how these relationships applied to political questions. That relationship of criticism to judgement is, of course, a very personal act of self-presentation on her part, but it clearly remains a distinctive element of the 'Reporter at Large' feature.

Arendt's essays, when published in book form, carried the subtitle 'the banality of evil' that made them infamous on a broader, more global scale than the more local disturbances among New York intellectuals that the magazine publication provoked. Her analysis of the Nazi bureaucrat has been incessantly studied ever since.[2] That subsidiary phrase had a less prominent position in the *New Yorker* text than it would subsequently claim in the book, though Arendt had written of Eichmann's stupidity, incapacity to think, and his terrifying ordinariness.[3] If the phrase alone sealed a dramatic fate for her text in the history of twentieth-century ideas, its equally polemical but not so stylised presentation in *The New Yorker* brought forth what most commentators refer to as a 'civil war' amongst the so-called 'family' of intellectuals and partisans from left and right in New York.[4]

Arendt had long been known as a political writer and journalist in New York. Shortly after her own forced emigration from Germany and escape from an internment camp in France, she had arrived in New York in 1941, writing and teaching to earn money. She covered topics from Zionism and the political ideas of Theodor Herzl, through to broader questions of politics and political commitment in a world still struggling to understand the nature of the totalitarian threat to modern representative democracy.[5] The two themes would occupy her political writing for several years, but are initially assayed in pieces written for magazines and periodicals that were often in direct competition with *The New Yorker*. For example, in the American-Jewish journal *Commentary* during the later 1940s and 1950s, she was publishing essays on the nascent Jewish homeland and politics in Israel, attacking the re-alignment of modern Zionism with modern nationalism, as well as reviewing contemporary political books quite extensively. In *Partisan Review*, however, she wrote about more general political subjects in the aftermath of war and destruction, even trailing her panoramic survey *The Origins of Totalitarianism* within its pages.[6] Calibrating the sorry future of political parties in an age of nationalism and national-chauvinism, focusing on the nature of political fear, and thinking about the relationship between understanding and politics, were central to Arendt's writing during this decade. In *Partisan Review* again, she wrote about the 'alien' prophecy inherent in the claims of history to provide causal explanations of past actions, when it is in fact only through the present that we can bring 'the past into being'.[7] From that premise, she tried to disentangle historical from political understanding. Because politics always involves the creation of something new, or is a new beginning, it is always uncertain and always requires imagination, sympathy and judgement. Furthermore, this

> understanding becomes the other side of action, namely that form of cognition, in distinction from many others, by which acting men [. . .] eventually can come to terms with what irrevocably happened and be reconciled with what unavoidably exists. As such, understanding is a strange enterprise.[8]

It is also a strange enterprise to the extent that our best guide to understanding our present political predicament has therefore to be grounded in larger, historically orientated claims about the development of modern politics and especially the development of modern political ideas. Understanding is never complete, because it is a human and therefore fallible enterprise, and history doesn't provide clear lessons. But if politics is about new beginnings whose understanding will only become clearer through activity and judgement, then politics is premised on the fact of human difference, or in Arendt's terms, plurality, which can be thought about historically. Plurality is threatened by the attempt to impose control, or to impose answers to political questions that claim legitimacy as truths about the world, or as being the only right answer; in part, this is the threat posed by modern totalitarianism. It was also the problem facing both Israel in a global system of states, and the European states-system threatened by 'civil war', as foreign and domestic politics merged into one another during and after the Second World War. Federation held the promise of a solution, but it couldn't be guaranteed whether in Israel and Palestine or in Europe.[9] In fact, by the time these early writings fused together, Arendt's writings combined a genealogy of nation-state violence in *The Origins of Totalitarianism*, tracing the emergence of totalitarian national politics out of anti-Semitism, nationalism and race-imperialism, with a philosophical critique of some of the dominant ideas of human agency and judgement, in particular those of Hegel and Marx, from *The Human Condition*.[10] On the basis of the wider successes these books and essays brought about, she would be able to pitch her idea to cover Eichmann's trial in Jerusalem to *The New Yorker* and be taken seriously.

Partisan Review was a more polemical and hard-nosed political magazine than *The New Yorker*, and Arendt had written much for it before 1963. When news spilled out that Mossad had captured Adolf Eichmann in Argentina in May 1960 and that he was to stand trial in Israel, its editor, Norman Podhoretz, hoped to send Arendt to cover the proceedings. However, the magazine couldn't afford the costs. Arendt pitched the idea to *The New Yorker*, and William Shawn decided to support and to fund the proposal. He took a particularly hands-on approach to coaxing out the eventual text of her essay, but remained lenient with deadlines (necessarily, since Arendt had had a car crash, and her husband was seriously ill, not long after the trial). Part of the generally accepted and publicly presented justification for her interest was personal; having written much about the Nazis, this would be a real chance to engage in an imaginative reconstruction of a judicial scene, focusing on the ideas and actions of a crucial cog in the bureaucratic machine that organised the death-transportations, and to think about how one might engage in the critical interpretative activity of understanding and judging him at all. Put in the retrospective terms of a reconstruction of Arendt's interests, there could hardly have been a more appropriate testing-ground for her own theoretical and political ideas, and perhaps this lies behind her oft-quoted and apparently odd-sounding remark, written to her close American friend Mary McCarthy about the work, that she wrote her text in a state of near 'euphoria'.[11] If she was euphoric, however, others were less so, particularly the rather acerbic Norman Podhoretz for whom this was a more obviously Jewish rerun of earlier substantial disagreements with both *The New Yorker* and Hannah Arendt about race.[12]

Many interpreters have noted the connections between what we might call the judicial imaginary of the trial and its reportage, which in combination with the emotional or affective politics that structured the enterprise from beginning to end made it such a highly charged affair.[13] Eichmann, arbiter-designer of the efficient networks that sent vast numbers of people to their deaths, sat on trial in front of three Israeli judges, from behind a bulletproof glass box where the spectacle of the trial was broadcast to the world's media. All in turn sat in judgement, but as the Israeli leader David Ben-Gurion famously noted, the 'fate of Eichmann, the person, has no interest for me whatsoever. What is important is the spectacle.'[14] That spectacle had its own unique procedural requirements (shortly before the trial, the 'Eichmann-law' was passed to allow a trial to continue even if the defendant was to plead guilty). It also had its own narrative logic, where according to Ben-Gurion, the new sovereign people of Israel could redeem 'the blood of six-million Jews'. As a show trial it was, of course, a highly political event, deeply bound up with a desire on the part of the Israeli political leadership to have Eichmann stand trial as a representative for the history of anti-Semitism generally, and the obscenities of Nazi ideology particularly.[15] The first thing that Arendt did, however, was to challenge this out loud. It brought her into clear conflict with the symbolic high-politics of Israeli statecraft when she claimed that as a single man, Eichmann could be neither the embodiment of an entire history of anti-Semitism, nor a placeholder for the entire Third Reich. To think he could be was a category mistake in terms of the relationship between understanding, judicial guilt and political judgement. To think that he should be was indicative of what Arendt thought of as a catastrophic failure of political understanding. It was a misunderstanding wrought by the violent ideological coagulant of totalitarianism.

From inside his glass box, Eichmann looked every inch the Vacuum Oil Company salesman he had been before accepting with such diligence his new vocation in the Nazi elite. The incongruity between his appearance, speech and guilt was indeed jarring, and brought home the disjuncture for Arendt between the man, his actions, and his understanding (or more pointedly, his utter lack of understanding) of those actions. His supremely bureaucratic banality had a deeper fascination for her, though, than the thought that his defence would be the Kantian-inspired claim that he was simply following orders. That was no defence at all. Eichmann was, rather, an unthinking individual. This is a highly charged criticism for Arendt, given that for her, thought is also a strange activity, requiring a sense of oneself as part of a world with others in it. That interconnectedness drives a certain way of being, or comportment, in the world and it motivates our action. And if thought becomes the necessary ingredient for activity, at the same time it is an active form of judgement about what one should do (it involves the imagination) and what one has done (it involves an unending quest for understanding). When applied to the sphere of open possibility that is the genuinely political realm, its expression is grounded by our connectedness as citizens who share a world together, who make claims by justifying thoughts and plans to one another through various institutions, and whose own plans and thoughts are rooted in the very messiness that is the activity of living together in communities. Eichmann's 'almost total inability ever to look at anything from the other fellow's point of view' was precisely the problem, just as it had been his problem while a travelling salesman.[16] To be able to think and act differently, and to remember shared histories if a political society or polity is to remain healthy and flourish, was absolutely necessary, and Eichmann's totalitarian mindset precluded such plurality. These were claims Arendt amplified elsewhere. For example, in 'Society and Culture', a contemporary essay from 1960 and published in *Daedalus*, Arendt explored the intersubjective foundations of all forms of judgement and reiterated what she saw as the 'public world' connections between artistic and political judgement. She considered them still further in 'Freedom and Politics', from the *Chicago Review* of the same year, emphasising even more emphatically her claims about the relationships between political thought, political action and political judgement.[17]

In 'Freedom and Politics', moreover, Arendt reprised her earlier claims about political agency. Politics, and hence the agonistic public sphere of competition, reputation, action and excellence, is simply action, and action always entails the conditions of rebirth ('natality'), or more prosaically, the possibility of always being otherwise. It has much in common with Aristotle's account of political deliberation. For deliberation, or more specifically, deliberative rhetoric and political persuasion, is what is required in public in order for politics to function adequately. Running these claims together means that freedom simply *is* politics. The relationship between the two spheres is not about freedom of the will, nor is it a claim about the truth of the relationship. Instead, it is about living together and acting together, where action is something that is imaginatively developed and considered in public, and which in turn is judged publicly. Politics and the political sphere are therefore explicitly opposed to both the private sphere and the 'social' question.[18] Politics is not principally concerned with questions of happiness or justice, for those are derivative upon the principal questions of politics, yet another thought that Arendt develops explicitly from the political philosophy of Immanuel Kant, who was so influential for her thinking about the nature of judgement from the 1950s through to the 1970s.[19] For both, in fact, this meant simply a reiteration of a classic position on the primacy of *salus populi* understood in the broadest possible history of western political thought. Public safety and political order first, justice, happiness and welfare second.

That we might now think the most precious political freedom we have is the freedom to withdraw from politics, to be represented (and to have our politics done for us by others, just as rich men might hire stewards), has been a conventional worry about the nature of modern political freedom at least since the French Revolution. Benjamin Constant outlined it very clearly in 1819.[20] Played out fully, it means we pay more attention to moral or economic freedoms, rather than political freedom. In the light of totalitarianism, however, Arendt finds this particularly troubling. She writes that it is more difficult to think rather than to act under totalitarianism because thinking requires the other to be present at least in the imagination, while acting without thinking is perfectly possible, easier even. This, after all, is what Eichmann illustrates. Anyone can be a murderer in the banal sense of just acting. What Eichmann could not see was the world from the perspective of other people, and that personal incapacity was the hook around which Arendt wrote up her pieces on the trial and its voluminous documentation, with reference to wider debates about the nature and extent of collaboration and resistance to the Nazi terror. Her text was delivered later than expected, after she had returned to New York and read through the vast transcripts of the trial, but still (given the amount of reading and given her other commitments), she filed relatively quickly, and as was common with Shawn, he hardly edited the piece at all once he'd taken delivery of it: indeed, 'there is no documented instance', writes Ben Yagoda, 'of Shawn ever reading a draft of an article and either cutting it himself or asking the writer to do so'.[21] Plenty of others would.

Gershom Scholem famously wrote that Arendt had gone too far, suggesting that she was like a self-hating Jew.[22] The point motivated her own development of the idea of the political theorist as pariah, offering uncomfortable judgements in the face of power. Many just found her a pariah.[23] Pilloried as an anti-Zionist Jew, the irony is that she had held that view for a long time, making things clear by 1948 in rejecting the idea of enforced statelessness for the Palestinian people. It was a role that forever tarnished her reputation amongst a certain staple of the New York 'family', and her 'Reporter at Large' pieces unleashed a purging, or a 'civil war amongst its Jewish intellectuals'.[24] Her sarcasm was taken as the sarcasm of the intellectual, which didn't play well with more overtly radical public moralists from other magazines.

Norman Podhoretz's response was a frustrated essay, which tried achingly to be original, subtitled the 'Perversity of Brilliance'.[25] Simultaneously Irving Howe, in his own response, 'Hannah Arendt and *The New Yorker*', worked up a stereotypical critique of the liberal elitism paraded by *The New Yorker*, although he did pause to wonder whether his own response wasn't equally just a knee-jerk cultural reaction.[26] Most other critics didn't even stop to think about how jerky their immediate replies were, even if a wider cognitive dissonance between the significance and substance of Arendt's subject matter and the glossy adverts that made up so much of the magazine was quite literally apparent. Contemporary readers may have skimmed over the adverts of *The New Yorker* just as the magazine's readers do today. It is perhaps historical distance that makes more noticeable the dissonance between Arendt's writing about the increasing zeal of Eichmann's transportation projects, and the one and a half pages of advertisements for high-end make-up and designer millinery that intrudes on her report.[27] Whether Arendt herself cared about the mixture of a serious editorial message and the glamorous advertising of *The New Yorker*, mixing 'a half page of crunchy goodness' after a page of 'thought', is another question.[28] But any historical reconstruction of Arendt's texts on these themes at least has to recognise the incongruity, just as she would have understood it given her account of the relationship between historical and political understanding.

In the archives at the New York Public Library, you can see the original drafts of Arendt's work for *The New Yorker*. The papers are the yellow sheaves that the typists sent to Shawn after manuscripts came in, and you can see Shawn's hand all over the text. But this is not present in such a way as to suggest radical editorial surgery. Unsurprisingly, both he and his editorial colleagues recognised the panoramic survey as well as the biting sarcasm and irony of Arendt's work, and they also of course picked up on the specific criticisms she had made of the Jewish Councils (*Judenräte*), directly claiming their complicity with parts of the Nazi transportation networks. What the editors proposed, and what Arendt accepted, were in most cases amendments to style rather than substance, with occasional modulations in tone. As the only other person to compare the manuscripts for the magazine with the published text in the book, *Eichmann in Jerusalem*, Allison Hoffman has noted that the *New Yorker* pieces are structurally clearer, and more tightly presented and argued, than the slightly baggier book. In part, this reflects Arendt's style too; once she had written a piece, she was reluctant to look at it again, so the changes made by *The New Yorker* were accepted while the script of the manuscript sent to the publishers didn't receive quite the same treatment.[29]

The sarcasm that is part of 'Eichmann in Jerusalem' has also often been misunderstood. For there is more than a hint of irony in Arendt's rendition of Eichmann's testimony about his relationship with Judaism, for example, when he avowedly became a 'convert' to the need for a Jewish cause, he said, after reading Theodor Herzl. All too quickly, however, this moved into another commitment, to bureaucratic efficiency in promulgating a violent final solution to the *Judenfrage*. Shawn obviously knew that the piece was going to generate controversy, but even if, as Yagoda has claimed, in the early 1960s he was explicitly trying to make waves with the 'Reporter at Large' features, he surely could not have expected quite the vitriolic attacks Arendt's piece received. Yet as an editor he had long given his charges their head, asking them specifically to speak about issues from their point of view, without pulling punches and without fear or favour. As I have suggested, his editorial notes do not often suggest cuts or extensions affecting substance at all, but only really concern some of the more aggressive forms of language that Arendt uses. It is possible to make much of this, but really it seems that Shawn was as willing to let Arendt's text stand in the round as he was for those of his other prized reporters. He liked it, admiring its conceptual focus and understanding its difficulties, and commending its cerebral focus on judgement, truth and political action. Shawn's obituary of Arendt reiterates his reasons for such support, seeing in her 'awesome mind' one of those great characters 'who are empowered to inch human thought forward'.[30]

For Arendt, of course, there was no question about Eichmann's guilt. It was straightforward and clear-cut. In the context of a political show trial as well as trial for manslaughter, though, she wondered whether the tactics of the Israeli state might come to backfire. She did so, moreover, from within the perspective of a long and deep-seated engagement with what she called the 'great tradition' of the history of political thought, and in particular the place of American development within that story. One might argue, in fact, that because her essay was written up specifically for *The New Yorker*, this American dimension formed part of her underlying assumptions about how to present her argument about totalitarianism and the problem of evil in Europe.[31] It would align well with her contemporary writing about the nature of politics, violence and sovereignty in America during the 1960s and into the 1970s, a period when the 'imperial republic' went to war, and *The New Yorker* 'became most overtly political'.[32] It is towards that development that my discussion now turns.

The 'imperial republic' for Arendt was a new species of American political development, one that signified how far the nation had come in forgetting its origins. Unlike the French Revolution, where a nation was constructed (she claimed) out of an abstract equation of absolute sovereignty with absolute equality and rooted in violence, the American construction of a new secular order (*novus ordo saeclorum*) had none of the so-called terror of natural right. In her equation of revolution with a process of gradual secularisation, the American creation of a new model of politics had a different character. The series of seminars she gave at Princeton in 1959, and published as *On Revolution* soon after, were her principal contribution to this key opposition between theory and practice. The American Revolution was exceptional, because it used little of European political theory about sovereignty. That which it did use, primarily Montesquieu, was itself an exception to the gradual development of the great tradition of political theory accounted for in her work. The French Revolution, by contrast, was exceptional in a different way, in terms of both its epic scale and force. The American rejection of sovereignty in favour of the creation of a federal nation, underpinned by a notion of the people, was the real novelty. The memory of that novelty bound its people together in a radically different way, but that rootedness would soon be under threat with the development of an 'imperial republic' engaged in warfare abroad, and large-scale corruption at home. The precipitant risks to the American polity in the later 1950s seemed to be over-determined by the threat of nuclear annihilation, while the period from Vietnam to Watergate told its own story. The basic problem of constitutional and political memory remained Arendt's focus in American terms, while her reconsideration of the French revolutionary legacy lay in the background, as both an explicit and implicit challenge to older German political theorists like Carl Schmitt, whom she thought the 'most consistent and most able defender of the notion of sovereignty'.[33] It was an account of American exceptionalism.

The risks posed to traditional models of politics that prioritised revolution (or rapid secularisation) were clear, so how did revolution make politics safe for democracy in the new federal nation? According to Arendt, through its unique process of secularisation. In the American case, the justification for revolution could be found in the religious covenants governing early settler communities. So how could covenants be made to overcome religion through revolution to bring into the world a secular form of American politics? The answer would come through a distinctively American defence of rights and liberties (and concomitantly, a concern with the issue of civil disobedience) as a new form of political theology, one made safe for secular-minded republican politics. The right to have rights in common was the paradigmatic political solution, and was a secularisation of the theological or covenantal foundation of the new republic. This American republican moment, according to Arendt, was unique precisely because it secularised politics on the basis of covenants that were originally based on mutuality and brotherhood, and not divine exclusivity. From that basis, her wider theory of revolutionary transformation towards modern secular politics therefore became possible, even if (as many have claimed) it is historically dubious in fact. Her normative concern with the fate of the imperial republic and its foundations in a process of secularisation shaped her analysis of contemporary American politics, giving it a distinctive texture into which more immediate issues could be folded.

The combination of technologies capable of mass destruction with an ideology of Cold War liberalism made Arendt's concern about the relationship between nuclear annihilation, foreign warfare and domestic politics a central background problem. As should now be clear, for Arendt, politics is a sphere of plurality rather than unitary sovereignty, and this opposition structures her account of the politics of the 1950s and 1960s, including the Hungarian Revolution of 1956 and the civil rights demonstrations at Little Rock. This is therefore the necessary background to understanding her wider claims in *The New Yorker* both about Eichmann, and latterly about truth and politics. When she noted that the sphere of the political was increasingly directed towards foreign affairs and war, she worried that this was a disaster waiting to happen for the American republic. Thinking about politics as the primacy of foreign policy was the legacy of the aggressive wars of defence undertaken by the French revolutionaries. But America had its own alternative intellectual sources for constructing a different form of 'realism' about politics. Somewhat counter-intuitively, in fact, Arendt sought to uncover a legacy of Roman thinking about politics that was plural and legalistically inclusive, claiming that America was the country that had updated a Roman politics of law based on citizenship, under a federal structure that avoided talk of sovereignty, and which, crucially, was anti-imperial.[34]

According to Arendt once more, the 'American Experiment' (the title of a lecture she gave in Boston in 1975, subsequently reprinted in the *New York Review of Books* as 'Home to Roost') was unique.[35] While it offered a pathway around European juridical-sovereign models of politics, Vietnam and Watergate threatened to short-circuit this domestic tradition, turning it into another form of anti-politics in which logics of warfare and corruption threatened to transform legitimate political criticism and judgement into a language of universal moral threat and moralised opprobrium. There could be no possible compromise or political disagreement between the friends and enemies of humanity, as the enemies of America were being presented, and the danger was that America would fall into the sort of moralised, utopian anti-politics that signified post-revolutionary European political thought, at least as she presented it.[36]

Arendt wrote about such political issues at the same time as she also recovered the lives and works of friends and comrades in *The New Yorker*. Her pieces on Brecht (5 November 1966) and Walter Benjamin (19 October 1968) bring together a political sensitivity and a talent for combining personal and biographical judgement with political critique. They worked well in the 'Reflections' category that Shawn had developed as a 'rubric' for essays in the magazine.[37] Her essays were interspersed with a more general theoretical attack on the fraught relationship between 'Truth and Politics', originally prepared for a meeting of the American Political Science Association, but which (and this must be a first for an academic conference paper) appeared in *The New Yorker* on 25 February 1967. It was in part reprised in a *New York Times* piece on American politics and violence the following April.[38] Her claims about 'truth' are interesting. Politics is not, and cannot be, about truth, because truth is an attempt to close down judgement by proclaiming ontological certainty, and politics is not about certainty. It is instead about persuasion and muddling through, trying to create and make the world new. That is the lesson of historically minded political theory as Arendt understood it.

She went further, because there is a sense in which for politics to be present at all, a genuine common sense, or *sensus communis*, must exist. Political judgement cannot be grounded in anything other than this shared, common life. Yet if this public life is eroded by an image-obsessed media politics on the one hand, and structurally compromised on the other by a focus on individual or social rights rather than the collective freedom of a political society, then the primacy of the social question will effectively dethrone politics completely. This is how she read the fate of nineteenth-century European politics, but her rather broad concern led to some perverse contemporary judgements, particularly about race and civil disobedience. If *The New Yorker* had been pilloried on the left for its apparently glib intellectualism concerning racism in the South, Arendt's take on race politics and violence sounds *prima facie* odd. The civil rights movement, Rosa Parks, and the events of Little Rock, are all 'social', rather than 'political' questions. Here Arendt's apparently heroic vision of politics as public practice seemed overly demanding for some, particularly at a moment where Ralph Ellison's *Invisible Man* (1952) and his wider commentary on the necessary qualities of visibility in the public sphere for a healthy political community,

seemed to offer a more profound vision. His was an account of citizenship based on the common interest of friends living well together, when
there is a bond of trust between citizens and state. It looks more prosaic
and certainly less heroic as a model for thinking about contemporary
politics.[39] But if there is a general sense in which Arendt seems to idolise
the polis as a model for modern politics, in a more conventional sense
her reflections on the civil rights movement again presuppose a distinction between Europe and America, which 'is not a nation-state in the
European sense and never was'.[40]

Arendt's point seems to be that compartmentalising racism as a
Southern problem and as a rights problem is foolish, because it is a
problem for America as a whole: the problem of how it is even possible
to think that you have a politics based on both plurality and political
equality, given the very visible segregation of huge swathes of the population. She wrote her own 'Reflections on Little Rock' for *Commentary*,
but it was thought too outré for publication there. *Dissent* printed it
instead, adding a critical preface, a year later. Visibility and audibility
are not the same, she writes, noting the political unimportance of voice
without presence. Being observed whilst simultaneously remaining invisible in the public realm is the strange position occupied by non-citizens
in a society predicated on equal citizenship for all. So, she writes, the
question of the colour line and race concerns 'not the well-being of the
Negro population alone, but the survival of the Republic'.[41] Legalistic
measures to enforce the claim rights of some citizens alone, however
well intentioned, are misguided because the problem goes deeper. In
a sense, civil rights are not enough, when what has gone wrong is
that 'moderate' and 'law abiding' citizens, hitherto the backbone of a
Republic, let the streets be governed by mob rule. This is the political
problem, because what 'equality is to the body politic, discrimination is
to society'.[42] Discrimination in the social sphere is in principle fine; in
the political sphere, it is a cancer, and the question of the boundaries of
public and private need to be carefully policed. That was (and is) a task
of the non-sovereign model of those checks, balances and boundaries
enshrined within the American revolutionary secular heritage. But that
was (and is) a task that has become confused.

For Arendt, there are various ways of learning these lessons and
keeping them in mind. Some 'outsiders' can show us the possibilities of
independence and creativity within political societies – one reason why
she cherishes, for example, the *sui generis* 'pearl diver' Walter Benjamin,
the unluckiest original in the rogues' gallery of critical theory. His essays
on collecting, on language and translation are lovingly touched upon by
Arendt in an essay that takes up over ninety pages (including adverts) of

The New Yorker.[43] The manuscript notes about her piece on Benjamin are available too, but as with most of Arendt's notes in *The New Yorker* archives, they turn out to add little to our knowledge of the formation of her ideas. Even when there are (as there are here) several versions of the text, Arendt's ideas were rarely transformed in the editorial process.[44] What her lack of attention to the specifics of the *New Yorker* demographic indicates, especially when seen in comparison with her numerous other essays, editorials and opinion pieces, is that she wrote however she wanted to, whatever the subject and audience. This makes it all the more important to think about her *New Yorker* writing from the perspective of the magazine itself, and of its editor. Hannah Arendt was, quite simply, admired and feted by *The New Yorker*. The only piece in the archives critical of her is a review of the curious book she wrote on Rahel Varnhagen, offered by George Steiner. That review was 'killed' – paid for, but never published.[45] In fact it seems that Arendt's connections to the local New York scene, when allied to the lustre of her European philosophical background, helped lay the groundwork for the increasingly highbrow and political stance the magazine would take from the later 1960s onwards. From her perspective, writing for *The New Yorker* allowed her to express her belief that the relationship between judgement and political critique could be very personal indeed. For instance, her focus on the 'pariah' frames a forgiving account of some of the crudities of Brecht's politics, while in remembering Auden, the subject of one of her last *New Yorker* pieces, his deep recognition of the distance between poetry and political consequence is flagged as a mark of his genius.[46] Both are models of a kind.

The principal way Arendt suggests that we should think about these lessons and issues, however, is to return to the history of political ideas. In terms of understanding America, that meant a return to Tocqueville, and in this she was in line with contemporary accounts of the 'Imperial Presidency' offered by Arthur Schlesinger Jr., and of the imperial age more broadly outlined by Raymond Aron. Schlesinger anatomised the increasing centralisation of presidential power, but offered reflections on the cycles of American history that were always ultimately grounded in Tocqueville.[47] What makes Arendt's insertion into this context interesting is that she too resorted to Tocqueville in order to understand the question of civil disobedience, and its peculiar status in America. This was the topic of a fifth piece for *The New Yorker* on 12 September 1970, soon republished in *Crises of the Republic*.

Keeping faith with her rejection of the concept of sovereignty as the foundation of American politics, she worried that the contemporary imperial republic was being discussed in terms of sovereignty and reason of state by the back door. The 'political question' had changed.[48] In her terms, though, civil disobedience remained a peculiarly American problem because of its unique political foundation. For Arendt, civil disobedience in the American context is simply an updating of Tocqueville's concern with vibrant associational life, in the form of crises and protests provoked by attacks on the constitution by an overbearing executive.[49] In this, again, the question of race and racial violence was paramount, as was the problem of Vietnam.

Arendt notes in the *Times* that American violence is not nationalistic, but that it is racist. Its racism feeds on impotence, and impotence stems from the decline of the public sphere. That slippery slope of decline endangers the very existence of the republic, and therefore the 'real danger', she thinks, is not violence itself, but a massive white backlash against legitimate expressions of frustration and rage at such impotence, whether black or white. That might roll back integration and lead to 'unmitigated disaster'. Violence, though, is simply what happens when legitimate political authority (as she understands it) begins to break down, and that is what has happened across European political space. America might provide an alternative to this pattern, but in order to do so it needs to regain its memorial grip and revive, rather than consign to history, its revolutionary tradition. The problem of slavery, however, present at the founding, means that racial violence will remain a problem until the colour line itself is removed, and all races and creeds are incorporated into the '*consensus universalis*' of the republic.[50] As with the majority of her *New Yorker* writings, Arendt often wrote with reference to deep themes in European political theory and history, but grounded them with reference to claims about American exceptionalism that gave her work an instinctive tractability with an American audience.

Arendt's last essays in *The New Yorker* go back to her intellectual beginnings in their concern with the relationship between mind, thought and action. These three pieces focus on 'Thinking', and its relation to acting and willing. Like her other *New Yorker* essays, they were also to be published as a book, this time as the incomplete text, *The Life of the Mind*. Her final article appeared in the 5 December 1977 issue, the day after she died, aged 69, and these contributions neatly close a broad intellectual circle. They take their cue from her particular and idiosyncratic interpretation of Kant that made its debut in the 1950s and which provided the basis for her account of political judgement over the next twenty years. But they close the *New Yorker* circle, because in returning to the problem of thought they reconsider once more the problem of Eichmann's thoughtlessness, first aired in the pages of the magazine.

While teaching at Berkeley in 1955, Arendt began the transition from thinking about Kant's philosophy as an exercise in 'worldlessness', focusing on an abstract, willing agent, to an understanding of Kant's account of judgement as presupposing a basic and shared common sense capable of grounding an account of political judgement as something that takes place in the real world between determinate, concrete individuals. This was what she began to work up for *The New Yorker* twenty years later. Beginning with a concern over the difficulties of judging politically that was developed through considering Aristotle and Cicero on rhetoric, persuasion and judgement, she came to a view that the communicability of ideas to the many, not merely the few, is the central puzzle for modern politics, and that judgement in general, and political judgement particularly, must be related to thinking.[51]

If thinking depends on the existence of others, then a Kantian form of 'common sense' looks like a prerequisite for explaining it, and one thing the *New Yorker* archives do show is Arendt struggling to find the source for a quotation from Kant about 'Das Land des Denkens' while she was writing up 'Thinking' from a house in Maine. Mary McCarthy was on hand to help seek it out.[52] But thinking 'out of the world', wrote Arendt, is a consideration whose origins lie in a broader 'intellectual history', and the source for that history is Cicero, himself a Stoic source of Kant's own cosmopolitanism.[53] So although consciousness is not the same as thinking, judging is thought made active through the force of imagination and persuasion, and Arendt simply alludes in the archival papers to this wider intellectual heritage here.[54] Her purpose in thinking about thinking, though, is to show how critique and judgement must aspire to enlarge both mentalities and horizons. Practising judgement is necessarily critical, and it is therefore inherently public, inherently political, and necessarily pointed. This cannot be avoided, and trying to avoid it would be a dereliction of the duty Arendt set herself as both citizen and political theorist. Her writings embody the challenge of how to make political thought as a form of political action usable for thinking about contemporary political judgement, and nowhere is this more obvious than in her combination of *New Yorker* articles, which conclude once more with the question of American foundations.[55] In sum, the *New Yorker* life of Hannah Arendt's mind has pride of place in her own intellectual development. Even if she got many of the historical details wrong about the subjects she wrote upon, as many have thought she did about Eichmann or about the nature of radical evil, she nevertheless saw more clearly than most what the big questions are.[56]

Notes

1. Ben Yagoda, *About Town: The 'New Yorker' and the World it Made* (New York: Scribner, 2000), pp. 76, 313.
2. For a good summary, see Seyla Benhabib, 'Arendt's *Eichmann in Jerusalem*', in *The Cambridge Companion to Arendt*, ed. D. Vila (Cambridge: Cambridge University Press, 2001), pp. 65–85.
3. 'The lesson of the fearsome, word-and-thought defying *banality of evil*' appears in Hannah Arendt, 'Eichmann in Jerusalem V', *The New Yorker*, 16 March 1963, pp. 58–134 (p. 101).
4. Thomas Bender, *New York Intellect* (Baltimore: Johns Hopkins University Press, 1987), chapter 8; Thomas L. Jeffers, *Norman Podhoretz: A Biography* (Cambridge: Cambridge University Press, 2010), pp. 75–6.
5. For example, Hannah Arendt, '*The Jewish State*: 50 Years After, Where Have Herzl's Policies Led?', *Commentary*, 1 (1946), 1–8.
6. Hannah Arendt, 'The Mob and the Elite', *Partisan Review*, 17.8 (1950), 808–19.
7. Hannah Arendt, 'Understanding and Politics', *Partisan Review*, 20.4 (1953), 377–92 (p. 388).
8. Ibid., p. 391.
9. Hannah Arendt, 'Parties, Movements and Classes', *Partisan Review*, 12.4 (1945), 504–13 (pp. 505–6, 512); *The Jewish Writings*, ed. J. Kohn (New York: Schocken, 2008), pp. 446–7.
10. Hannah Arendt, *The Origins of Totalitarianism* (New York: Harcourt Brace 1973 [1951]); Hannah Arendt, *The Human Condition* (Chicago: University of Chicago Press, 1958).
11. Carol Brightman, ed., *Between Friends: The Correspondence of Hannah Arendt and Mary McCarthy* (London: Secker & Warburg, 1995), p. 168.
12. For details, see Norman Podhoretz, *Ex-Friends: Falling Out with Allen Ginsberg, Lionel & Diana Trilling, Lillian Hellman, Hannah Arendt, and Norman Mailer* (New York: Free Press, 1999), pp. 143, 148–9, 151, 165; Nathan Abrams, *Norman Podhoretz and 'Commentary' Magazine: The Rise and Fall of the Neocons* (London: Continuum Abrams, 2010), pp. 38–9; Jeffers, *Norman Podhoretz*, pp. 86–7, 89–90.
13. See Lyndsey Stonebridge, 'Hannah Arendt's Testimony: Judging in a Lawless World', *New Formations*, 67 (2009), 78–90.
14. Ben-Gurion cited in Idith Zertal, *Israel's Holocaust and the Politics of Nationhood*, (Cambridge: Cambridge University Press, 2010), pp. 106–7.
15. Ibid.
16. Hannah Arendt, 'Eichmann in Jerusalem I', *The New Yorker*, 16 February 1963, pp. 40–113 (p. 100).
17. Hannah Arendt, 'Society and Culture', *Daedalus*, 89.2 (1960), 278–87, updated as 'The Crisis in Culture', *Between Past and Future* (London: Penguin, 1977), pp. 194–222 (pp. 214–16); 'Freedom and Politics', *Chicago Review*, 14.1 (1960), 28–46.
18. Arendt, 'Freedom and Politics', pp. 28–30, 41, 43, 45.
19. Hannah Arendt, *Lectures on Kant's Political Philosophy*, ed. Ronald Beiner (Chicago: Chicago University Press, 1992).
20. Benjamin Constant, 'The Liberty of the Ancients Compared with that

of the Moderns' [1819], in B. Fontana, ed. *Constant: Political Writings* (Cambridge: Cambridge University Press, 1999) pp. 308–28.

21. Yagoda, *About Town*, p. 326.
22. See Gershom Scholem, '*Eichmann in Jerusalem*: An Exchange of Letters between Gershom Scholem and Hannah Arendt', *Encounter*, 22 (1964), 51–6.
23. Judith Shklar, 'Hannah Arendt as Pariah', in *Political Thought and Political Thinkers*, ed. Stanley Hoffman (Chicago: Chicago University Press, 1988), pp. 362–75.
24. See Anson Rabinbach, 'Eichmann in New York: The New York Intellectuals and the Hannah Arendt Controversy', *October*, 108 (2004), 97–111; Michael Ezra, 'The Eichmann Polemics: Hannah Arendt and her Critics', *Democratiya*, 9 (2007), 141–65.
25. Norman Podhoretz, 'Arendt on Eichmann: A Study in the Perversity of Brilliance', *Commentary*, 36.3 (1963), 201–8.
26. Irving Howe, '*The New Yorker* & Hannah Arendt', *Commentary*, 36.4 (1963), 318–19.
27. See, for example, 'Eichmann in Jerusalem IV', *The New Yorker*, 9 March 1963, pp. 48–131 (pp. 50–2).
28. Mary F. Corey, *The World Through a Monocle: 'The New Yorker' at Midcentury* (Cambridge, MA: Harvard University Press, 1999), p. 194.
29. Allison Hoffman, 'Hannah Arendt's Draft of History', *The Tablet*, 11 April 2011, available at <http://www.tabletmag.com/jewish-news-and-politics/64097/arendt> (accessed 1 May 2014).
30. William Shawn, 'The Talk of the Town: Comment', *The New Yorker*, 22 December 1975, p. 27.
31. Peter Baehr, *Hannah Arendt, Totalitarianism and the Social Sciences* (Stanford: Stanford University Press, 2010), chapter 2.
32. Yagoda, *About Town*, p. 358.
33. Arendt, 'Freedom and Politics', p. 36.
34. Dirk Moses, '*Das römische Gespräch* in a New Key: Hannah Arendt, Genocide, and the Defense of Republican Civilization', *Journal of Modern History*, 85.4 (2013), 867–913.
35. Hannah Arendt, 'Home to Roost', *New York Review of Books*, 26 June 1975, pp. 3–6.
36. Hannah Arendt, *On Revolution* (New York: Viking, 1965), pp. 42–4.
37. Yagoda, *About Town*, p. 316.
38. Hannah Arendt, 'Truth and Politics', *The New Yorker*, 25 February 1967, pp. 49–88; 'Is America by Nature a Violent Society?' *New York Times*, 28 April 1968, p. 24; cf. *On Violence* (New York: Harcourt Brace, 1969).
39. Danielle Allen, *Talking to Strangers* (Chicago: University of Chicago Press, 2005), pp. 25–7.
40. Hannah Arendt, 'Reflections on Little Rock', *Dissent* (1959), 45–65 (p. 47).
41. Ibid., p. 47.
42. Ibid., p. 51.
43. Hannah Arendt, 'Walter Benjamin', trans. Harry Zohn, *The New Yorker*, 19 October 1968, pp. 65–156 (pp. 153–6).
44. New Yorker Records, box 1497, Essays III and IV.

45. New Yorker Records, box 1606.

46. Hannah Arendt, 'Remembering Wystan H. Auden, who Died in the Night of the Twenty-Eighth of September, 1973', *The New Yorker*, 20 January 1975, pp. 39–46 (p. 45); cf. 'What is Permitted to Jove', *The New Yorker*, 5 November 1966, pp. 68–122.

47. David Bates, 'Enemies and Friends: Arendt on The Imperial Republic at War', *History of European Ideas*, 36 (2010), 112–24.

48. Hannah Arendt, 'Civil Disobedience', *The New* Yorker, 12 September 1970, pp. 70–105 (p. 100).

49. Hannah Arendt, *Crises of the Republic* (New York: Harcourt Brace 1972), p. 96.

50. Ibid., pp. 90–1.

51. David Marshall, 'The Origin and Character of Hannah Arendt's Theory of Judgement', *Political Theory*, 38.3 (2010), 367–93 (pp. 380–2).

52. Hannah Arendt, letter to Mary McCarthy, letter 2, 10 August 1977, p. 2, New Yorker Records, box 1621.

53. Martha Nussbaum, 'Kant and Stoic Cosmopolitanism', *Journal of Political Philosophy*, 5.1 (1997), 1–25.

54. New Yorker Records, box 1621, Galley 18.

55. Hannah Arendt, *The Life of the Mind* (New York: Harcourt Brace, 1978), p. 211.

56. Tony Judt, 'Hannah Arendt and Evil', repr. in *Reappraisals* (London: Vintage, 2009), pp. 73–92 (p. 90).

Chapter 11

On Blustering:
Dwight Macdonald, Modernism and
The New Yorker

Tom Perrin

'Masscult and Midcult', the midcentury US critic Dwight Macdonald's celebrated two-part hatchet-job on so-called middlebrow culture, loses its edge when it comes to assessing *The New Yorker*, the middlebrow magazine for which Macdonald, at the time he wrote the articles in 1960, had been a staff writer for eight years. 'Masscult and Midcult' is filled with the zingers for which Macdonald was known: 'the beatnik's pad is the modern equivalent of the poet's garret in every way except the creation of poetry'; Midcult's 'cakes are forever eaten, forever intact'.[1] But when it comes to *The New Yorker* they desert him in favour of vacillation: on the one hand, *The New Yorker* is not 'another Midcult magazine', rather, it is 'quite different'; on the other, just a few lines earlier, it *is* 'a Midcult magazine', albeit one 'with a difference'.[2] Macdonald goes on to say feebly that his positive view of the magazine is 'not without criticism'.[3] Like all middlebrow products, Macdonald says, *The New Yorker* is produced to a 'formula' that makes it 'monotonous', except that its formula is better than the one used in editing its 'Midcult brethren' (its fellow middlebrow magazines? or its brother-magazines that are middlebrow, as opposed to whatever *The New Yorker* is?). Plus, it is 'personally edited', leading to the frequent appearance of 'extra-formula happy accidents'.[4] This treatment of *The New Yorker*, largely extraneous to Macdonald's argument, takes up a page of his article, and a forty-six-line footnote in which, protesting too much, he tells the story of how 'Masscult and Midcult' was rejected by the *Saturday Evening Post* (it eventually appeared in *Partisan Review*) because of the editor's view that Macdonald was 'going easy' on the magazine for which he worked.[5]

It is easy to suspect that the *Post* editor who rejected the article was right: Macdonald could not see straight when it came to his employer. This essay, however, argues that something more is going on. Macdonald's prose emblematises a midcentury middlebrow literary mode to which I want to give the name *blustering*.[6] Blusterers, who appear all over middlebrow US prose of the early Cold War, aim to talk with the appearance of forthrightness, but they get so bogged down that they end up muddled and mired in self-contradiction. Macdonald's subject, *The New Yorker*, is not incidental to this mode, and nor is high modernism, the movement that functions as a kind of hero in 'Masscult and Midcult'. Blustering, I suggest, is a formal response on the part of middlebrow culture to a rupture within modernist ideology – to the way in which modernism could seem to function not only as culture's most valuable form of capital but also as a zone of pure art, secluded from the cultural marketplace. In addition, the chapter gives a new gloss on the well-known spat between Macdonald and Tom Wolfe that occurred in the pages of *New York* and the *New York Review of Books* in 1965–66. We intuitively see Wolfe's satire on *The New Yorker*, and Macdonald's responses to it, as a microcosmic paradigm shift, the moment when Macdonald the high modernist is symbolically bested by Wolfe the postmodernist. By contrast, I read Macdonald's contribution to the argument as arising from middlebrow culture's defining ambivalence towards modernism. I go on to argue that blustering might itself be seen as an example of the modernism seemingly conspicuous by its absence from *The New Yorker*. I want to claim blustering as a variety of what Miriam Hansen calls 'vernacular modernism', an example from the expanded repertoire of modernist cultural productions that has been assembled in the new modernist studies over the last fifteen years or so. Hansen suggests that vernacular modernism comprises 'cultural prac-tices' outside the traditional modernist canon 'that both articulated and mediated the experience of modernity'.[7] Macdonald's blustering in *The New Yorker* is an exemplary instance of such a practice – a modernist and middlebrow mode mediated by modernism's self-contradictory and competing ideologies that at the same time attempts to articulate those ideologies.

Blustering in the broadest sense, of course, predates Macdonald, modernism and *The New Yorker*. Shakespeare's Polonius might, for instance, be justifiably identified as a blusterer without arguing that Polonius has some kind of relationship with modernism *avant la lettre*. In addition, blusterers are almost invariably male, and in the US midcen-tury blustering is surely rooted to some extent in the jittery masochism of that moment's conception of masculinity.[8] One might, for instance, draw parallels between Macdonald's prose and the downtrodden men of James Thurber's sketches. The relationship between blustering and gender is nicely brought out in Woody Allen's famous 1974 *New Yorker* story 'The Whore of Mensa', in which call-girls rent themselves out to frustrated men looking for 'pseudo-intellectual' discussions; seren-dipitously the story involves one girl offering to procure for the private-detective narrator 'photographs of Dwight Macdonald reading'.[9] Here, however, I want to focus on the specific mode of blustering that arises from the tension between modernism and the middlebrow at a particu-lar historical moment when high modernism's incoherence is forced into view by the particular editorial viewpoint of *The New Yorker*.

Mark McGurl has written that twentieth-century literary culture pos-sesses 'a tripartite structure in which moron, bourgeois moralizer, and modernist intellectual revolve in a shifting set of ideological dependen-cies'.[10] We can see this going on in the self-contradictions of midcentury middlebrow writing as it vacillates between imitating and resentfully dis-missing high modernism. Indeed, Allen's joke about 'Dwight Macdonald reading' depends on precisely this structure: as a modernist intellectual, Macdonald is supposed to equate reading with masturbation. Reading is pleasurable because it allows him to experience intellectual mastery, but it is also shameful, it exposes him to blackmail, because it threatens to expose him as McGurl's bourgeois, a figure who *has to read* in order to attain the cultural capital that provides his livelihood only as long as he can be imagined as not having to work – that is, to read – for it. The modernist intellectual at whose reading we peep thereby loses his elbow patches. Blustering is desperate to prove its intellectual serious-ness even as it dismisses intellectuality as empty pretentiousness. It uses self-consciously ordinary language in order to guarantee the authenticity of ideas whose authenticity is the means by which they seek to transcend the ordinary. Using *The New Yorker* as its prime example, this chapter outlines the formal contours of blustering as an aesthetic mode that such revolving and shifting produces.

By contrast with its competitor *Vanity Fair*, modernist artwork, prose and poetry rarely appeared straightforwardly in *The New Yorker*. The magazine never published such authors as James Joyce, William Faulkner or Gertrude Stein, and gave cursory or unflattering reviews of their work.[11] Modernism was more commonly represented through parodies such as E. B. White's 'Across the Street and Into the Grill', the imitation of Hemingway's style that severely damaged his reputation in 1950, or the anonymous parody of a fraud modernist artist, 'Mr. Swackhammer', that appeared in 1925.[12] Such parodies are, as Daniel Tracy has pointed out, ambivalent. On the one hand they represent a 'normative backlash' against new modes of aesthetic production; on the other, they flatteringly assume fluency with modernism among *New Yorker* readers – they 'signal [. . .] a genre of middlebrow mastery and playful display of expertise in a variety of forms[,] communicat[ing] the sense of a circle of well-informed friends'.[13] Parodying modernism, as Faye Hammill argues in the opening chapter of this book, was thus part of *The New Yorker*'s central investment in sophistication. Expecting *New Yorker* readers to laugh at modernism meant expecting them to possess a high degree of knowledge about the avant-garde. Blustering, though, its prose torqued and fragmented by backtracks, qualifications, apologies and dodges, might be considered another place in which modernist prose, freighted like the parodies with ambivalence, found its way into the magazine.

In addition, the magazine's prose style, its layout, and its contents, convey a similar ambivalence. By midcentury *The New Yorker* had a long history of distaste for the formal complexity that marked modernist texts. From one direction, founding editor Harold Ross was determined to keep the magazine both light and comprehensible. Macdonald recalls him asking of difficult pieces, 'do we have to run that in our funny little magazine?'[14] James Thurber complained that Ross 'sometimes seemed to be editing [. . .] for a little boy or an old lady whose faculties were dimming' and had a 'profound uneasiness with anything smacking of scholarship or specialized knowledge'.[15] Gertrude Stein was told in a rejection note from fiction editor Katharine White that 'she was not allowed to buy anything [Ross] didn't understand'.[16] The magazine's house prose style, into which every article was infamously translated, was strongly influenced by long-time contributor E. B. White, champion of plainness and simplicity. The 'List of Reminders' that White added in his revision of William Strunk's famous primer *The Elements of Style* gives a sense of White's priorities: 'Do not be tempted by a twenty-dollar word when there is a ten-center handy, ready and able'; 'Write in a way that comes easily and naturally to you, using words and phrases that come readily to hand'; 'Rich, ornate prose is hard to digest, generally unwholesome, and sometimes nauseating'; 'Use orthodox spelling'.[17] In addition to the double-edged 'sophistication' that Tracy discusses, then, a culture based on such priorities helped keep high modernist authors largely out of *The New Yorker*.

At the same time, however, looked at as a whole, *The New Yorker*'s styles and makeup clearly bear the imprint of the social forces that produced modernism. For instance, Saul Steinberg, the artist who drew *New Yorker* cartoons and covers for six decades, including surely the most recognisable of all the magazine's covers, *View of the World from 9th Avenue*, often pastiched modernist styles in his *New Yorker* work; yet this in no way indicated hostility – much of Steinberg's other work was straightforwardly cubist in nature. In the mid-1960s both Samuel Beckett and André Breton were approached to write the introduction to a book of his work, and he was friends with many canonical modernist artists, including Alberto Giacometti and Jackson Pollock.[18]

As 'Masscult and Midcult', among many other documents, makes clear, one of modernism's main concerns was to represent and redeem the individual, threatened with fragmentation and insignificance in an era of mass entertainment, multinational companies and weapons that would destroy millions in a moment. Formally, *The New Yorker* is, like many modernist texts, fragmented, a mass of contradictions: Macdonald could condemn middle-class blindness to poverty next to a puff for luxury cars; John Hersey's 'Hiroshima' could be bathetically interrupted by a full-page ad directed at 'those few men in each community who want a finer hat'.[19] The magazine both celebrated and critiqued cultural norms, and was saturated with, while at the same time critiquing, advertising.

Moreover, individual pages sometimes juxtapose competing elements in a way that appears to create a modernist work of art. For instance, a long review by Macdonald of Richard Ellmann's *James Joyce* lionises Joyce as 'A Hero of Our Time' for his rugged individualism in columns that are, in a serendipitous metaphor for modernist anxiety over the eclipse of the individual by mass culture, seemingly squeezed thin on both sides by advertisements for the products of large corporations. As Tom Wolfe has it, 'running between these tropical forests of ads is a single thin gray column of type, editorial matter' that 'seem[ed] to grow paler and paler' amid the 'beautiful lush ads', a description that takes on an added piquancy in the context of Macdonald's essay on Joyce.[20] Elsewhere on the page we see a cartoon where a firm rings up an employee during his free time to check that he is still thinking about his job, and later in the article an advertisement for a book on the threat of 'the new Super-science'.[21] Without discussing Joyce's prose, and, indeed, explicitly dismissing the question that he ought to discuss it, Macdonald is sure that Joyce's heroism lies in his demonstrating the power and freedom of the individual. 'Whatever one's estimate of "Finnegans Wake"', Macdonald writes, Joyce's 'carrying it through' is 'certainly heroic'. This is because, in a bland world of organisation men, where 'people [. . .] go walkin' up and down the street and they don't know what they want', Joyce alone has been 'stubborn enough to know his job and stick to it'. For Macdonald, the very act of writing a modernist epic like *Ulysses* or *Finnegans Wake* is enough to render the individual 'heroic' whatever the text's content, since writing a difficult 'eight-hundred-and-forty-two-page' novel, and 'devot[ing] several hours a day to correcting misprints', constitutes a heroic act of 'will'.[22] While few individual elements in *The New Yorker* were stamped with the hallmarks of modernism, the magazine as a whole, albeit unintentionally, often was.

As I argue below, such ambivalence towards modernism made *The New Yorker*, especially the writing of Dwight Macdonald, an emblematically blustery location. In order to articulate the force of such a claim, it is worth first contextualising Macdonald's blustering within midcentury literature more generally. Blustering aims for forthrightness, but is so unsure of its position that it contradicts itself constantly. It attempts to employ plain language but comes out jagged and contorted. It wants to be short and to the point, but goes on far too long. It seeks to demonstrate its author's strength but showcases only his weakness. Moses Herzog, eponymous protagonist of Saul Bellow's 1964 novel, writes blustering letters to anybody and everybody, dead or alive, as a symbol of his castration – abandoned by his harpy of a wife, he is 'cracked', 'going to pieces', 'breaking up'; blustering and cuckoldry go hand in hand: 'his former friend, Valentine, and his wife, his ex-wife Madeleine, had spread the rumor that his sanity had collapsed'.[23] Herzog's rationale for the letters drips with tragic irony; he feels 'the need to explain, to have it out, to justify, to put in perspective, to clarify, to make amends' – to put to rest every anxiety that dogs his life.[24] But the process he believes will demonstrate his strength of character ends up revealing nothing but his willingness to be stepped on – something he realises when (surprise) the new love affair whose success provides the novel's closure enables him to stop writing them.

Another midcentury blusterer appears in Herman Wouk's *Marjorie Morningstar* (1955): Noel Airman, a superficially fascinating but ultimately banal songwriter, is explaining to the protagonist the philosophical doctrine he has invented, 'that the force that moves the world is a desire for Hits'.[25] The idea, he explains, is breathtaking in its simplicity, a 'white-hot fragment' that will revolutionise the discipline of philosophy. Yet as he explains it, it becomes clear to the reader that this idea is nothing but 'the vapidest college-boy philosophizing'.[26]

It is Noel's style, more than anything, that makes his vapidity clear. He switches violently between dismissing the academy and aspiring to belong to it. His idea, he says, is different from the 'academic verbiage' he reads in journals; he has no time for 'college boy[s]'; he faults philosophers for a solipsistic 'love [of] words' and '[t]hinking'.[27] His speech is self-consciously informal, seeking to bolster its authenticity by, for instance, associating philosophy – or, rather, 'the old philosophic puzzlers' – with what is supposed to be a list of everyday concerns: '"What restaurant shall I eat at tonight? How can I get this girl into bed? Where can I get hold of some more money?" – the questions people really spend their time trying to answer.'[28] At the same time he dreams of his theory being an academic totem of some kind, 'a book – rather short, but rather difficult – or a long Socratic dialogue, or a series of connected essays'. His hauteur towards academic philosophy is, like *New Yorker* parodies, designed to convey both disdain and a superiority based on weary familiarity – Noel's work 'reintroduces teleology as a major concept in dialectical analysis', it will be 'Santayana tinctured with James', 'a mishmash of Adler, Nietzsche, La Rochefoucauld, and who knows what else'.[29] More than anything, it is Noel's inability to explain his 'white-hot fragment' with any concision or clarity that reveals its fraudulence. For one thing, his explanation goes on for eleven pages. For another, it is filled with moments of distraction and threads lost. Noel often 'seemed to be talking to himself': 'I'll eat when I'm *bloody* good and ready'; 'I'm tense and tired'; 'Isn't it just a question of projection, isn't the externalizing just a secondary mechanism? – No, no.' The speech ends with Noel trailing off as he tries to salvage his idea from Marjorie's tepid reaction to it: 'The feminine reaction always has its cold-water validity, tempering if nothing else –'.[30]

The examples from the work of Bellow and Wouk involve a degree of distance between implied author and character – as readers we intuit that we are not supposed entirely to sympathise with these characters at these moments. Macdonald's blustering, as we will see, is essentially unironic. In this, too, he has peers. For example, Jack Malloy, the philosopher-criminal who inhabits the moral centre of James Jones's 1951 blockbuster *From Here to Eternity*, is presented to the reader as a secular saint, with 'unembarrassed dreamer's eyes', a mastery of left-wing theory, a 'perfect [. . .] physique' and a 'kingly', 'awesome' bearing.[31] Yet, when he, like Wouk's Noel Airman, attempts to marry his authentic, working-man's language to his highbrow philosophising, the effect is as long-winded as in Wouk:

> You see what that implies? If God is Instability rather than Fixity, if God is Growth and Evolution, then there is no need for the concept of forgiveness. The mere concept of forgiveness implies the doing of something wrong, Original Sin. But if evolution is growth by trial and error, how can errors be wrong? since they contribute to growth? Does a mother feel called upon to forgive her child for eating green apples or putting his hand on the stove? Did you ever truly love some body, or some thing? A woman; did you ever love a woman? If you ever really truly loved a thing, you never even considered forgiving it something, did you?[32]

Malloy's capitalisation of key concepts such as 'Instability', 'Fixity', 'Growth', and 'Evolution' – implied, like his salt-of-the-earth refusal of apostrophes, since this is a transcription of his speech – does nothing to clarify what these terms are supposed to denote. As in Wouk, heterosexual love is brought in as a guarantor of Malloy's authenticity, with the word 'woman' repeated as if to insist on his auditors' confirmation of his point. Again, as in Wouk, scholarly concepts are invoked but dropped in a quasi-casual manner that suggests easy familiarity – 'something wrong, Original Sin'. And again, as in Wouk, the whole thing takes a painfully long time to expound – eight pages of small type in the 1998 Delta reprint.

These examples, in addition to demonstrating blustering as a form, reveal its entanglement with modernism. In *Marjorie Morningstar* Noel invokes modernism without performing its style. He attempts to demonstrate his authority by dropping names that Wouk elsewhere clearly associates with empty modernist relativism, Adler and Nietzsche. Yet, as with Macdonald, his speech painstakingly avoids the imagined pretentiousness of modernist difficulty with its casual, conversational style. In *From Here to Eternity*, modernism's primitivist fascination with authenticity is at issue. Jack Malloy is an autodidact genius, taught to read by IWW members jailed by his county-sheriff father. His lack of privilege guarantees the authenticity of a love of literature signaled via proto-modernism: 'The first book he had bought for himself, with the money from the first job, was Walt Whitman's *Leaves of Grass*.'[33] His education has come via manual labor, rather than through the academy: 'harvest fields and timber camps', 'South American freighters out of Frisco'.[34] The novel's championing of Malloy is part and parcel of a wider primitivism: Jones seeks to create sympathy for his working-class soldier characters by printing pages on end of their 'bull sessions', thrilled with the notion that non-normative speech patterns and vocabularies might possess a richness of their own, a 'lovely beautiful brilliant shuttling' of phrases back and forth between the men.[35] *From Here to Eternity*'s protagonist, Robert E. Lee Prewitt, writes a song, 'Re-enlistment Blues', part-way through the novel, which is printed for the first time in its entirety as a postscript to the main text, raising Prewitt up to stand with, or perhaps displace, Rudyard Kipling, who provides its epigraph. The naming of Prewitt's text as a 'Blues' can also be understood in terms of Jones's attempt to set it outside the sphere of bourgeois cultural capital, specifically locating it within (in Jones's view) an authentic jazz tradition that can contain 'the whole feel and pattern of the joyously unhappy tragedy of this earth'.[36]

Yet if Jones engages in the modernist project of cannibalising working-class culture to lend his text the cultural capital its authenticity provides, he angrily disavows this same project. When Prewitt and his friend Maggio are picked up by a pair of 'pseudo-intellectual [. . .] queers' – prostitution being one of the GIs' main money-making side-projects – one of the queers, Hal, turns out to be the mirror-image of Malloy, expounding a blustering doctrine that 'the rise of the Industrial Revolution' shows that 'Sin, per se, is not a self-evident phenomenon but a thing deliberately constructed for the mechanical control of society.'[37] Unlike Malloy, however, Hal's philosophy is shallow – 'half-assed', 'fake', Prew calls it.[38] As readers we are encouraged to side with Prewitt's judgement because Hal (ironically, like Jones himself) has a love for the primitive, patronisingly calling Prew a 'little savage' and a 'simple child of the primitives'.[39] Blustering and ambivalence towards modernism go hand in hand.

Given the widespread blustering in middlebrow cultural production at midcentury, why focus on Dwight Macdonald, a critic who wanted to be anything but middlebrow, and why especially on his writing for *The New Yorker*? The answer is that *New Yorker* writing on culture, and Macdonald's blustering in particular, is a textbook example of what happens when prose that strives to be plain attempts to engage an aesthetic philosophy – high modernism – riven with self-contradiction. In the first place, Macdonald strove for forthrightness in his prose. His speciality was what the critic Jennifer Szalai has called, in an essay on Macdonald entitled 'Mac the Knife', 'the ruthless takedown'.[40] Today such takedowns are what he is best remembered for – 'Masscult and Midcult', or his scathing review of James Gould Cozzens's bestseller *By Love Possessed* from the January 1958 issue of *Commentary*. His work is filled with barbs. On Cozzens: his writing is 'about as bad as prose can get';[41] on Dorothy L. Sayers: 'There is nothing more vulgar than sophisticated *kitsch*.'[42] He slashes at the 'folk-fakery of *Oklahoma!*', 'the orotund sentimentalities of *South Pacific*', and Hemingway's prose in *The Old Man and the Sea* ('the drone of the pastiche parable, wordy and sentimental').[43] He associates mediocrity with obfuscation, prose that is 'shallow and muddy', and talent with the ability to write in a way that is 'clear and deep'.[44] Perhaps because of this, Macdonald's own prose, like Wouk's and Jones's, has a painfully self-conscious informality. Breaking one of Strunk and White's most famous rules from *The Elements of Style*, Macdonald continually 'affect[s] a breezy manner': Plato was 'essentially a literary man'; 'Chaucer stuck on a five-line moral at the end' of 'The Reeve's Tale'.[45] When Macdonald did imitate modernist style it was as parody, as in an ultimately unpublished review for *The New Yorker* of the avant-garde anthology *New Directions 14*:

13 stories
  5 essays
    67 prose poems
      32 poemy poems
        425 pages
and pages
and pages
    pullulating   crepitating   ululant with
words words words
breaking   breaking   breaking   on
cold
grey
stones

GRANDIOSE DIARRHEA OF LANGUAGE

The bread and butter of 19th century writing, how nourishing compared to these hors d'oeuvres from the literary deep-freeze!

Those eminent Victorians, long of wind and flat of foot, how terse, how direct compared to All the Sad Young Middle aged Men exacerbating their insensibilities and taking their time about it.[46]

Macdonald's parody displays his ambivalence just as well as his other writing: he imitates not just the midcentury modernist poetry he means to satirise, but also the manifesto language of high modernist periodicals like Wyndham Lewis's *BLAST*. Compare Lewis et al.'s 'VICTORIAN VAMPIRE, the LONDON cloud sucks the TOWN's heart' with Macdonald's 'how nourishing compared to these hors d'oeuvres from the literary deep-freeze!'[47] Furthermore, while he contrasts the *New Directions* writers unfavourably with their Victorian predecessors, he lambasts those predecessors also ('long of wind and flat of foot'), and with a phrase from another set of high-modernist fellow travellers, the Bloomsbury Group, Lytton Strachey's 'eminent Victorians'. In general, however, Macdonald stayed firmly away from writing in such a mode.

Macdonald's passion for clarity, then, leads him into an ambivalent relationship with modernism. On the one hand, like most of the other New York Intellectuals, Macdonald admired nothing more than high modernism, which was for him the polar opposite of the mass culture he deplored, and the middlebrow culture that was the same mass-cultural wolf in the sheep's clothing of sophistication. During Macdonald's long involvement with *Partisan Review*, modernism was the keystone on which the journal's anti-Stalinist leftism was built: Stalin's preference for mass-cultural socialist realism in art and literature symbolised, for Macdonald, Phillip Rahv, Clement Greenberg, Mary McCarthy and others, the totalitarian turn that Soviet Communism had taken from the 1930s onwards.[48] Indeed, the best-known articulation of *Partisan Review*'s left-wing defense of modernism, Greenberg's 1939 essay 'Avant-Garde and Kitsch', was based on an exchange of letters between Greenberg and Macdonald; Louis Menand refers to the essay as more truly a 'collaboration' between the two than Greenberg's own work.[49] Macdonald's admiration for modernism was not entirely bound up with his leftism, however. He idolised T. S. Eliot, with whom he kept up an adulatory correspondence for many years, and he had tremendous admiration for James Joyce, who professed to have no interest in politics.[50] Rather, modernism represented for Macdonald art for art's sake – a pure and authentic pursuit by contrast with the inauthentic, market-driven dross of masscult and midcult. The modernist avant-garde, he wrote, was based not on a desire to be rich or popular but on:

> a shared respect for certain standards and an agreement that living art often runs counter to generally accepted ideas. [. . .] Its significance was simply that it refused to compete in the established cultural marketplaces. It made a desperate effort to fence off some area within which the serious artist could still function.[51]

In his 1959 piece on Joyce, Macdonald writes that Joyce 'was a hero because he was courageous about the one great thing in his life' – a good summary of his attitude in general: Macdonald's work focuses less on modernism's politics or its products than on its integrity.[52]

This attitude proved problematic, especially for a critic invested in the notion that great ideas were fundamentally simple and could be expressed in simple terms. For modernism, as the term was understood in Macdonald's circle during the midcentury, was marked not only by authenticity but also by complexity. As middlebrow authors like Wouk, Robert Ruark, James Michener and others never tired of pointing out, high modernism's formal difficulty made it just as susceptible to charges of pretentious cultural-capital-generation masquerading as art as Macdonald's hated Midcult. The egotistical and shallow modernist writer is a stock figure in middlebrow novels of the period – a prime example might be the character Tom Keefer from Wouk's 1952 novel *The Caine Mutiny*, a smart-ass novelist 'too clever to be wise', whose arrogant disregard for the good of society is revealed when he foments a mutiny onboard the warship on which he serves. Keefer is a modernist author whose novel (entitled *Multitudes, Multitudes* in allusion to Faulkner's *Absalom, Absalom!*) is described as 'sort of a jumble of Dos Passos and Joyce and Hemingway and Faulkner', and his modernism clearly symbolises his empty-headed contrarianism.[53]

As is now well known, Macdonald's insistence that modernist high art was a sacred wood that could be 'fence[d] off' from the rest of culture, like that of many midcentury critics, was a self-serving misprision; rather, modernism was part and parcel of a larger cultural field – a small but pertinent example of which fact might be Daniel Tracy's pointing out that it was middlebrow magazine culture that was responsible for organising 'modernism' into a quasi-coherent movement in the first place.[54] Because of this, when Macdonald's writing addresses issues of formal complexity or difficulty, blustering is frequently the result. His famous takedown of Cozzens accuses the novelist, among other things, of being a blusterer, his prose exemplified by its 'needless qualifications, its clumsiness, its defensive qualifications'.[55] Yet this is exactly how Macdonald writes when he attempts to split the non-existent hairs that separate middlebrow formal complexity from modernist. In 'Masscult and Midcult', when Macdonald attempts to explain what is bad about Hemingway's prose in the middlebrow *The Old Man and the Sea*, he ends up writing in circles. Macdonald's ostensible problem with Hemingway's novella is that its action is all-but-explicitly marked as allegorical, rather than its universal significance arising out of a naturalistic, concrete situation. Thus Hemingway's story 'The Undefeated' is good because it 'has four people in it, each with a name and each defined through his words and actions; *Old Man* has no people, just two Eternal, Universal types'.[56] However, having made this claim, Macdonald appears immediately to realise that many successful modernist texts employ just such an allegorical mode, and is forced to employ one of his hated defensive qualifications: 'Perhaps a Kafka could have made something out of' *The Old Man and the Sea*, but not Hemingway, because Hemingway writes in a 'realistic manner' – except, apparently, when he doesn't.[57] If Macdonald has any idea about what formal differences make Kafka's allegories successful and Hemingway's unsuccessful, he does not say.

Elsewhere in this essay the need for qualification even jeopardises Macdonald's putdowns: his attack on Thornton Wilder's play *Our Town* is based on the idea that Wilder has taken modernist theatrical innovations – Brecht's *Verfremdungseffekt* and Westernised elements of Chinese theatre – and popularised them. However, once again Macdonald pulls his punches when he needs to explain the difference between a good Brechtian *Verfremdungseffekt* and a bad Wilderian one: 'I agree with everything Mr. Wilder says,' he writes, 'but I will fight to the death against his right to say it' – he goes on – 'in this way'.[58] The 'way' to which Macdonald objects is the folksiness of Wilder's dialogue, especially that of the Stage Manager, the character in the play who breaks the fourth wall, but he cannot explain why a folksy manner should subvert this modernist theatrical technique. Instead he resorts to mere parody to make his point: 'Guess there just hasn't been anybody around for years as plumb mellow nor as straight-thinking neither, as Mr. Wilder's stage manager. Nope.'[59]

Finally, in characterising Macdonald as an exemplary blusterer, we might point to his inconsistency, references to which are the most consistent thing about later writing on him and his work. 'He changed his views about as often as Paris realigns skirt lengths';[60] he 'exasperated his left-wing friends by changing his political views unpredictably and abruptly, sometimes between soup and dessert'.[61] His ideas often appeared self-contradictory – his biography is entitled *A Rebel In Defense of Tradition*, and his biographer, Michael Wreszin, writes there that 'the major consistency in the man and his life was paradox and contradiction'.[62] Reviewing that biography in an article titled, after Emerson, 'No Foolish Consistency', John Elson suggested in *Time* that Macdonald 'wrote too much and sometimes too carelessly, left many projects half finished and was variously a Trotskyite, a socialist, a pacifist, an anarchist and an aging camp follower of the student lefties of '68'.[63] His nickname was reportedly 'flighty Dwighty', and Leon Trotsky allegedly once told him that 'every man has a right to be stupid on occasion but Comrade Macdonald abuses it'.[64]

If midcentury middlebrow literary culture took an inconsistent attitude towards modernism, that attitude was both amplified and emblematised by *The New Yorker*, with its particular mix of liberalism and conservatism, lightness and hauteur, gravitas and humour. As a result, it was Macdonald's work in and in relation to the magazine that led to his most blustery writing. In the December 1937 issue of *Partisan Review*, Macdonald wrote a sustained attack on *The New Yorker* that skewered the magazine's 'elegant-trifler pose' as the worst kind of aspirational decadence.[65] For Macdonald, the magazine's celebrated humour was priggish – it could 'be read aloud in mixed company without calling a blush to the cheek of the most virtuous banker'.[66] But, worse, its ostensible neutrality from politics was itself profoundly oligarchic, 'a form of upper class display, since only the economically secure can afford such Jovian aloofness from the common struggles' – an attitude that Macdonald denounced as 'monstrously inhuman' during the decade of the Depression.[67] Yet by 1937 Macdonald had already published two pieces in *The New Yorker* – a 'Talk of the Town' and a fascinated Profile of Leonor F. Loree, President of the then-powerful Delaware and Hudson Railroad. Indeed, this was not the only admiring piece the lifelong leftist wrote about a capitalist magnate. In 1952 he wrote a two-part Profile on Richard Weil, Jr., CEO of Macy's New York – the company where Macdonald had in fact begun his own career. Despite his politics, the admiration for 'hero[es]' and great men he articulated in his review of Joyce's biography evidently also extended to captains of industry. Macdonald continued to publish in *The New Yorker* through-out the ensuing decades, and in 1952 the then new editor William Shawn brought him onto the magazine as a staff writer, a position he held until 1974.

During the mid-1960s Macdonald had moved so far from his younger self that he unwillingly became a totem of the New Journalism's anxiety of influence. In 1968, Norman Mailer used Macdonald's involvement with *The New Yorker* in order to rewrite the critic's leftism as an empty gesture: 'although Macdonald would not admit it, he was in secret carrying on a passionate love affair with *The New Yorker* – Disraeli on his knees before Victoria'.[68] The former leftist gadfly had come to repre-sent all that was most genteel about old New York, and writing for *The New Yorker* was that gentility's symbol. In 1965 and 1966, on behalf of Shawn, he wrote a rebuttal of two articles Tom Wolfe had written for *New York* magazine, then still a supplement of the *Herald Tribune*. To Wolfe's portrayal of *The New Yorker* as a zombified relic of the 1930s staffed by a crew of self-important litterateurs he named '[t]iny [m]ummies', Macdonald produced a tone-deaf response.[69] Macdonald's long, pettifogging pair – pair! – of essays spends pages addressing minor inaccuracies of Wolfe's ('Manuscript paper used to be "maize-yellow" (or orange) but was changed to white a year before Wolfe's articles appeared') and spinning out long-winded Classical etymologies:

> 'parajournalism,' from the Greek *para*, 'beside' or 'against': something similar in form but different in function. As in parody, from the *parodia*, or counterode, the satyr play of Athenian drama that was performed after the tragedy by the same actors in grotesque costumes. Or paranoia ('against/ beside thought') in which rational forms are used to express delusions.[70]

The effect of reading Macdonald's rebuttal is to be convinced that Wolfe took liberties with small truths about *The New Yorker* in order to capture a larger one: the magazine really did seem to be staffed by dreary fogies like, in Wolfe's words, 'the testy but lovable Boswell who annotates my old laundry slips, Dwight Macdonald'.[71]

We can read the episode, too, as another instance of Macdonald's ambivalence towards modernism generating middlebrow blustering. He seems to have found nothing in common between the high modernism of the 1920s and '30s and its midcentury incarnation. Revering Picasso, he dismissed Jackson Pollock as a member of the 'Drip and Dribble School'.[72] Finding Joyce to be 'great', 'a hero', creator of 'high art', he found in Wolfe's Joycean prose ('Wh-wh-wh-wh-wh-whoooaaaaaaugh! – piles of whichy whuh words – which, when, where, who, whether, whuggheeee, the living whichy thickets') nothing but the language of the 'toy catalogue', that is, of mass culture.[73] Yet his intended dismissal of Wolfe is shot through with envy. Macdonald refers repeatedly and unnecessarily to 'Laugh and Lie Down', the critique of *The New Yorker* he had written thirty years earlier, when he was a young Turk:

> In the December, 1937, *Partisan Review* I published a ten-page critique of *The New Yorker* that was not marked by humility. Its [. . .] line was: '*The New Yorker* is the last of the great family journals. Its inhibitions stretch from sex to the class struggle. It can be read aloud in mixed company without calling a blush to the cheek of the most virtuous banker.'

'A sensible critique of *The New Yorker* would be useful for there is much to criticize. Many of the complaints I made in *Partisan Review* still seem to me valid'; Wolfe 'was thirty-three when he wrote it while I was thirty-one when I wrote mine'.[74] So there. Macdonald's prose wants to have it both ways, at once attacking Wolfe for being an irresponsible provocateur and mourning his own usurpation from that same role.

When Macdonald writes in *The New Yorker* about other subjects his prose is much more straightforward than when he writes about modernism. Other well-known articles of his – for example, a *New Yorker* Profile of Dorothy Day and the Catholic Workers, or the long review of Michael Harrington's *The Other America* that has been credited with influencing John F. Kennedy's and Lyndon B. Johnson's anti-poverty programs – are models of clarity:

> The problem is obvious: the persistence of mass poverty in a prosperous country. The solution is also obvious: to provide, out of taxes, the kind of subsidies that have always been given to the public school (not to mention the police and fire departments and the post office) – subsidies that would raise incomes above the poverty level, so that every citizen could feel he is indeed such.[75]

When Macdonald's drive to write simple, forthright prose is not skewed by his ambivalence about the subject at hand, he does not bluster.

Compare this with his Profile of Alfred H. Barr, director of collections at MoMA, from 1953. MoMA, as well as Barr himself, were subjects about which Macdonald had reason to feel a good deal of ambivalence. On the one hand, MoMA established modernist art – Picasso, Cézanne, Van Gogh – as part of the canon. Such artists were members of the avant-garde that Macdonald claimed had produced 'most of the major creations of the last seventy years'.[76] For Macdonald, the museum is, at its best, a 'model [. . .] of how to popularize without vulgarizing'.[77] In addition, Barr possessed the dynamism and willpower that Macdonald admired in his pieces on figures as diverse as Day, Joyce and Weil. He tells with delight the story of Barr spearheading the museum in its early days, during which it administered ten shows for 204,000 visitors out of a single office shared by the top four directorial staff answering five telephones and writing correspondence on two typewriters.[78] Barr inhabited two personae Macdonald liked: he was both a 'nice old absent-minded professor' and 'more than something of a politician'.[79]

On the other hand, the museum was a prime example of middlebrow culture, turning high art into 'show business' with 'a curious combination of scholarship and showmanship'.[80] The influential exhibition catalogues Barr writes are sufficiently formulaic that Macdonald cannot resist having fun with them. Barr has, for Macdonald, a series of set modes for explaining art to the masses: 'his [. . .] In a Nutshell [. . .] style [. . .] his Reassuring Expository, or This May Hurt Just a Little, style [. . .] his Freewheeling, Rhetorical style [. . .] his High Level style, [. . .] the Popular Punchy Style'.[81] More than this, however, Macdonald has difficulty reconciling the museum's deliberate populism with the space 'fence[d] off' from the 'cultural marketplace' that is, for him, modernism's defining feature. His writing on MoMA often employs the weasel words with which he defended *The New Yorker* itself: he justifies the museum's attempts to attract the *'hoi polloi* [. . .] with snob appeal, along the lines of the "Men of Distinction" whiskey ads and the Aqua Velva After-Shave Club' as 'a peccadillo in a good cause'.[82] Of the museum's vigorous public promotion of its exhibitions, he writes:

> There was once some truth in the charge of publicity-seeking, but the Museum's showmanship can be defended, in general, as a means of getting the public interested in modern art, and in the Museum's early years could be defended specifically as necessary for its economic survival. It is true that *Direct Advertising* in 1950 called it 'our most promotion-minded institution,' but there is promotion and promotion.[83]

Vacillating between disdain for MoMA's pandering to the masses and admiration for its success, Macdonald blusters. His contrast between 'publicity-seeking' and legitimate 'promotion' initially backtracks with a double qualification – MoMA's showmanship can be defended 'in general', or, at least, in general for the museum's 'early years'; subsequently, he abandons substantive contrast entirely in favour of an ironic distinction without a difference – 'there is promotion and promotion'. The phrase masks its lack of content with a characteristic *New Yorker* move: shifting the burden of interpretation onto the reader by flatter-ingly hailing him as an insider, one who has such good taste that he does not need to be told what the difference between 'promotion and promotion' is, since, surely, he already knows. Modernism's equivocal signification of both *l'art pour l'art* and culture-as-capital, as ever, brings out the blusterer.

Anxiety over cultural capital ran especially high in the midcentury US during the post-Second World War boom, with the rapid growth of a professional-managerial class whose prosperity depended to a new extent on the possession of such capital.[84] Modernism, as hegemon of the postwar cultural field, both possessed and disavowed its possession of the majority of that capital, and the proliferation of blustering as a mod-ernist mode of middlebrow writing was one result. Macdonald, modern-ism and *The New Yorker* formed a combination ideal for producing this mode: modernism's conceptual incoherence produced ambivalence in a writer who prized the clear definition of cultural concepts, and whose ambivalence strikingly short-circuited his prose, writing in a magazine already defined by its own ambivalence towards modernism. On the one hand, then, this chapter has identified blustering as a new variety of vernacular modernism that appears throughout middlebrow culture; on the other, it has enabled us to see the proliferation of such a modernist mode in the pages of a middlebrow magazine typically associated with plain style, *The New Yorker*.

Notes

1. Thanks for their help with various aspects of this chapter are due to Lauren Berlant, Hillary Chute, J. D. Connor, Mary Esteve, Kate Gaudet, Mollie Godfrey, Elizabeth Hutcheon and participants in the 2013 Post45 confer-ence. Dwight Macdonald, 'Masscult and Midcult', in *Against the American Grain* (New York: Random House, 1962), pp. 52, 57.
2. Ibid., pp. 69, 68.
3. Ibid., p. 69.
4. Ibid., p. 68.
5. Ibid., p. 69.
6. I say 'I'. In fact I am indebted to Mollie Godfrey for coming up with 'blus-tering' as a name for the phenomenon I identify.
7. Miriam Bratu Hansen, 'The Mass Production of the Senses: Classical Cinema as Vernacular Modernism', *Modernism/Modernity* 6.2 (1999), 59–77 (p. 59).
8. One colleague suggested 'mansplaining' as an alternative to blustering; the complexities involved with applying this twenty-first-century term to the mid-twentieth century have dissuaded me from using it.

9. Woody Allen, 'The Whore of Mensa', *The New Yorker*, 16 December 1974, pp. 37–8 (pp. 37, 38).

10. Mark McGurl, *The Novel Art: Elevations of American Fiction after Henry James* (Princeton, NJ: Princeton University Press, 2001), p. 110.

11. Although other modernists, such as William Carlos Williams and (especially) Vladimir Nabokov, were published. See Ben Yagoda, *About Town: 'The New Yorker' and the World it Made* (New York: Scribner, 2000), pp. 173, 206; on this topic also see Faye Hammill and Karen Leick, 'Modernism and the Quality Magazines: *Vanity Fair* (1914–36); *American Mercury* (1924–81); *New Yorker* (1925–); *Esquire* (1933–)', in *The Oxford Critical and Cultural History of Modernist Magazines*, ed. Peter Brooker and Andrew Thacker, 3 vols (New York: Oxford University Press, 2009–13), vol. II, North America: 1894–1960 (2012), pp. 176–96; Daniel Tracy, 'Investing in "Modernism": Smart Magazines, Parody, and Middlebrow Professional Judgment', *Journal of Modern Periodical Studies* 1.1 (2010), 38–63.

12. E. B. White, 'Across the Street and Into the Grill', *The New Yorker*, 14 October 1950, p. 28; Corey Ford, 'Probing Public Murals', *The New Yorker*, 23 May 1925, p. 22.

13. Tracy, 'Investing in "Modernism"', p. 38.

14. Dwight Macdonald, 'Parajournalism II: Wolfe and *The New Yorker*', *New York Review of Books*, 3 February 1966, available at <http://www.nybooks.com/articles/archives/1966/feb/03> (accessed 12 May 2014).

15. Quoted in Yagoda, *About Town*, p. 204.

16. Quoted in Hammill and Leick, 'Modernism and the Quality Magazines', p. 187.

17. William Strunk, Jr., and E. B. White, *The Elements of Style, with Revisions, an Introduction, and a Chapter on Writing*, 2nd ed. (New York: Macmillan, 1972), pp. 69, 63, 65, 67.

18. On Steinberg, see Deirdre Bair, *Saul Steinberg: A Biography* (New York: Nan A. Talese, 2012).

19. Dwight Macdonald, 'Books: Our Invisible Poor', *The New Yorker*, 19 January 1963, pp. 82–132; 'Rover', *The New Yorker*, 19 January 1963, p. 88; John Hersey: 'Hiroshima', *The New Yorker*, 31 August 1946, pp. 15–68; 'Our Custom Is Limited to Those Few Men in Each Community Who Want a Finer Hat', *The New Yorker*, 31 August 1946, p. 29. See Yagoda, *About Town*, pp. 239–40, for an excellent account of *The New Yorker* as a mass of contradictions.

20. Dwight Macdonald, 'Books: A Hero of Our Time', *The New Yorker*, 12 December 1959, pp. 201–22 (p. 201); Tom Wolfe, 'Lost in the Whichy Thickets: The New Yorker', in *Hooking Up* (London: Picador, 2010), p. 267.

21. 'Daniel Lang's Superb Stories of Lives Dramatically Affected by the New Super-Science', *The New Yorker*, 12 December 1959, p. 207. See Chon Day, Cartoon, *New Yorker*, 12 December 1959, p. 201.

22. Macdonald, 'Books: A Hero of Our Time', pp. 207, 202, 211, 221, 207, 221.

23. Saul Bellow, *Herzog* (New York: Viking, 1964), pp. 1, 7, 2.

24. Ibid., p. 2.

25. Herman Wouk, *Marjorie Morningstar* (Garden City, NY: Doubleday, 1955), p. 336.

26. Ibid., p. 342.
27. Ibid., pp. 334, 335.
28. Ibid., p. 333.
29. Ibid., pp. 334, 343.
30. Ibid., pp. 338–9, 342, 343.
31. James Jones, *From Here to Eternity* (New York: Delta, 1998 [1951]), p. 634.
32. Ibid., pp. 640–1.
33. Ibid., p. 635.
34. Ibid., pp. 636, 637.
35. Ibid., p. 173.
36. Ibid., p. 465.
37. Ibid., pp. 375, 367, 373.
38. Ibid., p. 373.
39. Ibid., pp. 376, 377.
40. Jennifer Szalai, 'Mac the Knife: On Dwight Macdonald', *The Nation*, 21 November 2011, available at <http://www.thenation.com/article/164752/mac-knife-dwight-macdonald> (accessed 1 May 2014).
41. Dwight Macdonald, 'By Cozzens Possessed: A Review of Reviews', *Commentary* (January 1958), 31–47 (p. 42).
42. Dwight Macdonald, 'A Theory of Mass Culture', in *Mass Culture: The Popular Arts in America*, ed. Bernard Rosenberg and David Manning White (New York: The Free Press, 1957), p. 64.
43. Macdonald, 'Masscult and Midcult', pp. 39, 42.
44. Macdonald, 'By Cozzens Possessed', p. 40.
45. Strunk and White, *Elements of Style*, p. 66; Dwight Macdonald, 'Books: The Book-of-the-Millennium Club', *The New Yorker*, 29 November 1952, pp. 171–92 (pp. 172, 186).
46. Quoted in Michael Wrezsin, *A Rebel In Defense of Tradition: The Life and Politics of Dwight Macdonald* (New York: Basic Books, 1994), p. 294. Wrezsin conjectures that Shawn must have rejected the poetic version of this review; Macdonald's ms. appears in *The New Yorker*'s archives, but the published version of the review is written in conventional prose. See Dwight Macdonald, 'Books: Two Acorns, One Oak', *The New Yorker*, 23 January 1954, pp. 92–100.
47. Wyndham Lewis et al., 'Manifesto', *BLAST* 1 (1914), 9–43 (p. 11). Quoted in Wreszin, *A Rebel In Defense of Tradition*, p. 294.
48. See, for example, Alan M. Wald, *The New York Intellectuals: The Rise and Decline of the Anti-Stalinist Left from the 1930s to the 1980s* (Chapel Hill: University of North Carolina Press, 1987).
49. Louis Menand, 'A Critic at Large: Browbeaten: Dwight Macdonald's War on Midcult', *The New Yorker*, 5 September 2011, pp. 72–8 (p. 74).
50. See, for example, Dwight Macdonald, *A Moral Temper: The Letters*, ed. Michael Wreszin (Chicago: Ivan R. Dee, 2001); Macdonald, 'Books: A Hero of Our Time', pp. 201–2.
51. Macdonald, 'Masscult and Midcult', p. 56.
52. Macdonald, 'Books: A Hero of Our Time', p. 211.
53. Herman Wouk, *The Caine Mutiny* (Garden City: Doubleday, 1952), p. 468. Also see Tom Perrin, 'Rebuilding *Bildung*: The Middlebrow Novel

of Aesthetic Education in the Mid-Twentieth-Century United States', *Novel: A Forum on Fiction*, 44.3 (2011), 382–401.

54. Tracy, 'Investing in "Modernism"', p. 58. Also see, for example, Andreas Huyssen, *After the Great Divide: Modernism, Mass Culture, Postmodernism* (Bloomington: Indiana University Press, 1986); McGurl, *The Novel Art*; Andrew Ross, *No Respect: Intellectuals and Popular Culture* (New York: Routledge, 1989).
55. Macdonald, 'By Cozzens Possessed', p. 41.
56. Macdonald, 'Masscult and Midcult', pp. 376, 377.
57. Ibid., p. 42.
58. Ibid., p. 40.
59. Ibid., p. 44.
60. John Elson, 'No Foolish Consistency: Biographical Sketch of Dwight Macdonald', review of Wreszin, *A Rebel In Defense of Tradition*', available at <http://kenrahn.com/JFK/History/WC_Period/Reactions_to_Warren_Report/Reactions_of_left/Bio_of_Macdonald.html> (accessed 12 June 2014).
61. Edward Mendelson, 'Dwight, the Passionate Moralist', review of Dwight Macdonald, *Masscult and Midcult: Essays Against the American Grain*, *New York Review of Books*, 8 March 2012, available at <http://www.nybooks.com/articles/archives/2012/mar/08> (accessed 12 June 2014).
62. Wreszin, *A Rebel In Defense of Tradition*, p. xiv.
63. Elson, 'No Foolish Consistency'.
64. James Wolcott, 'Dwight Macdonald at 100', *New York Times*, 16 April 2006.
65. Dwight Macdonald, 'Laugh and Lie Down', *Partisan Review* 4.1 (1937), 44–53 (p. 50).
66. Ibid., p. 48.
67. Ibid., p. 50.
68. Norman Mailer, *The Armies of the Night: History as a Novel, the Novel as History* (New York: Penguin, 1994), p. 26.
69. Tom Wolfe, 'Tiny Mummies! The True Story of the Ruler of 43rd Street's Land of the Walking Dead', in *Hooking Up*, p. 239.
70. Macdonald, 'Parajournalism II'; Macdonald, 'Parajournalism, or Tom Wolfe & His Magic Writing Machine', *New York Review of Books*, 26 August 1965, available at <http://www.nybooks.com/articles/archives/1965/aug/26> (accessed 12 June 2014).
71. Tom Wolfe, letter, *New York Review of Books*, 17 March 1966.
72. On Picasso, see Macdonald, 'Masscult and Midcult', p. 20; Wreszin, *A Rebel in Defense of Tradition*, p. 292.
73. Macdonald, 'Books: A Hero of Our Time', pp. 201, 211; Dwight Macdonald, 'Books: The Bible in Modern Undress', *The New Yorker*, 14 November 1953, p. 207. Wolfe, 'Lost in the Whichy Thickets', p. 257. Macdonald, 'Parajournalism'.
74. Macdonald, 'Parajournalism II'.
75. Macdonald, 'Books: Our Invisible Poor', rev. of Michael Harrington, *The Other America*, *The New Yorker*, 19 January 1963, pp. 82–132 (p. 132).
76. Macdonald, 'Masscult and Midcult', p. 56.

77. Dwight Macdonald, 'Action on West Fifty-Third Street: I', *The New Yorker*, 12 December 1953, pp. 49–82 (p. 61).
78. See Dwight Macdonald, 'Action on West Fifty-Third Street: II', *The New Yorker*, 19 December 1953, pp. 35–72 (p. 36).
79. Macdonald, 'Action on West Fifty-Third Street: I', p. 75.
80. Ibid., p. 68; Macdonald, 'Action on West Fifty-Third Street: II', p. 40.
81. Macdonald, 'Action on West Fifty-Third Street: I', p. 77.
82. Macdonald, 'Action on West Fifty-Third Street: II', p. 66.
83. Ibid.
84. See especially Janice A. Radway, *A Feeling For Books: The Book-of-the-Month Club, Literary Taste, and Middle-Class Desire* (Chapel Hill: University of North Carolina Press, 1997).

Index

Illustrations are indicated by *italics*.